Modernising Work in Public Services

# Modernising Work in Public Services

## Redefining Roles and Relationships in Britain's Changing Workplace

Edited by

Pauline Dibben, Phil James, Ian Roper and Geoffrey Wood

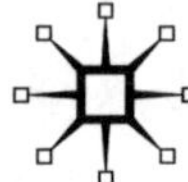



First published 2007 by
PALGRAVE MACMILLAN
Houndmills, Basingstoke, Hampshire RG21 6XS and
175 Fifth Avenue, New York, N. Y. 10010
Companies and representatives throughout the world

PALGRAVE MACMILLAN is the global academic imprint of the Palgrave Macmillan division of St. Martin's Press, LLC and of Palgrave Macmillan Ltd. Macmillan® is a registered trademark in the United States, United Kingdom and other countries. Palgrave is a registered trademark in the European Union and other countries.

ISBN-13: 978–1–4039–9859–0      hardback
ISBN-10: 1–4039–9859–0      hardback

This book is printed on paper suitable for recycling and made from fully managed and sustained forest sources. Logging, pulping and manufacturing processes are expected to conform to the environmental regulations of the country of origin.

A catalogue record for this book is available from the British Library.

A catalogue record for this book is available from the Library of Congress.

10   9   8   7   6   5   4   3   2   1
16   15   14   13   12   11   10   09   08   07

Printed and bound in Great Britain by
Antony Rowe Ltd, Chippenham and Eastbourne

*This book is dedicated to:*

*Peter, Shaun and Carina, Coralie and Brian; Caroline and Nathaniel; and Vicky and Alice. With thanks for the lifelong support of Win and Ralph Stevens, George and Doris James, Rita Evans, and Bob and Van Wood.*

# Contents

**Part III   The Dynamics of Collective Employment Relations and the Performance of Services**

# List of Tables

# List of Figures

# List of Contributors

**Philip Beaumont**, Professor of Employment Relations, School of Management, University of Glasgow

**Susan Corby**, Reader in Employment Relations, Business School, University of Greenwich

**Ian Cunningham**, Senior Lecturer in Human Resource Management, Department of Human Resource Management, University of Strathclyde

**Pauline Dibben**, Lecturer in Human Resource Management/Organisational Behaviour, Management School, University of Sheffield

**Moira Fischbacher**, Senior Lecturer in Strategy, School of Business and Management, University of Glasgow

**John Grahl**, Professor of European Integration, Middlesex University Business School, Middlesex University

**Damian Grimshaw**, Professor of Employment Studies, Manchester Business School, University of Manchester

**Phil James**, Professor of Employment Relations, Oxford Brookes University Business School

**David Marsden**, Professor of Industrial Relations, London School of Economics

**Miguel Martínez Lucio**, Professor of Industrial Relations and Human Resource Management, School of Management, University of Bradford

**Catherine Needham**, Lecturer in Politics, Department of Politics, Queen Mary, University of London

**Judy Pate**, Lecturer in Strategy, School of Business and Management, University of Glasgow

**Ian Roper**, Principal Lecturer in Human Resource Management, Middlesex University Business School

**Mark Stuart**, Professor of Human Resource Management and Employment Relations, Leeds University Business School

**Noel Thompson**, Professor of History, School of Humanities, University of Wales, Swansea

**Geoffrey Wood**, Professor of Human Resource Management, Management School, University of Sheffield

# Introduction: Is 'Modern' Necessarily Better?

*Pauline Dibben and Phil James*

The British public sector, from its expansion under the first post-war Labour Government as an accompaniment to the establishment of the Welfare State, to the present day has never been immune from change. However, the pace and scale of it has arguably never been greater than that which has occurred over the last quarter of a century. Indeed, 'modernisation' has become effectively the central theme of government approaches towards the sector during this period.

According to the post-1997 Labour administrations, the process of modernisation they have overseen has provided the basis of a more cost-effective, efficient and responsive public sector. To its critics, however, the current direction of reform embodies a number of problematic employment-related consequences which lead it to be marked by highly dysfunctional outcomes. These consequences are seen to include lowered levels of job security, work intensification, the delivery of public services by ill-trained and poorly rewarded contractor staff who do not have access to effective collective representation and the widespread destruction of the 'public sector ethos' that has traditionally supported the carrying out of public sector work in a responsible, accountable and efficient way.

Which of these interpretations is most correct is a matter of profound policy importance, given the implications that they carry for future public welfare, particularly among the more vulnerable sections of the population, and for the health and more general well-being of those engaged in public sector work. To date, however, systematic and rounded analyses of the employment-related effects of recent government reforms are rare. Moreover, few have embodied both a micro- and macro-level focus and been informed by a detailed consideration of the philosophical, regulatory and institutional forces that have shaped them. This is despite the fact that Britain has played a pioneering role in re-configuring the boundaries of 'the public sector' and re-shaping its internal managerial structures and processes and, in doing so, often provided a 'modernisation template' for other nations (Bach *et al.*, 1999). The present volume has been compiled to address these gaps in the currently extant literature.

In what follows in the remainder of this introductory chapter the main elements of recent public sector modernisation are initially highlighted by locating the reforms pursued by the post-1997 Labour governments in the context of those initiated by the successive Conservative administrations during the period from 1979. Following this, details are provided on the volume's organisation and content.

## Public service modernisation under New Labour: how new is it?

The modernisation of the public sector constituted a central plank of the policies of the Conservative governments led by Margaret Thatcher and John Major. This process of modernisation, which evolved over the years between 1979 and 1997, came to encompass three distinct *foci*.

One focus of reform centred on the re-drawing of the boundaries of government involvement in the economy and society *via* an expanding remit of privatisation into increasingly controversial aspects of public life. Commercial organisations such as British Leyland, Amersham International, Rolls Royce, ICL and TSB formed one category of privatised organisations. Another was the more contentious area of the water and electricity utilities – since there is a public aspect to this activity. Further to this, came the privatisation and deregulation of bus companies (see for example Dibben, 2006) and the railways. Then, central to the concerns of this volume, the adoption of mechanisms, notably compulsory competitive tendering and the Private Finance Initiative, aimed at increasing private sector engagement in the delivery of public services – areas which are arguably too sensitive for outright privatisation, but nevertheless seen as amenable to marketisation.

The second line of reform entailed taking action to make labour markets more competitive and 'free' and increasing the freedom of 'managers to manage' in both the public and private sectors. This action included the introduction of a range of anti-union laws, the prohibiting of public bodies from imposing employment-related conditions into tendering processes, the rescinding of the fair wages resolution under which government contractors were obliged to provide recognised terms and conditions, and the encouragement, both ideologically and symbolically, of non-union-based employment regimes – encouragement most graphically illustrated through government decisions to de-recognise unions at Government Communication Headquarters (GCHQ) and withdraw pay bargaining rights from teaching unions.

Finally, a third strand of reform involved the introduction of mechanisms aimed at more directly engendering changes in the way that public sector bodies were managed; changes that, in large part, sought to create systems of management accountability and managerial systems of control akin to those found in the private sector. These mechanisms included the use of the Audit Commission to assess the value for money of public services, the adoption, notably under the Major Governments, of target setting and associated auditing processes, the decentralisation of management structures and collective bargaining in the civil service, the creation of an internal market in the National Health Service (NHS), and the encouragement of individual performance-related pay systems.

Subsequent developments since the coming to power of New Labour in 1997 have in many respects continued these three lines of reform. For example, privatisation has continued, albeit on a much lower scale, partly for the simple reason that the scope for it was much reduced. Competitive tendering and market testing have also remained of importance. For example, despite Best Value removing the compulsory element from the tendering process, a range of mechanisms are employed under it that effectively retain very strong pressure to outsource services (Higgins *et al.*, 2004). In addition, there has been a massive expansion of 'public-private partnerships' under the umbrella of the Private Finance Initiative (PFI).

Meanwhile, attempts to reform public sector management processes and structures have, arguably, intensified through the ever greater usage of government imposed targets and related mechanisms of audits, and more recently, through the pursuit of greater consumer choice. This last objective has, strikingly, led to the reintroduction of an internal market in the NHS following the earlier abolition of the one put in place during the period of Conservative rule.

At the same time, and in sharp contrast to what went before, the Labour governments since 2001 have dramatically increased public sector expenditure. They have also pursued labour market policies which have attempted to combine the improvement of public sector performance with the creation of greater 'fairness' at work. Thus, while most of the anti-union laws that Labour inherited have remained, a new statutory union recognition procedure has been put in place and 'partnership' has been encouraged between unions and employers. In addition, individual employment rights have also, in part as a result of European directives, been considerably expanded, perhaps, most notably, through the introduction of a National Minimum Wage. Most critics would argue that many of these regulatory changes have been made as a result of union pressure, and that European Union (EU) initiatives have been watered down as a result of lobbying from employer organisations, such as the Confederation of British Industry. Nevertheless, insofar as this is true, the fact remains that these concessions would probably not have occurred under a Conservative administration. It is also important, in the current context, to acknowledge that, in combination, they have acted to reduce the extent to which the contracting out of public services can lead to a driving down of terms and conditions.

It is in the area of public expenditure and labour market policy, then, that New Labour's reform agenda could claim to be a departure from the policies of the Thatcher and Major Governments, leading to the description of a 'third way' approach (Giddens, 1999). How far this agenda provides for a productive combination of 'fairness' and other forms of organisational modernisation therefore represents the fundamental test of its validity and utility.

This test, in turn, raises a host of related questions. For example, to what degree have recent processes of reform embodied a mutuality of interest between public sector bodies and their workforces? Have employer-worker and employer–union relationships improved since the election of the first Blair Government in 1997? And how far in practice has it proved possible to combine a commitment to fair employment practices with a continued emphasis on marketisation? It is questions such as these that the contributions within this volume seek to address.

## Modernising work in Britain's public services: an overview

Against the background of the debates outlined above, this volume focuses on three broad and distinct themes: the underlying drivers of change in public services; the implications of these changes for the individual work experiences of workers; and the way in which the reforms concerned have impacted on the dynamics of collective employment relations and the performance of services. To this end, contributions were sought from leading academics who, in combination, could shed important light on these issues. The book is also systematically divided into distinct parts, addressing each of these aspects of 'modernisation' in turn. While attention is focused on public services in Britain, this is contextualised within more general debates about changes to the public sector, and includes reflection on the nature of policies and practices within other states.

### The underlying drivers of change

Government ideology is arguably intangible and multifaceted, and composed of various strands of both academic and popular thought. Thus pinning it down is likely to be a difficult task. It is also difficult to judge the extent to which ideology informs behaviour, or whether it is merely rhetoric. Nevertheless, an ideological discourse can be used to justify policy choices and can pervade changes to working practices. In examining changes to public service work, a prior investigation of how ideology might influence behaviour is therefore essential.

In recent years, attention has been paid to how a neoliberal ideology has informed new public management practices during the 1980s and 1990s.

This has been the subject of debate both in Britain and further afield (see, for example, Dibben *et al.*, 2004; Minogue *et al.*, 1998). Different countries, and their Welfare States, have been conceptualised as falling either closer to, or further from, a model of neoliberalism. Movement in either direction has, in turn, been seen to have variously stemmed from attempts to address social needs or to meet political exigencies.

In the case of Britain, a key issue which merits attention in this regard is the extent to which British governments since the late 1970s have rejected post-war Keynesianism and moved toward a more neoliberal position; an examination that, of necessity, requires an exploration of how, and why, concepts such as public choice have informed the political economies of successive Conservative and Labour governments. In Chapter 1 Noel Thompson examines the nature of the challenges that have been made to the Keynesian social democratic consensus, and investigates the extent to which New Labour is characterised by a new ideological underpinning.

Another important factor that has influenced work and employment in Britain's public services is employment regulation. Whether popular or not with political bodies, business, and the broader population of public service consumers, employment regulation within Britain has been informed by supranational regulation, and in particular by the directives put forward by the European Commission. Therefore, this subject forms the central focus of Chapter 2 of this volume. In it, John Grahl posits that the European Commission's proposed Directive on Services in the Internal Market (Bolkestein Directive) attacks both the social models of Member States and worker rights. He further traces the ideological thinking that informed the directive's development and highlights how the European Parliament has sought to place limits on these potential consequences as well as its more general implications for the effective delivery of social welfare through public services.

In the long period of growth between the 1950s and 1970s, various sets of institutions and practices were set up under the remit of a Welfare State. These have been subject to attack since that time, with the deregulation of product and labour markets and cutbacks to the role of the State, including the scope and nature of social services offered. In Chapter 3, Geoffrey Wood examines the forces and dynamics that have contributed toward such changes, and then moves on to assess the extent to which factors such as corruption in decision-making, labour repression and changing demographics present continuing threats to public service provision.

The final chapter in this part examines the composition and trends of public sector work, focusing on public services in both England and Scotland, the latter country forming a useful comparator due to its political and legal autonomy from England since devolution. In Chapter 4, Philip Beaumont, Judy Pate and Moira Fischbacher explore the extent to which levels of employment have grown or declined, and show how an understanding of the causes of this are key to understanding the changing nature of public service work. They further go on to examine how these trends have existed alongside parallel actions to improve the performance of public services *via* changes in respect of pay, retention and the management of absence.

## The consequences of public service 'modernisation'

Having investigated the potential drivers of the modernisation process, the second part of the volume explores the consequences of these influences for workers. Arguably, one of the consequences of ideological, regulatory and social change has been a declining public service ethos. But this assumes that such an ethos is distinctive to the public sector more broadly, and public services in particular. Moreover, it implies that it is possible to define what such a concept means in practice. Chapter 5, by Catherine Needham, critically evaluates this amorphous concept in the context of Britain's reform agenda. In doing so, she draws on the arguments advanced by various proponents of the concept, and reveals how it has been used at different times and for different purposes. Nevertheless, the chapter shows how understanding the way in which the 'public service ethos' is positioned is vital to making sense of the shifting priorities of reformers and to gaining an understanding of the implications that recent reforms have for the future of public services.

Recent policy developments aimed at enhancing equality and diversity among those employed in public service work form the focus of Susan Corby's contribution in Chapter 6. More specifically, the chapter explores the rationales underling these developments, examines how public sector practice in the area compares with that in the private sector, considers how progress has been hindered by legal weaknesses and cultural, organisational and financial barriers and, more generally, discusses whether arguments for equality based on the business case and social justice are complementary.

Chapter 7 then tackles fairness and equity in payment systems. David Marsden examines the erosion of long-established salary systems which embodied grade and seniority increments through the introduction of individual performance-related pay arrangements. In doing so, he probes beneath the surface of these new systems, and evaluates the extent to which they provide the basis for procedural justice.

The final chapter in this part addresses the notion of employment security in public services. In Chapter 8, Pauline Dibben argues that 'employment security' and 'job security' should not be used interchangeably, and that clearer distinctions should be drawn in defining this concept. She develops a framework that distinguishes between the macro- and micro-level, evaluates the current status in Britain's public services, and argues for more focused action on this issue by both State and trade unions.

## The dynamic nature of employment relationships

Trust and cooperation are vital ingredients for partnership. Yet these are difficult to achieve in the initial stages of a relationship, and even more difficult to sustain over the longer term. Couple this with the changing dynamics of public services, and immediately it is possible to see weaknesses in the concept.

The 'partnership' ideal has been used in a variety of contexts, and Chapter 9 of this volume tackles it in respect of industrial relations. Miguel Martínez Lucio and Mark Stuart argue that the development of partnership in employment relations has been a central feature of New Labour's policy for the public sector and represents an attempt to move away from conflictual relationships towards greater consultation and engagement. However, even where it appears that partnership might be feasible, such as in local government where union recognition exists, membership is high and collective bargaining well-established, their analysis indicates that a number of strategic and structural challenges confront the establishment of long-term reciprocal relationships in a sector confronted by marketisation and other forms of fragmentation.

Further complications arise for public service employment where services are contracted out to other bodies such as the private sector or not-for-profit organisations under market-based competition. In such circumstances, although trade union membership, recognition and organisation are common features in the public sector, the reach of their influence is limited. In Chapter 10, Ian Cunningham and Phil James examine the dynamics of employment relations within this context, undertaking an analysis of the institutional position and role of trade unions in the public sector and then drawing on empirical research to evaluate the ability of trade unions to regulate employment relationships when services are outsourced to the voluntary sector.

The subject of partnership is returned to in Chapter 11, but this time in order to investigate inter-organisational relations in public service delivery. Damian Grimshaw and Ian Roper highlight tensions in the 'public-private partnership' approach advocated by the current and previous governments. They challenge the assumptions underpinning such partnerships, and raise serious concerns about the individualisation of service users, the costs of separating policy from implementation, and the problems inherent in applying a principle-agent model to public service provision. In developing their arguments, they refer to recent empirical research which explores contractual relations in public services.

The concluding chapter, Chapter 12, by Geoffrey Wood and Ian Roper, reflects on the British experience in a comparative context. The inter-related strands of analysis within the volume are drawn together in order to assess the implications of recent reforms for public service workers. At the same time, the benefits and disadvantages of reform for the other 'partners' of public service delivery – the not-for-profit organizations and private sector – are addressed and the likely nature of future reform trajectories explored.

## Acknowledgement

With thanks to Anil Verma for his useful comments on the structure and focus of this volume.

# Part I

# Underlying Drivers of Change in Public Services

# 1
# From Hayek to New Labour: The Changing Ideology of Public Sector Provision

*Noel Thompson*

The changes that have occurred in public sector employment over the last three decades stem, in large measure, from ideological shifts that have affected governmental perceptions of the nature of public sector bodies, the role that they can and should play and the manner in which they should be managed and made accountable. It is the purpose of this chapter to discuss these, beginning with the post-war Keynesian social democratic consensus, before moving on to consider the multifarious challenges to this and the impact that these have had upon the political economies embraced by Thatcherite Conservatism and New Labour.

## The Keynesian social democratic consensus

The Keynesian social democratic consensus that emerged in the post-war period delineated a role for the State that remained essentially uncontested for almost two decades. The *White Paper on Employment Policy* of 1944 committed it to maintain a high and stable level of employment; the *Beveridge Report on Social Insurance and Allied Services*, 1942 outlined its responsibilities as regards welfare provision, while the Attlee Government established the parameters of a mixed economy whose margins might be debated but whose substance was largely undisputed. Full employment ensured that the Welfare State rested on financially sound foundations, while public ownership, in theory, gave the State control over sufficient of the commanding heights of the economy to enable it to provide strategic leadership. Moreover, the public institutions these responsibilities engendered were seen as being operated by a Civil Service characterised by its permanence, its neutrality, its integrity, its independence, its industry, its expertise and above all its capacity to work altruistically for the public good. Underpinning much of this was a Fabian belief in the possibility of a science of public administration whose practitioners would bring a new professionalism to bear on the business of public management and whose conduct would be informed by a sense of public service.[1] It was a Civil Service too which was characterised, as were public services more generally, by hierarchic organisational structures, a paternalistic management style, collectivised industrial relations, and standardised employment practices, and which sought to be a model employer in setting standards to which the private sector should aspire.

## The challenge to consensus

The late 1960s and 1970s saw a conjuncture of economic developments which threatened to undermine the central components and institutional characteristics of this post-war settlement. The economy moved from a position of full or near-full employment, while at the same time inflation accelerated to double-digit levels by the mid-1970s. Public expenditure underwent a seemingly inexorable rise, while the quality of public services came under increasingly critical scrutiny from both the Left and the Right of the political spectrum. In this period too there was growing concern about the efficiency of public enterprises, while, more generally, Britain's mixed economy was distinguished by periodic balance of payments crises and relative economic decline (Conservative Party, 1976: 32).[2]

It is not surprising therefore that it was during this period that there occurred a fundamental, multifaceted and well-orchestrated, ideological challenge to the post-war Keynesian social democratic settlement. Of course some of the key elements of this critique had an earlier provenance. Specifically, the *fons et origo* of much of what was to become, by the 1970s and 1980s, a comprehensive assault upon the contemporary role of the State and public services in post-war western societies was to be found in the political economy of Friederich Hayek; in particular in works such as *The road to serfdom*, 1944 and *The constitution of liberty*, 1960. In the 1930s Hayek, carrying the torch lit by Ludwig von Mises, had denied the possibility of economic rationality in the context of a planned socialist economy. By 1944 he was not only arguing the case for the impossibility of rational economic calculation under socialism but also argued further that the 'collective and conscious direction of all social forces to deliberately chosen goals', which socialism implied, necessitated the progressive abandonment of 'that freedom in economic affairs without which personal and political freedom have never existed in the past' (Hayek, 1986: 10).

A free economy, by which Hayek meant a market economy, was the *sine qua non* of a free polity. This did not preclude State intervention; indeed it did not preclude an extensive system of social services, as long as these did not operate as a significant constraint upon market competition. However, the primary role of the State should be 'to create conditions in which competition will be as effective as possible' and 'to supplement it when it cannot be effective' (*ibid.*: 29). Furthermore, if the market economy and associated freedoms were to flourish, State action and State intervention must also be predictable. Economic actors could not operate to best advantage in a context of arbitrary, discriminatory and coercive State activity. State action should therefore be governed by 'rules fixed independently of…concrete circumstances' (ibid: 56).

Hayek's strictures on the role of the State under socialism did not stop short at the totalitarian '"hot" socialism' of the communist bloc but extended to what he termed the '"cold" socialism' of western social democracy and, in particular, its manifestation in the Welfare State; a State which in consequence of what he referred to as Britain's post-war 'plunge into her socialist experiment', represented a critical threat to political and social freedoms, with 'the greatest danger to liberty' 'com[ing] from…the efficient, expert administrators exclusively concerned with what they regard as the public good' (Hayek, 1960: 253, 262). Social insurance in particular had come to mean 'compulsory membership in a unitary organisation controlled by the State', while its administration had become 'a self-willed and uncontrollable apparatus' and had transmuted itself into an instrument 'for determining the relative incomes of the great majority and thus for controlling economic activity generally' (*ibid.*: 303). The Welfare State had in effect become a 'substitute for old-fashioned socialism' with all the coercive consequences which the *Road to serfdom* had detailed (*ibid.*: 289).

These themes of freedom against tyranny, choice against coercion, competitive as against monopolistic provision, individual initiative *versus* collective uniformity and the market against planning, represented, for a time, a thin, blue, lightly-manned, ideological line thrown up to prevent the seemingly inexorable advance of the 'cold socialism' of Keynesian social democracy.[3] However, by the late 1960s, a critical view of the role of the State, public services and their bureaucracies was emanating from new quarters and, in particular, from the Virginia School and public choice theory. Underlying this theory was a methodological individualism which saw politicians, bureaucrats and interest groups as self-interested utility maximisers driven by motives comparable to actors in the economic drama of the marketplace (Buchanan, 1972: 16).[4] In that regard it involved the importation of 'the general analytical framework of economics into political science' (Tullock *et al.*, 2000: 5). From this perspective 'bureaucrats normally ha[d] several private motives…not to work too hard…to expand the size of [their] own department and in the process of so doing being willing to go along with the expansion of all the rest' and, in addition, to maximise their own 'perks' (Niskanen *et al.*, 1973: 27; Tullock, 1998: 1043). As to politicians, their primary objective was to maximise the votes they attracted, thereby maintaining and strengthening their hold on political power.[5] And as for interest groups, these sought to maximise their share of national resources.

Such a position clearly underpinned a particular perception of government bureaucracy and, more generally, public sector employees, fundamentally different from that 'Fabian' conception that, as noted above, informed the optimistic rationalism of Keynesian social democracy. In contrast the Virginia School saw 'bureaucrats' as being 'much like other people and, like people...[as] more interested in their own well-being than in the public interest.' They might 'to some extent...attempt to do what is right' but 'in modern societies, where civil service legislation makes it all but impossible for the superiors either to dismiss them or reduce their salaries, the degree to which bureaucrats are so compelled is moderate'. 'The student of public choice [was therefore] unlikely to believe that government officials are overly concerned with the public interest' (Tullock, 1998: 1042; Tullock *et al.*, 2000: 15; Tullock *et al.*, 2000: 55).

In the Virginia view of things, both politicians and bureaucrats were also seen as having a strong motive to take account of, or even collude with interest groups both within and outside the public sector; groups that sought 'to enlarge their resources not through higher efficiency but through campaigning for more public money' (Howe, 1982: 19). Indeed public choice theorists identified a formidable conjuncture of interests, with politicians, public sector unions, local and central government employees, large corporations and particular economic interests often forming a interlinked constituency whose interwoven aspirations it was mutually advantageous to accommodate. The public sector in particular boasted 'very large numbers of organised groups operat[ing]... according to their own interests (miners, first division civil servants, and teachers)...The incentive for each [being] to treat the income of the private sector as a "common property resource"' (Burton, 1984: 100). This was a view echoed by Keith Joseph.[6] 'Where', he asked, 'are these firms or industries with politically powerful union groupings to squeeze public money out of the government to maintain economically unjustified jobs?'; 'they tend to be where large concentrations of union labour exist, particularly the nationalised industries' (Joseph, 1976: 41). But even outside the public sector there existed a 'para-government' that included private-sector unions, trade associations and claimants' unions. And the pressures which such interest groups could exert, and the political advantages in accommodating them, were seen as resulting, almost inevitably, in an excessive growth of public expenditure and a greater than optimal supply of public goods (Thompson, 1990: 26). Thus bureaucrats often took the initiative in 'form[ing] mutually beneficial alliances with pressure groups' (Tullock *et al.*, 2000: 63); pressure groups having an interest in the expansion of those elements of the public bureaucracy that represented and defended them (Brittain, 1973: 242; Shearmure, 1984: 80). Further, the large numbers employed by central and local government and organised in professional associations and trade unions meant that, in terms of vote maximisation, the bureaucracy had become a significant constituency in its own right and one whose interests politicians ignored at their peril.

What also militated in favour of the strengthening of this unholy alliance was the fact that while the costs, in terms of the inexorable rise of rapidly increasing government expenditure, accelerating inflation, a 'bloated bureaucracy', public and private sector inefficiency and institutional sclerosis, were increasingly manifest, they were spread across the nation as a whole.[7] In contrast the benefits of such an alliance were highly concentrated. This therefore made for more powerful imperatives from special-interest groups to defend their gains, than those emanating from the general public to oppose their demands, or to press for a dismantling of interest-group alliances (Hayek, 1979: 13–17). As one commentator put it, 'modern democratic governments long ago discovered that, to stay in power by currying the support of a majority of the electorate, it is necessary to construct a plethora of interventions to retain the backing of important groups of beneficiaries, while hiding the cost to the losers – *by dispersing them as widely as possible even to generations yet unborn*'[8] (Burton, 1984: 96, my emphasis).

The Institute of Economic Affairs (IEA) provided an important conduit for these ideas. From the 1960s the IEA was publishing works by James Buchanan and Gordon Tullock, the two founding fathers of public choice theory. And, by 2000, 'the ideas of the public choice school ha[d] so permeated the Institute's publications that virtually every monograph has for many years had those ideas at its heart' (Seldon, 2000: xiii, v). Such views also rapidly found their way into the speeches and literary output of the Conservative Party leadership (Thatcher, 1977).

The Virginia School therefore contributed key elements to what was to become the New Right critique of government, the public sector and the bureaucracies which serviced them; a critique that also furnished a compelling narrative of Britain's poor, post-war economic performance and relative economic decline. Thus public expenditure was portrayed as having risen inexorably as private and public special interests had superseded the more general interest of the nation in guarding against waste and inefficiency. Moreover, political competition had fuelled this process as politicians sought to purchase the median voter and acted in a manner that accommodated that voter's rising material expectations.

Such increasing public expenditure was also seen as theoretically underpinned by a crude Keynesianism that celebrated the virtues of deficit financing and further fuelled an inflationary spiral that effected a redistribution of wealth in favour of central and local government without overt recourse to punitive taxation. In this latter respect Keynesian 'deficit spending and inflationary finance tended to undermine whatever resistance there was to the expansion in the size of public budgets' (Buchanan and Wagner, 1977: 69).

In its critique of crude Keynesianism and its separation of the wheat of private sector endeavour from the chaff of public sector inefficiency and waste, public choice theory also enjoyed a symbiotic relationship with other components of the New Right critique of Keynesian social democracy. Thus Keynesian demand management implied the competence of the State, with the requisite expert guidance, to secure the full employment on which social progress, and certainly an expanded Welfare State, was predicated. However monetarism, as articulated in the 1960s by Hayek, Friedman and their British acolytes, called that fundamentally into question. In his Presidential Address to the American Economic Association in 1967, Friedman posited the idea of a natural rate of unemployment at which the economy would normally settle because of imperfections in the labour market; imperfections which were seen as resulting in large measure from the power of trade unions, particularly those in the public sector. Unemployment could not be reduced permanently below this by a government-induced expansion of aggregate demand. And any short-run, positive impact on employment would only occur to the extent that a rise in prices lowered real wages; something labour would act to redress should it occur, with unemployment once again increasing to its 'natural' rate, but at a higher level of price inflation. There was therefore no so-called Phillips-Curve trade-off between unemployment and inflation. In this context the accelerating inflation of the 1970s resulted from a doomed attempt to force unemployment below its natural rate. As David Laidler, one of the leading British monetarists of the 1970s put it, 'the basic error committed has been to neglect to control the money supply while pursuing an unrealistically low unemployment target, primarily by fiscal means. Monetary expansion, largely a by-product of full employment fiscal policies, has been responsible for the British inflation rate in the 1970s' (Laidler, 1976: 52).[9]

So monetarism too was informed by a general suspicion of the utility of the role the State was playing. And here again the expertise and indeed the hubris of public officialdom was called into question. Those who sought to manage the macroeconomy in the public interest were not the cure: they were the disease – a very British disease that included accelerating inflation, a stagnating economy, relative economic decline, rising unemployment, and the increasing attenuation of the manufacturing sector.

Public choice theory also dovetailed with, and was reinforced by, three other components of the New Right critique of the public sector and the growth of public sector employment, namely 'crowding out', 'overload' and welfare dependency. Central to the first of these was the distinction between productive and unproductive activity that informed the hugely influential, *Britain's economic problem, too few producers* (Bacon and Eltis, 1976); a distinction which rested on an attempt to differentiate between labour that did, and labour that did not, produce a marketable output. Into the latter category fell the greater part of employment in the public services which had expanded rapidly in the 1960s and early 1970s,[10] appropriating resources otherwise available for the expansion of the traded goods sector; something which had consequences for Britain's general economic performance and, in particular, her export industries and balance of payments position. As Bacon and Eltis saw it, 'most of the extra goods for the consumption of the vastly larger numbers of teachers, social workers and civil servants, and the extra buildings to house them could only be supplied by building fewer factories in industry itself…by exporting less or importing more' (Bacon and Eltis, 1976: 17). Moreover 'the extra taxes needed to take these vast extra resources away from those who produced marketed goods and services must hit incentives' which also adversely affected national economic performance.[11] For Keith Joseph, 'the public sector, including central and local government, and more accurately named *state-sector, or wealth-eating sector*; was bound to spread like bindweed at the expense of the *non-state sector, the wealth-creating sector*, strangling and threatening to destroy what it grew upon' (Joseph, 1976: 22, my emphasis). In effect public and private sectors were participating in a zero-sum game with the gains of the former inevitably eroding the prosperity of the latter.

The crowding out of the tradable activity of the private sector was also effected through the medium of the capital market as rapidly rising public expenditure was financed by resorting to public sector borrowing. So, for Keith Joseph, 'the state sector bids up interest rates, [and] bids off funds'; 'state borrowing from the public by government and local authorities competes for limited funds with borrowing by private firms. The State, central and local, is in a strong position. It is a safe borrower…and it can push up interest rates knowing that the public will pay the extra in the form of taxes and rates' (Joseph, 1975: 17; Joseph, 1976: 39). Moreover the expansion of the non-tradable goods sector was also seen as further exacerbating inflationary pressures.

So again the narrative was one of a bloated public sector with a workforce that was expanding exponentially, appropriating a disproportionate share of resources, contributing little to economic performance and aggravating the economic difficulties which Britain confronted in the 1960s and 1970s; in particular balance of payments crises, inflation, relative economic decline and a shrinking manufacturing base. And it was a narrative increasingly articulated within, and by, the Conservative Party. For Keith Joseph 'the public sector utterly depends upon the efficiency of private enterprise'; 'profit-making free enterprise [was] the base on which all our public services rest' (Joseph, 1976: 61). For Margaret Thatcher, it was 'private industry that creates wealth – governments, on the whole, do no more than spend it' (Thatcher, 1977: 58). Indeed '*industry and trade* [were] *the basic social service*, because they provide[d] a large number of jobs. They also provide, through taxation, the resources to educate our young people and care for the weak, the sick and the elderly' (*ibid*.: 82, my emphasis). The public sector, or a significant part of it, was essentially parasitic and like all parasites it damaged the health of its host.

Interwoven with these ideas of constraining and crowding out was the notion of overload (see King, 1975). Not only was the State doing more and at greater cost, it was also doing what it did less and less well and preventing the individual or private enterprise from doing it better. For Harris, in his IEA pamphlet *The end of government*, 1980, 'the larger the government grows, the more crippling its diseconomies of scale.' The government in the 1960s and 1970s had become '"overloaded" with more tasks than it could competently carry out' (Harris, 1980: 25). 'It is a bitter irony that as government has aspired to do more it has become unable to discharge its basic functions' (Thatcher, 1977: 74). Some wrote in this period of the crisis of the State, anticipating that as 'western societie became overburdened with welfare and other statist commitments, they would ultimately collapse' (Barry, 1984: 50); largely from the cost of fulfiling them.

Further, the assumption of an increasing range of responsibilities were not only seen as overburdening the State but also producing the inexorable growth of a dependency culture; an idea that became a fundamental component of New Right thinking. Such a view of what the Welfare State had become was integral to the political economies of monetarists, public choice theorists, those who adhered to notions of institutional sclerosis and those who articulated a narrative of contemporary moral decay. The existing tax and social security system was seen as 'positively encourag[ing] dependence on the State' (Conservative Party, 1976: 11) 'By enlarging the role of the State and diminishing the role of the individual', Conservative and Labour post-war governments had 'crippled the enterprise and effort on which a prosperous country depends,' (Conservative Party, 1979: 6) both undermining competitiveness and demoralising the population by eroding, 'the values of prudence and foresight and independence' (Willetts, 1992: 147). As John Gray put it 'the development of the post-war Welfare State in Britain, Europe and America has produced a servile psychology' and also 'a lack of initiative and entrepreneurship' (Gray, 1984: 39). More worryingly, welfare-related expenditure also created, and was seen as being used to induce, political dependency.[12]

The 1970s and 1980s therefore witnessed a well-articulated, well-organised and, one might also add, a well-resourced assault upon the Keynesian social democratic conception of the role of the State, local government and public services within the British polity. And the ideas of the Virginia and Chicago Schools, mediated by organisations such as the IEA, the Centre for Policy Studies and the Adam Smith Institute, iterated in publications such as the *Journal for Economic Affairs*, popularised by journalists such as Paul Johnson, Samuel Brittain in the *Financial Times* and Patrick Hutber in the *Sunday Telegraph*, and championed by New Right politicians such as Keith Joseph, Nicholas Ridley and Margaret Thatcher, undoubtedly did substantial and lasting damage to it. The public sector was portrayed as having grown to proportions that threatened individual freedom, choice, initiative and independence. It was serviced by a utility-maximising bureaucracy whose agenda and objectives only rarely meshed with public needs and whose increasing cost eroded the resources available to the private sector. This in turn jeopardised Britain's economic performance as a comparatively poor rate of economic growth, the intensification of balance of payments crises, growing international indebtedness and stagflation made all too apparent. Keynesian demand management had proved ineffectual at best and destabilising at worst, while the progressive globalisation of economic activity was seen as confirming that impotence, as well as intensifying the imperatives to reduce a burdensome public sector that undermined competitiveness and acted as an incentive to corporate exit and disinvestment.

Much has been written on the limitations, tensions and inconsistencies of this New Right vision. Amongst other things 'economic freedom' required the creation of a strong and coercive state as the legislative and other assaults upon trade unions in the 1980s made clear (Gamble, 1994). There was tension too between the rhetoric of a supply-side revolution and a monetary policy which sought to squeeze inflation from the system. For the latter strategy produced a rapid rise in interest rates and a consequent appreciation in sterling which, in the early 1980s, destroyed a substantial proportion of British manufacturing capacity, turning the West Midlands into the poorest region in England and provoking Terence Beckett, Director of the CBI, to threaten 'a bare knuckle fight with the government' (Smith, 1987: 98). In effect the monetarists' Medium-Term Financial Strategy did greater damage to the 'marketable' sector of the economy than could have been envisaged in the wildest nightmares of Bacon and Eltis. And, as to the crowding out of the private sector, in the first three years after 1979 real public spending actually increased from 40.5 per cent to 44 per cent of GDP (*ibid.*: 105). Moreover, the attempt to curtail public spending by reducing the expenditure on nationalised industries and local authorities involved higher charges and rates, putting further pressure on industry to shed labour and scale back its activities.

## Thatcherism and the rise of marketisation

However, while monetarism and other elements of New Right political economy were theoretically and prescriptively bankrupt by the mid-1980s (Jenkins, 1989: 378) ideas both when they are right and when they are wrong are often as powerful as Keynes opined. For these powerful ideological currents and economic imperatives fundamentally altered the popular, the academic and, even within elements of the Left, the political perceptions of the utility of the public sector and public sector employment. They also called into question the mode of public service delivery, the traditional public service ethos, the use of resources by the public sector, its size, its management structure, its responsiveness to users and consumers and what that sector should and should not be in the business of doing. And, in the Thatcher era and beyond, they underpinned and informed a philosophy of marketisation; a philosophy claimed to be able to deliver the prescriptive agenda embraced by the New Right – slowing the growth of government expenditure, reducing it as a percentage of GDP, providing better value for money from the expenditure of public funds, subjecting public officials and employees to market or quasi-market imperatives, shrinking public bureaucracies, dismantling concentrations of administrative power, prioritising the interests of the service user over those of the service provider and engendering entrepreneurialism on the part of the public services and public service employees.

This philosophy of marketisation had a number of dimensions. To begin with it scripted the service user as consumer. This allowed the New Right to appropriate the language of democratisation, choice and individual empowerment and to conceptualise the users of public provision as wielding power in the marketplace. Thatcherism could therefore pose as the champion of individual freedom against the coercive authority of large and insensitive bureaucratic battalions; offering in particular the freedom to hold service providers to account by steering resources to or from them on the basis of choices made. In effect there was here an attempt to alter the perception and self-perception of both users and providers, with the public no longer being viewed, or viewing themselves, as passive clients to be treated at best with benevolent paternalism and at worst authoritarian resentment. 'In hospitals, schools, housing schemes, advice and information services and many other aspects of public administration managers are being exhorted to pay more attention to consumer wishes, offer consumers wider choice, and develop techniques for marketing their particular service' (Pollitt, 1987: 43). This, it was argued, would help to democratise service provision, enhance the sovereignty of the user/consumer, limit the power and discretion of the public service bureaucracy and reduce the costs and enhance the quality of the services provided.

Choice, of course, implied multiple providers and thence competition and this is what the Thatcher Government of the 1980s and early 1990s sought to deliver through privatisation, and deregulation. Indeed it was this process 'in areas of employment, health care, housing, education, transport and other sectors of social infrastructure, together with the progressive contracting out of some of the regulatory functions of local government and the passing of broad areas of publicly-funded activity (such as training) to quango-style bodies', that 'represent[ed] the operational triumph of what, in the late eighties, became known as Thatcherism' (Brereton and Temple, 1999: 456). It was also the practical expression of what has sometimes been referred to as 'the new institutional economics';

an economics that sought to embed quasi-market incentive structures into public service provision (Rhodes, 1996: 655); structures that militated in favour of 'disaggregated bureaucracies, greater competition through contracting-out and quasi markets and consumer choice', with an increasing and inevitable shift to public service organisations being generally more contract-based (Deakin and Walsh, 1996: 36).

And if these developments made for greater choice and efficiency, they also made for a general downsizing of the public sector and thence, in theory, a diminution of public expenditure on service provision. As Bacon and Eltis had put it in *Britain's economic problem*, 1976, 'the most fundamental way of reducing the size of the non-market sector is to use the price mechanism to allocate resources which are now given away'; or, in the words of Geoffrey Howe, 'state ownership and control should be displaced or supplemented, wherever sensibly possible, by the discipline and pressure of the market place and by some degree of private ownership' (Bacon and Eltis, 1976: 79; Howe, 1982: 20). Discipline and choice were the mantra when the virtues of the market were discussed and trumpeted; something redolent of the kind of liberal authoritarianism that has been remarked on by other commentators as a distinguishing characteristic of the New Right project (Gamble, 1994).

In part marketisation would be effected through privatisation but other expedients were mooted and adopted. There was, for example, the proposed utilisation of quasi-markets in relation to Welfare State provision, particularly in the late 1980s and early 1990s;[13] markets which were to take a number of forms. Sometimes the idea was that the 'consumer power' of service users would be deployed by a single purchasing agency; sometimes it was to be distributed to users by way of vouchers and sometimes it was to take the form of non-profit and profit organisations competing for public contracts (Le Grand and Bartlett, 1993: 10). As one commentator saw it in 1993, 'soon the vast majority of civil service work will be carried out by semi-autonomous agencies working with business-like contractual frameworks, or by full private organisations' (O'Toole, 1993: 5).

In addition, market imperatives were applied by such means as the introduction of Compulsory Competitive Tendering for services previously provided in-house by local and central government; thereby, as one public choice theorist put it, 'providing the service at a price known to the representative of the average voter from a source that is not administratively dependent on the bureaucracy'[14] (Niskanen *et al.*, 1973: 54). As with quasi-markets this put constant and intensifying pressure on public sector managers to slim down bureaucracies and reduce labour costs in order to deliver value for money.

Also integral to the philosophy of marketisation was a change in attitude to the role and conduct of public service managers. Initially, this took the form of a generalised exhortation for them to emulate their private sector counterparts. And, indeed, a number of such counterparts were imported into the public sector; the expectation being that they would infuse the public organisations which they joined with a spirit of entrepreneurialism, a respect for efficiency and a concern for the bottom line (Brereton and Temple, 1999: 5). Such 'new wave' management, 'New Public Management' or 'New Managerialism' was most apparent in the 1980s and early 1990s and received a particularly powerful exposition in Peters and Waterman's *In Search of Excellence* (Peters and Waterman, 1987). Underpinning it was the belief that scientific and effective management was something that transcended the public/private sector divide and that 'an influx of managers from the private to the public sector, and greater interchange of staff between the sectors' (Boyne *et al.*, 1999: 407) was something that would be relatively unproblematic. In such a context it was almost inevitable that things like performance-related pay, tightening labour discipline, cutting labour costs, decentralised pay bargaining and many of the other appurtenances of flexible labour markets should have come to the fore. More generally, and consistently with this, the kind of developmental humanism that previously characterised the management of staff in public service employment was transmuted into something more nearly resembling utilitarian instrumentalism. In this regard, it has been suggested that these developments fundamentally altered the traditional public service ethos and values that had characterised public administration since the late nineteenth century, but a discussion of this is beyond the remit of this chapter (Bevir and Rhodes, 2003; Brereton and Temple, 1999).

## The political economy of New Labour

To what extent, then, has New Labour embraced the new philosophy and the new ethos of public service organisation and management, along with the more general ideological foundations that underpin it? To begin with, New Labour's position on public expenditure, prudent financial management and its rejection of the 'tax and spend' neo-Keynesianism attributed to Old Labour has militated in favour of a value-for-money emphasis and a predilection for market or quasi-market incentives and disciplines. This has been expressed and reinforced by an acceptance, and a continuation, of the privatisation process set in motion in the Thatcher years. And while there has been no explicit embrace of the Virginia School and public choice theory, the impact that such ideas have had on the conduct of public administration has not been challenged but rather, with certain refinements, was actually accommodated. It can also be argued that in its pre-1997, prawn cocktail offensive, and in its subsequent attitude to private enterprise and an enterprise culture (Thompson, 2002: 252–5), New Labour has, with certain provisos, bought into the dichotomy of wealth-creating and wealth-consuming activities – the former largely equated with the private and the latter with the public sector. In short, for both political and economic reasons, New Labour has been relatively at ease with many aspects of the ideological and institutional hollowing out of the State, and has even hollowed a little further.

It has also embraced the idea that the State in general, and public services where possible, should be in the business of ensuring the market's more effective operation. This was particularly so with the labour market and, in that regard, New Labour has been as critical of the emergence of a dependency culture as the New Right. Thus, government has been seen as having a responsibility to provide assistance in finding work, in skilling for employment and in structuring the tax and benefit system in such a way as to make work pay. Everything should be done to incentivise participation in the labour market and the labour market itself should be made flexible; a market free from restrictive practices, overweening trade union power and the kind of rigidifying labour market legislation that characterised increasingly sclerotic economies such as those of Germany and Japan. In this regard the minimum wage has had to be at a level, and kept at a level, that did not dissuade employers from taking on labour.

More positively in this regard, making the market work has also led to a particular emphasis on the State's responsibility for the provision of education and training (Blair, 1998: 10). A flexible labour force must be a skilled and polyvalent labour force. Education should, in part at least, be about enhancing job-related capacities and also about inculcating the values and attitudes of an enterprise culture. In this way, the State and public services could have a positive supply-side impact on the quality of what was, in the 1990s, increasingly seen as the crucial factor input – namely labour. For while finance was mobile, labour was less so. What differentiated successful from less successful economies was therefore the quality and flexibility of their labour forces.[15]

In general terms, New Labour has embraced the individualistic, entrepreneurial and consumerist ethos which informed the political economy of Thatcherism. Thus the role of the State has been to intensify competition, not soften its imperatives and the Victorian values of Samuel Smiles and Herbert Spencer were to be celebrated not eschewed. As Gordon Brown put it, competition 'forces producers to be efficient, extending the choices available to consumers and opening up the opportunity for the ambitious and risk takers. Instead of being suspicious of enterprise and entrepreneurs, we should celebrate an entrepreneurial culture, encouraging and rewarding the dynamic' (Brown, 2003: 271). And he has been clear too that this was the ethos which should infuse the public sector. Universities, for example, should operate in a context where they became 'in effect the seller, setting [their] own price for [their] service [with] the prospective buyer the graduate of higher education at the going rate' (*ibid.*: 266). Moreover he has argued for the need 'to look at services to consumers where traditionally

the public sector has been used and where markets are seen to have failed –
but where, in future, markets with their dynamism, capacity for innovation
and enhancement of choice, can better respond to new technology and
rising aspirations than a public sector context' (*ibid.*: 276). New Labour
might move to dismantle the internal market in the National Health
Service (NHS) but it has still been committed to an intensification of
private sector involvement in public services through the promotion of
Public Private Partnerships (PPPs) and Private Finance Initiatives (PFIs); and
this despite the concern of many commentators as to the long-terms costs
and implications of the latter. For as J.K. Galbraith wrote in 2004, 'as the
corporate interest moves to power in what was the public sector, it serves,
predictably, the corporate interest' (Galbraith, 2004: 58). And if New
Labour is still committed to 'fairness' it has to be efficient fairness, with the
latter becoming a means to an end and not, as with Keynesian social
democracy, an end in itself.

There are, therefore, significant similarities between the ideas of New
Labour and those of the New Right as to the role the public sector, and
those employed in it, should play, and how best they could play it. Of
course it is the case that in its reforms of the public services New Labour
has not embraced the Thatcherite legacy uncritically, but, as one commentator has put it, many believe 'that the new reforms are still couched in the
1980s ideological revival of *laissez-faire* economic thinking, which reflects a
lack of confidence in the ability of the State to solve economic problems
and, instead, proclaims the virtues of private ownership and market incentives as more cost-effective media of service delivery' (Grimshaw *et al.*,
2002: 476). And certainly New Labour has not retreated from the privatisation of direct service delivery, the embedding of market-based principles in
public management practice and the replacement of hierarchical command
structures by contractual relations, with all the market imperatives that
flow from these things. Thus in addition to the transfer of enterprises and
activities to the private sector, New Labour has also enthusiastically
pursued the idea of PPPs and the injection of private sector capital into the
public sector by way of PFIs. In part, these have been justified in terms of
curbing the growth of public expenditure and the financial expediency of
keeping certain items off the government's balance sheet, but clearly there
has also been an expectation that, where private meets public, the values of
the former will infuse the activities of the latter and the imperatives driving
private sector activity will be felt, and even embraced, by public sector
employees. Under New Labour the language of public service management
has remained that of efficiency, competition, value for money and entrepreneurialism; an entrepreneurialism that emphasises the importance of
making money as well as spending it (see *ibid.*: 478). It is also the case that
private sector activity is frequently taken as a benchmark of efficiency
against which the performance of public sector provision is assessed.

Yet if New Labour has used the language of competition and individual choice, it has also used the discourse of community and that certainly was a fundamental component of the Third Way which Giddens and other New Labour theorists articulated (Giddens, 1998; 2000). In that and other respects the Party has sought to put clear pink water between itself and the Thatcherite notion that there was no such thing as society. Such collectivist and communitarian rhetoric has informed its approach to social welfare. The language of rights and obligations to the community has been used to justify coercive pressures on individuals to re-enter the labour market but likewise to justify social investment in their employability. As Brown stated 'where there are barriers to the unemployed getting back to work, it is right to extend *both the opportunities and the compulsion of the New Deal*' (Brown, 2003: 274, my emphasis). One can also see the minimum wage as a collective limitation on the operation of the labour market; the legislative enforcement of society's view as to what constitutes a level of remuneration which will permit social inclusion. Further, New Labour must be credited with a programme of employment law reforms that have constrained the extent to which competition can drive down the terms and conditions of labour: a position that would be anathema to anyone subscribing to a Thatcherite agenda.

And as regards the philosophy of marketisation, what might also be averred is that New Labour has been less dogmatic about the virtues of market solutions and less festishistic about the qualities that markets and market competition possess. For example, in the provision of services the Labour Government replaced Compulsory Competitive Tendering (CCT) with Best Value; the latter necessitating neither privatisation nor competitive tendering but simply that public-sector organisations should not deliver services where more efficient deliverers were available. It is also the case that New Labour has instituted a wide range of benchmarks or tests of efficiency that have included, but also transcend, narrowly market criteria, though the use of Charter Marks which benchmarked service provision according to criteria such as access, choice and fair treatment, but were still very much customer oriented.

Also, in relation to this less rigid application of the principles of marketisation to the provision of public services, New Labour has developed the idea of networks, partnerships, cooperation and trust: seeing these as the accumulation of a kind of social capital which represents an investment as consequential as that in bricks, mortar and personnel. Within the NHS, for example, such mutually-supportive networks were seen as superseding the Conservative idea of an internal market and, more generally, New Labour has favoured partnerships between public service stakeholders rather than competitive contracts. As one commentator put it, the 'British government now works through networks characterised by trust and mutual adjustment to provide welfare services. The shifts from hierarchies to markets and then to networks involved changing the boundaries between the State and civil society' (Bevir and Rhodes, 2003: 43). Yet, it should be stressed that networks and partnerships have not necessarily superseded a reliance on market imperatives and have often worked in conjunction with them in the drive for allocative efficiency and improved productivity.

More generally one might argue too that, as regards public expenditure, New Labour has been willing to depart significantly from the Thatcherite agenda by 'promising better public service for the many not tax cuts for the few' (Fielding, 2003: 109). And substantial increases in public expenditure have indeed eventuated. Moreover, and with whatever stealth, there has, in marked contrast to the Thatcher years, been a measure of redistribution in favour of the poorer sections of society. This must be set too in the context of a rhetoric of social justice and social inclusion. Whether all this merits Gidden's categorisation of the New Labour project as 'modernised social democracy' is, of course, another matter, but it would seem to make an unqualified neoliberal categorisation untenable.

## Conclusion

Courtesy of free market economics, public choice theory, the Chicago School, the critics of welfare dependency and the work of those, such as Bacon and Eltis who have seen expenditure on public services crowding out the production of tradable goods, the last four decades have witnessed a kind of ideological hollowing out of the role of the State. *Pari passu* with this has gone the erosion and sometimes the demise of the principles and practices that traditionally underpinned public policy. Thus the State has been conceptualised as an economic burden, a sclerotic obstacle to enhanced performance, a source of waste and inefficiency, unresponsive to the needs of the population and hostile to the entrepreneurial spirit and the existence of an enterprise culture. In line with this critique, public sector employees have been seen as self-interested utility-maximisers more concerned with the size of their desks and empires than with the needs of those whom they putatively serve. It is in such a context that the philosophy of marketisation has emerged and triumphed and it is against this ideological backdrop that the treatment of public sector employees has evolved; evolved in ways which later chapters will analyse and discuss.

This, of course, raises the question as to why neoliberalism, even if transmogrified for New Labour purposes, continues to exert the kind of influence which it does; a question made all the more pertinent and acute by its frequent failure to deliver on its prescriptive agenda. Here one is tempted to say that, for some time, it has been the only show in town. While a residual Keynesianism can be detected in the present macro-economic management of the economy, and while there has been some redistributive progress, there has been no reconstitution of the Keynesian social democratic consensus to which the public sector was integral. More generally the Left lacks a coherent political economy on the basis of which any substantial ideological challenge to neoliberalism might be mounted (Thompson, 2002). And, related to this absence, the seeming triumph of the Anglo-American model of capitalism over its competitors has militated against this; a Left alternative which would re-position and re-imagine the public sector's role in a manner that would be prescriptively convincing and electorally successful. In short, the Anglo-American model itself has made for a barren soil in which to root such a social democratic political economy. In Gramscian terms a negative and critical view of public services and public expenditure remains the prevailing common sense, and the perceived fiscal threat they pose to that culture continues to be a compelling narrative for those who enjoy its perquisites.

## Notes

1. On this see, for example, Doig, 1995: 194. Such a bureaucratic ideal has sometimes been traced back to Confucius and Plato, see W. Niskanen *et al.*, 1973.
2. 'Quality of service has in many cases deteriorated, massive financial losses have been accumulated and morale has declined to dangerously low levels.'
3. Enoch Powell, Geoffery Rippon, Angus Maude, John Jewkes and, at a more profound philosophical level, Michael Oakeshott were among those few in the 1950s and early 1960s who sought to stem the tide and to reconstitute a free economy.
4. 'The economic model of behaviour is based on the motivational postulate of individual utility maximisation.'
5. Some traced the origins of this idea to Joseph Schumpeter who they saw as having begun the business of 'analys[ing] the political system as a market place in which entrepreneurs bid for the citizens vote instead of for the consumer's dollar', Brittain, 1973: 241. On this see also Tullock, 1976.
6. Keith Joseph had been Secretary of State for Social Services in the Heath Government 1970–4. However, under the influence of figures such as Arthur Seldon, Ralph Harris and Alfred Sherman he delivered a series of speeches in 1974–5 which attacked the Keynesian consensus, condemned the economic record of the Heath Government and his share of the responsibility for its failures, and embraced monetarism and liberal economics. He was one of the founders of the right-wing think-tank the Centre for Policy Studies in March 1974. On this see in particular Cockett, 1995: 236–42.
7. Olson, 1982, saw such sustained pressure from organised interests as resulting in an institutional sclerosis that militated against the kind of adaptivity needed for a strong economic performance.
8. On this see also Harris, 1980: 20 and more generally, Stigler, 1975.
9. For a fuller account of monetarism and its impact on public policy in Britain see Smith, 1987.
10. Thus in the period 1961–75 'employment by local authorities rose 70 per cent, and that of central government rose 27 per cent', Bacon and Eltis, 1976: 12.
11. Thus 'the non-market sector took 62 per cent of the marketed output in 1975 in place of 41.5 per cent in 1961', *ibid.*: 87.

12. In his autobiography, Nicholas Ridley provided an extreme but not untypical Conservative expression of this view when he wrote that Labour councillors would pay grants out of ratepayers' money to lesbian and gay groups and to many others such as ethnic minority groups, on the assumption that they too would become dependent and vote for the council, Ridley, 1991: 80.
13. For proposals for an NHS internal market see the White Paper, *Working for patients*, 1989.
14. Thus 'the White Paper *Competing for quality* introduced the concept of market testing as a means of exposing existing government programmes to direct competition', Deakin and Walsh, 1996: 34.
15. For the origin of such ideas see in particular Reich, 1993 and Pfeffer, 1994.

# 2
# Lisbon, Bolkestein and the Service Economy[1]

*John Grahl*

> Making Europe the best place in the world to do business in before this decade is out – the target our Heads of State and Government committed themselves to in Lisbon in 2000 – is one ambition we cannot afford to fail. It is the best – and probably only – guarantee for maintaining and improving our quality of life and social model, particularly against the background of an ageing population.
>
> This is a key message – I think we should admit it openly that has not yet hit home with our citizens, who still often regard 'competitiveness' and 'social protection' as two contradictory goals, whereas they are two sides of the same coin...
>
> Ladies and gentleman, as parents tell their children, you won't get any pudding if you don't eat your spinach.
>
> (Frits Bolkestein, 2003)

In Britain and other Member States, employment conditions in the private sector are constrained by the competition rules of the European Union (EU), because these rules prevent national governments from intervening to maintain employment or from using public funds to support wages and working conditions.

Until recently, however, the impact of these rules on public service workers has been much more limited, because national governments have been able to declare that certain activities, such as healthcare, (activities denoted, in EU jargon, as 'services of general interest') give rise to public benefits which justify the limitation or even the suppression of competition among suppliers.

Increasingly, however, the EU has tried to extend the scope of its competition rules to cover public services. The opportunity for this challenge arises out of the privatisation and outsourcing initiatives of the national governments themselves, because these policies either move whole sectors into the private sector or introduce private sector provision even though the service as such remains in the public sector (see Leys, 2001). In both cases the European Commission has tended to press for the application of its competition rules on the grounds that all market activities should be subject to Europe-wide competition and that suppliers from other Member States must be allowed to contest the markets of domestic suppliers.

The consequences for public service workers can be serious because competition among supplier firms implies, at least indirectly, competition among their work forces. Especially when firms in low-wage countries, or firms with access to unorganised labour, are allowed to compete in this way to carry out public service activities, the position of public service workers may be completely undermined.

Recently, however, there has been a drastic increase in the pressure from the EU to intensify competition in the provision of both public and private services. The European Commission's proposed Directive on Services in the Internal Market (Bolkestein Directive) was an astonishing attack on the social models of the Member States in general and on the rights of workers in particular. Although some of its teeth have now been drawn by the European Parliament (after a massive and almost universal campaign against it) the Directive is still a threat to the effective regulation of market economies. The Commission's advance of this extreme proposal, together with the fate of the draft Constitutional Treaty, testifies to what has become an unbridgeable gap between the ideology of official Europe and the perceptions of European citizens. Without a change of course by EU leaders, there must now be a real danger that the integration achieved over the last six decades will start to be eroded.

The present chapter discusses first the Lisbon strategy in the context of which the Bolkestein proposals were developed; it then examines these proposals and their implications; it suggests that the economic integration so far achieved in the EU may be put in danger unless a genuine turn towards social Europe takes place; and finally it looks briefly at the consequences for public sector employees in Britain.

## Lisbon

The Lisbon strategy, the project for a decade of rapid growth of the EU economies adopted by the European Council in 2000, has already been the target of more than enough irony. The laudable objective of full employment was to be achieved by a swift transition to a knowledge-based economy, which would make full use of the possibilities being opened up by new technologies. This transition in turn depended on market-oriented reforms, which would both sweep away obstacles to full economic integration in the EU and provide the flexibility required for a more dynamic and innovative economic system.

The economic expansion envisaged in Lisbon did not have a macro-economic dimension – there would be no attempt to increase aggregate demand to release the potential supplies identified by the strategy. On the contrary, the restrictive macroeconomic regime – with the Stability Pact limiting public sector deficits and the European Central Bank setting monetary policy with the overriding priority of price stability – was said to provide the necessary framework for adaptation at the microeconomic level.

The Lisbon strategy did nothing to correct the long-standing bias of European integration towards market-creating rather than market-correcting policies. The central measures of the strategy – for market-led integration in service activities and, especially, in finance – were accompanied by considerable reference to the 'European Social Model' (ESM) but not by any concrete initiatives in the field of social policy. The best way to defend the Social Model was, it was claimed, to generate high levels of output and employment and the best way to do that was, in turn, to promote flexible markets. The theme of 'financing the European Social Model' was given a certain prominence – this actually referred to the reduction of public sector pension liabilities – sometimes by methods that might seem opposed to the values of the ESM.

## Services

The growing importance of services in economic life results directly from their growing weight in output and employment. Services raise particular difficulties for the project of international trade liberalisation because often they cannot be delivered from a distance but require the presence of the service supplier in the country which makes use of them. Thus it is not usually possible to separate trade issues from issues of international investment and the international movement of labour.

A closely related difficulty is that many service activities are subject to regulation and other forms of social control. The production of a material good, at least by modern mechanical methods, can be separated from the conditions under which the good is used; this can be more difficult with a service which is often produced and consumed at the same time. Thus, while the international movement of material goods may be subject to control at frontiers themselves but otherwise be largely unregulated, the movement of services raises policy issues within importing countries and not just at their frontiers.

Public services raise further difficulties for the liberalisation agenda. Services have a public dimension when they are seen as involving public goods. In economic theory a public good is one for which there are beneficiaries who do not pay on the market. For example, inoculation against a contagious disease makes the recipient safer and this benefit can be priced as a private good. At the same time, however, it makes everyone else safer because they will not be infected by the recipient and this benefit is a public good for which it is impossible to charge a market price.

This text-book example may suggest that one can decide on the public nature of a good or service in an objective way. This is not the case, because such a decision depends on the concept one holds of individual and social welfare. For example, if a group of people are relatively indifferent to the quality of their physical environment, they will not recognise public goods which are readily identified by a group of people who are more sensitive to such issues. The same applies to the much more complex issues of the urban and social environments. To what extent is poverty a social as well as an individual misfortune? The question will be answered differently in Europe and in the US, in Ireland and in Denmark. Public goods are socially constructed.

Likewise, they may be socially deconstructed. It is a key part of the neoliberal project to deny or diminish the public character of those service activities which it seeks to privatise, liberalise and deregulate. At the same time, the notion of public goods (and by extension and generalisation, of *the* public good) is perhaps the weakest point in neoliberalism since this notion establishes clear limits to the role of markets.

## Services in world trade

Along with the closely related issue of international investment the liberalisation of service activities, often seen as necessitating their deregulation or privatisation, has been a key theme of the Northern countries within the World Trade Organisation (WTO) and the Doha Round of trade negotiations which the WTO is currently trying to conclude. Major concessions were made by developing countries during the 1990s, in the form of the General Agreement on Trade in Services (GATS) which often had the most severe consequences for their populations. Public goods have a particular role in low-income countries as they are often the only possible form of social policy: a government may be quite unable to indemnify the urban poor against unemployment; it might nevertheless attempt to provide them with clean water.

Western corporations, using the GATS and supported by both their own national governments and international institutions, have obtained lucrative contracts for the supply of previously public services, in a situation highly exposed to corruption. The countries which have seen their public services penetrated in this way have often suffered declines in service quality at the same time as higher charges are imposed on low-income groups (Wesselius, 2002).

The EU has tended to make common cause with the US on the issue of service liberalisation – in effect giving priority to contract-hungry European corporations rather than to the needs of the developing countries. As will be seen, the same interests were closely linked to the attempt at a radical deregulation of service activities within Europe itself: the Bolkestein

Directive, in fact, was supported only by big business and retail and whole-sale distribution – every other interest group and lobby, from small business through the cooperative sector to the unions rejected it.[2]

## Services in Europe

The Lisbon strategy drew on a specific type of diagnosis of the economic problems of Germany, which sees its relatively small service sector as a structural weakness. There is some danger of exaggeration in such a view: because German industrial companies make less use of outsourcing, activities are subsumed under manufacturing which would be treated as business services in Britain or the US; Germany's consumption of services is much higher than its production because of very high tourist expenditures, covered by industrial exports; lags in the development of service activities, to the extent that they exist, may relate as much to a relatively slow feminisation of the workforce as to the much discussed rigidities and regulations.

Fascination with the perceived 'new economy' of the US distorted the thinking behind the Lisbon strategy. For example, it was thought that Europe, by imitating the American system of financial markets, could rapidly obtain more dynamic and innovative investment. An overestimation of the potential of service activities was part of the same mindset. It was thought that structural change in the US, supported by new technologies, was generating massive productivity gains which could only be reproduced in Europe through a vast programme of deregulation to remove obstacles to structural change.

In retrospect, the view of productivity taken at Lisbon seems close to a moral panic. There are massive measurement problems with the productivity data. It cannot be denied that the sectors producing Information and Communication Technology (ICT) are registering big productivity gains, especially when one allows for quality improvements in computers. But these gains, in the Electronic Equipment and Office Equipment sectors, are found in all advanced economies. Outside these two sectors, there is little sign of the fabulous gains anticipated at Lisbon – only retail distribution, in the US, has been making exceptional advances in productivity and this is on the basis of huge megastores which would be neither feasible nor desirable to replicate in the EU (Gordon, 2005).[3]

In this and other respects, the thinking of Lisbon can be seen as subject to the same 'irrational exuberance' which, according to the then Chair of the Federal Reserve Alan Greenspan, had seized stock market investors at the same time.[4] A drive for further integration of the service sectors would have been at any time the kind of policy initiative one would expect from the Commission. The extreme and reckless form which the actual initiative took, however, may owe a great deal to the spirit of Lisbon.

## The Services Report

It is important to note that the Bolkestein Directive was produced by the Directorate-General for the internal market (of which Frits Bolkestein was Commissioner between 1999 and 2004). The issues concerned the functioning of markets which have already been fully liberalised in principle; they are therefore EU issues to be determined by qualified majority vote in the Council and with full co-decision powers for the European Parliament. However, the actual draft Directive made such vast incursions into Member State autonomy that it might well have been challenged on these grounds, had the Parliament not drastically reduced its scope and impact.

The specific character of Frits Bolkestein, a convinced Neoliberal, may also have influenced the course of events. He is an economic liberal of very long-standing, having represented the *Volkspartij voor Vrijheid en Demmocratic* (VVD) in the Dutch Parliament for some 20 years. He takes a robust view of the need for market-oriented reforms in the European economy. For example, he takes a clear position on the European variant of capitalism:

> [the trade unions] cling to traditional rights as though these were valid for ever, regardless of economic conditions. They want to remain within the comfortable and secure boundaries of what has been referred to as the Rhenish model of capitalism, where stakeholders are pampered instead of shareholders, and where consultations take place on numerous round tables. However, if Europe really wants to become the most competitive and most modern economic area, it must leave the comfortable setting of the Rhenish model and subject itself to the harsher conditions of the Anglo-Saxon form of capitalism, where the rewards, but also the risks, are higher.
>
> (Bolkestein, 2002a, cited by Callaghan and Höpner, 2005)

And likewise, he is very clear about the European Social Model:

> The Netherlands in company with other Member States, such as Germany, are finding out the hard way what it means to lose one's competitive edge in today's global economy. Painful measures can no longer be postponed. Belts need to be tightened. Social protection systems are turned again into safety nets where in some cases they had become hammocks.
>
> (Bolkestein, 2003)

Most of this is quite dubious, especially the reference to the supposed 'loss of competitiveness' by Germany, which had in 2005 a current account surplus equal to 4.1 per cent of its GDP, but the standard diagnosis is put forward with considerable force just because there is a complete disregard of qualifications and opposing arguments.[5] In any case, the European Commission (2002), in pursuit of the Lisbon objective of service sector liberalisation, produced a report on the 'State of the Internal Market for Services'. Although the Commission shares the Neoliberal *Zeitgeist* of most ruling groups in Europe, it is often more royalist than the king. Most proponents of the market economy recognise that many conceivable markets do not exist because there is little or no need for them. To the Commission on the other hand, the absence of any Europe-wide market is usually taken as a highly damaging consequence of non-tariff barriers.

So it was with the Report's identification of barriers to the cross-border movement of services. These relate to the fact that it is often necessary to have a presence in the importing country in order to deliver a service there. Thus service suppliers might need to establish themselves in that country, obtain inputs there, carry out marketing, distribute and sell the service concerned, and perhaps provide further services after sale. Each step could involve difficulties. Not all such difficulties relate to regulation of the activities concerned – some are the simple consequence of language and cultural differences, but the emphasis of the Commission report was very definitely on regulation and its supposed costs.

Bolkestein himself offers a characteristically robust diagnosis:

> The reason for the segmentation of the markets for services is simple. It is bureaucratic obstacles of a protectionist nature (Bolkestein, 2005).

This seems to be a wild assertion, even for someone who has never shown much fear of simplifications. Governments and other authorities regulate service activities for many reasons: public health, protection of the natural and urban environment, promotion of cultural policies, consumer and investor protection, health and safety of workers, promotion of better working conditions, efficient collection of taxes and public charges, suppression of fraud and other forms of criminality, and the defence and the finance of public goods of all kinds.

Of course, some regulation is essentially protectionist – but as such it is already contrary to EU law (Dräger and Wagenknecht, 2005) and would seem to require detailed identification followed by challenge in the courts rather than the blanket attempt at legislative suppression which in fact followed.[6] There are combined cases – where a regulation or procedure which is certainly justified on other grounds is operated in a protectionist or discriminatory way, but these cases again are exposed to legal challenge.

## The bonfire of controls[7]

On the basis of the report on barriers to trade in services, Bolkestein's Directorate-General for the Internal Market prepared a draft Directive on

Services in the Internal Market (European Commission, 2004). This had two outstanding features. Firstly, it sought to apply the principle of home country control to all transactions in services.[8] That is, service providers operating in another Member State would not be subject to regulation, of any kind, by that State, but would remain under the exclusive supervision only of their home country.[9] Now, since the 1980s, home country control has been successfully used to facilitate trade in goods. The notion is that a product which is regarded as safe in its country of manufacture is regarded as safe in all other Member States. But note that this use of home control reinforces, rather than subverts, the regulatory regime of the country in which production takes place – because it ensures that a country's manufacturing regulations apply to all output on the national territory, including that destined for export. Note also that in the case of trade in material goods, this mutual recognition of safety regulations was preceded by a phase of 'approximation' where regulatory requirements of each Member State were brought into broad equivalence. This approximation secured substantial equality in regulatory standards without the need for uniformity of procedures and also worked to avoid competition among regimes.

The same principle of home country control had also been applied to certain service activities, notably banking. However, this also was preceded by careful approximation of regulatory standards and, in the case of banking, was subject to important exceptions: it was recognised that the central bank of the host country would need to impose controls on foreign banks in order to operate monetary policy.

The allocation of exclusive regulatory power to the 'country of origin' in the Bolkestein Directive did not meet either of these conditions. The actual service provision activity would usually take place, in whole or in part, in the host country but would somehow be regulated, at a distance, by the home country. It was never made clear, in any of the discussions, how this could work – except by miracles of administrative 'cooperation' by the governments of the Member States concerned. Nor was there to be any attempt at approximation of regulatory standards – rather, mutual recognition of regulatory regimes was to be, as far as possible, 'automatic.'

The legal chaos threatened by this approach to integration deprived the proposal of support from jurists. In essence the rules applicable to a service activity would become not only arbitrary – any one of 25 regimes might apply depending on the origin of the provider – but also potentially compound – if a dentist and an anaesthetist came from two different Member States, the service activity they provided together might be governed by two different regulatory systems, both of them external to the country where the service was being provided, that is, that of the patient.

Secondly, and in order to consolidate the regulatory disarmament of service-importing countries, the draft directive specifically outlawed a whole range of regulatory procedures. According to Article 16 host governments would not be allowed to:

- oblige a service provider to be established on their territory
- require a service provider 'to make a declaration or notification to, or to obtain an authorisation from, their competent authorities, including entry in a register or registration with a professional body or association in their territory'
- require the service provider to have either an address or a representative in the host country
- oblige the provider to comply with national requirements for service providers
- restrict the use of self-employed workers by a service provider
- require the service provider to possess an identity document issued by host authorities.

It can be seen that supervision of service providers by host country authorities would be made objectively impossible by such restrictions. Further, Section 2 of the draft imposed drastic limits on the supervision of service activities in general, *whether the provider was domestic or external*. It did permit authorisation procedures for services where there was an 'overriding' reason of public interest, but even these exceptional procedures prevented host authorities from using many measures. For example, they were not permitted to:

- require a service provider to be resident on their territory
- make service provision subject to a demonstration of economic need
- require a financial guarantee
- require registration for a period of time prior to service provision
- restrict the freedom of a service provider to choose between presence as branch, subsidiary or agency.

In addition, a large number of administrative requirements would be made subject to strict limitations – that is, they would be permitted only if they could be shown to be non-discriminatory, justified by an 'overriding' public interest and 'proportional' (that is, not more stringent than was required to meet their objective). The requirements so limited included:

- the imposition of territorial or quantitative limits on service providers (such as a minimum distance between them)
- restrictions on the legal form of a service provider (for example, require the provider to be non-profit-making, or a limited company)
- requiring minimum capital to be held by the provider, or require the management of a service provider to have specific qualifications

- requiring minimum or maximum prices for the service
- requiring a service provider to offer specific other services with the service concerned
- require a certain number of workers to be employed
- restrict specific providers for any other reason than lack of professional qualifications

Further, no new restrictions of such a nature were to be introduced without the Commission being informed and given reasons for their introduction. The Commission would then have the power to strike down such rules or regulations.

The cumulative effect of these proposed restrictions would be to render it extremely difficult and often impossible for governments or other authorities to control service activities. They would, in fact, find it difficult even to inform themselves about what service activities were taking place on their territory without breaking these rules. At the same time, the only authorities left with any regulatory powers, those of the state of origin, were enjoined to exercise extra-territorial supervision in the host country. Article 34 ran:

**Effectiveness of supervision**
1. Member States shall ensure that the powers of monitoring and supervision provided for in national law in respect of the provider and the activities concerned are also exercised where a service is provided in another Member State.
2. Member States shall ensure that providers supply their competent authorities with all the information necessary for monitoring their activities.

It was not made clear how Member State governments could carry out such monitoring in other countries (potentially, 24 other countries) or how they could effectively obtain such information on the external activities of their own service providers. They could hardly obtain the information from the host country authorities because the latter were expressly forbidden to obtain it by the same directive.

This astonishing concept represents the *reductio ad absurdum* of Neoliberal Europe. In order to bring about market integration of very dubious value it would subvert the entire regulatory structure of every Member State and replace these relatively coherent structures, rooted in specific social histories, with the most complete anarchy.

The immediate and massive opposition to Bolkestein certainly contributed to the climate in which the EU suffered a drastic loss of legitimacy, demonstrated by the rejection, in France and the Netherlands, of the Constitutional Treaty.

## Healthcare, posted workers, services of general interest

To illustrate the intended content of the Bolkestein Directive three specific aspects can be dealt with in a little more detail.

Healthcare provision was, from the start, a key target of the Bolkestein initiative. The context was established by Member State policies opening up public sector systems to private provision. This in itself is a highly questionable move, driven by the lobbying power of contract-hungry corporations rather than by the preferences of patients or by any real efficiency gain (see Leys, 2001).

The Bolkestein proposal saw here an opportunity to promote a Europe-wide healthcare market. For non-hospital care it would permit patients to shop for services throughout the EU. Their home governments would pick up the bill – any service available to patients at home could be purchased elsewhere in the EU. The standard Bolkestein device was used to reinforce this patient's right to roam. Member States could not make their assumption of the costs involved 'subject to the granting of an authorisation'; they would simply have to pay up. For hospital care, the draft was a little more circumspect – costs of treatment in another Member State would only have to be covered if it were not readily available at home. Without this condition governments might have faced massive bills for treatment in countries with better standards of comfort or higher levels of public provision.

In any case, the open market in healthcare services aimed at by Bolkestein would obviously generate considerable costs for public systems, and the most likely response of governments would be to transfer more of the responsibility for costs onto individual patients: liberalisation would drive forward privatisation. Given his preference for safety nets over 'hammocks', the Commissioner himself would probably have welcomed such an outcome.[10]

Late in the day, when the scale of resistance to his directive was quite apparent, Bolkestein denied that it had any implications for employment rights:

'Let me now say where the proposed directive does **not** apply.

1) It does not apply to black labour (sic), which is a matter for national administrations to address;
2) It does not apply to employees. Polish workers who cross the German border to work in a German slaughter-house fall within the Collective Bargaining Agreement that applies to their employer. They do not perform a service. Wherever there is a sub-ordination there can be no service.
3) According to the Posted Workers Directive of 1995, workers who are posted to an establishment in another Member State must follow the employment conditions of the host country.'

(Bolkestein, 2005)

In this account, the directive only concerned the liberal professions and self-employed craftworkers; a minor measure really, hardly worth all the fuss.

However, it is clear that the draft directive did have very serious implications for employment rights and that these were intentional. The situation for a worker who takes up indefinite employment in another Member State is clear; the employment relationship is governed by the employment rules of the host country and the worker receives the full social security rights of the host country. This approach was firmly established at a time when the European social models were perceived as the political basis for the market economy, not as hindrances to it; failure to give full national treatment to migrant workers was seen at that time as a barrier to integration.

At an advanced stage of integration, however, increasing difficulties resulted from temporary movements of workers, often linked to the provision of services. These 'posted' workers might have employment contracts in their countries of origin (or in third countries) but they spent short periods of time in another Member State. A notorious example of these problems arose from the presence of British construction workers in Germany in the first half of the 1990s, during the reconstruction boom in the Eastern Länder. Supplied by Dutch intermediaries, these workers broke every rule of the German employment regime, from limitations on hours of work, through health and safety regulations to basic compliance with the tax laws.

The 'Posted Workers' Directive of 1996 attempted to bring some order to this chaotic situation (Cremers and Donders, 2004). It specified that workers temporarily active in another Member State (usually in order to provide some service) would be covered by a core of basic employment rights laid down by the host country, even though this might fall well short of full 'national treatment.' Thus the host country's maximum working periods, minimum rest periods, minimum rates of pay, health and safety rules, and equal opportunities rules would all apply, even though, for example, such workers would not be integrated into the host country pension system. The directive was not a full solution to the problem; it was affected by the recent tendency to minimalism in EU employment legislation (Grahl, 2006) and left an enormous amount of discretion to Member States (including the definition of 'posting' and 'worker').

However, even this very limited constraint on the employment of workers in other countries was seen as a barrier in the Bolkestein proposal. The draft recognised, in Article 24, that the host country authorities would have to be responsible for ensuring that the posted worker was actually accorded national treatment. In the same Article, however, it proceeded to tie the hands of these authorities by forbidding them:

- to require posted workers to be authorised or registered
- to require their employer to have a representative in the country

- to require either employer or employee to hold or keep employment documents in the country

Effective enforcement of employment law could not possibly be secured under these conditions. Once again, the 'cooperation' of the country of origin is invoked. If the host country authorities, for example, wish to know such details as the identity of the posted worker, the period over which he or she was on host territory, or the employment conditions which were obtained, then the country-of-origin authorities must provide this data – 'within two years of the end of the posting'. Rapidly shifting temporary employment markets cannot be regulated with a two year delay.

Even apart from the problem of enforcement it was the view of the jurist Niklas Bruun (2004) that the Bolkestein draft completely changed the meaning of the Posted Workers Directive, the provisions of which would cease to represent minimum employment standards for these workers and be turned into maximum standards.

The provision mentioned above, that host governments could not object to service workers having self-employed status is also very relevant in this context. The Bolkestein Directive, by ruling out this type of control while obstructing effective supervision of posted workers was in fact encouraging pseudo-self-employment with all its corrosive effects on labour standards.

As a third illustration of the scope of Bolkestein, there is the issue of services of general interest, which is the term often used in the EU to refer to various forms of public good. There is an abstract but extremely important debate around this issue in the EU, because, as was suggested above, the recognition of public goods sets limits to the role of markets and, of course, the EU leadership is committed to a market-led integration strategy. The position taken by the European Commission (2004a) in its recent White Paper on the issue was to emphasise the distinction between a public service *mission*, which Member States retained the right to define and the process of service *provision*, where there would be an attempt to apply EU competition rules.

The Bolkestein draft was extremely ambitious in the same direction, since it was to apply to all services of general *economic* interest and implied a definition of the latter which included all public services where the service was paid for, even if, as in the case of healthcare discussed above, it was the authorities and not the recipient who paid for the service. It was not intended to apply the principle of home country control in these cases, but access for providers from other Member States was to be guaranteed.

Bolkestein himself asserted that the introduction of market-based provision could only improve the quality of public services and make them more efficient, but he did not want to consider the full range of evidence arising from such reforms. Reference to the railways in Britain, or to electricity supply in California, was, he insisted, 'pure demagoguery.' It is not clear, however, why these negative examples of deregulation of public services were not relevant to the Service Directive.

## Amendments proposed by the European Parliament

The European Parliament (EP) considered the draft directive in detail in the autumn of 2005 and voted on it in February of 2006. By this time, the Constitutional Treaty had fallen victim to the massive loss of legitimacy of the European project even in countries, such as France and the Netherlands, where the traditional view had been very much in favour. By this time, also, the negative verdict on Bolkestein of all organisations except those of big business had become extremely clear. Even with its current conservative majority there could be no question of the Parliament simply endorsing Bolkestein.

There is no doubt that the amendments passed by the European Parliament (2006) would significantly dilute the directive and reduce its impact on the regulation of service provision. The impact of Bolkestein's proposals is reduced firstly by the exclusion of a wide range of services from the directive: healthcare is removed,[11] as are some social services and several others. Secondly, the EP states that the established legal position in several fields must not be changed by the directive. This is, in particular, the case for both labour law and social security so that the original provisions of the Posted Worker Directive, as establishing minimum conditions, remain in force. Similarly, it is made clear that regulations designed to ensure cultural pluralism are unaffected by the services directive. Throughout the amended document, it is insisted that there are many reasons which will justify regulation of service activities, including regulation by the obligatory registration and authorisation of providers. For example, it is stated that:

> The notion [of 'overriding public interest'] covers at least the following grounds: public policy, public security and public health within the meaning of Articles 46 and 55 of the Treaty, the maintenance of order in society, social policy objectives, the protection of the recipients of services, including patient safety, consumer protection, the protection of workers, including the social protection of workers, preservation of the financial balance of the social security system, maintaining a balanced medical and hospital service open to all, the prevention of fraud, cohesion of the tax system, prevention of unfair competition, maintaining the good reputation of the national financial sector, the protection of the environment and the urban environment, including town and country planning, the protection of creditors, safeguarding the sound administration of justice, road safety, the protection of intellectual property, cultural policy objectives, including safeguarding in the audio-

visual sector the freedom of expression of various elements, in particular social, cultural, religious and philosophical, in society, the maintenance of press diversity and policy for the promotion of the national language, the preservation of national historical and artistic heritage and veterinary policy (European Parliament, 2006: 26).

However, Dräger (2006a) warns that not all the teeth of the Bolkestein Directive have been drawn. Although the general requirement for regulation of service providers by their 'country of origin' is removed, there is no clear assertion that regulation will be by the host country; rather there is asserted a general 'freedom to provide services.' And the relevant Article 16 is little changed. It still contains a list of requirements and procedures which the service-receiving country *must not impose*. These still include: a requirement not to use self-employed workers, a requirement to be legally established in the host territory, a requirement to be registered, a ban on the setting-up of offices or other infrastructures by non-established providers, and the requirement of specific identity documents for service providers. And it should be noted that, for the purposes of this key Article 16, the grounds for exceptional requirements do not correspond to the long list above. They include 'public policy or public security or the protection of the health and the environment' but exclude consumer protection and employment regulation. This was insisted on by the conservatives (European Peoples' Party) in their negotiations with the social-democrats.

Although the EP has sought to exclude the purely fictitious establishment of service providers in the country of their choice (establishment by letter-box only), it reasserts a general freedom to 'establish' in all Member States which is bound to encourage tax- and regulatory-avoidance and hence regime competition. And although the Parliament asserts in principle that labour law is not to be affected by the directive, both laxity towards self-employment and barriers to registration of service providers will make the enforcement of labour law more difficult.

Nor is the draft directive as amended by Parliament the last word. There must still take place an attempt to get agreement between parliament and the council of ministers, with the latter heavily influenced by the Commission. Bolkestein's successor as Commissioner for the internal market, Eddy McCreevy, has already laid down some markers. There will be an attempt to widen again the scope of the directive by including some of the sectors excluded by the EP. And further measures are to be proposed to counteract the EP's position on posted workers (a new directive to prevent the provisions for posted workers becoming obstacles to trade in services) and on healthcare (a new directive on patient mobility) (all details from Dräger, 2006a).

It would be complacent, therefore, to think that the EP has blocked the Bolkestein initiative. The attempt to drive through a widespread deregulation of economic and social life on the basis of free competition in service sectors is still a central component of the current strategy of EU leaderships.

## The meaning of Bolkestein

Neoliberal principles, as such, have little appeal to the populations of the EU. As Frits Bolkestein himself admits, this 'key message' has not 'yet hit home with our citizens.' As a surrogate for a radically deregulated, privatised and liberalised economy, these citizens are therefore offered a utopia of services, the 'knowledge-based' economy, where abundance flows from the integration of technically dynamic service sectors across the EU. It is simply the case that the reforms necessary for this integration coincide with the radical deregulation of economic life.

The notion of a service-based, 'post-industrial', economic system may itself be greatly exaggerated, or even misconceived (for a critique, see Wilensky, 2003). It may be more logical to interpret many current developments in the productive system as a transformation of the industrial system rather than its displacement (Veltz, 2000).

On the other hand, the vision put forward by EU leaderships today, although completely unrealistic in some respects (such as the drive to overtake the US by 2010) is in other respects very impoverished. The Lisbon agenda comes close to a slavish imitation of the current US economic model, and this markedly narrows the possibility for new forms of service and of service employment. In practice, emphasis falls either on cheap consumer services, notably in the retail sector, based on low wages and employment deregulation (the Walmart/McDonalds service economy which is seen as the solution to Germany's unemployment) or on business-related services, driven forward by outsourcing, which may sometimes offer better employment conditions but adds little to individual or social well-being (for the standard view, see OECD, 2000).

A whole world of possible services is neglected in this market-centred vision (Dräger, 2006) – environmental services, services aimed at healthier lifestyles and better provision for the young and the old – which would contribute as much to employment and much more to well-being than the current business-led model of the service economy. The experience of the Nordic economies in developing comprehensive childcare services is of great significance here, an experience deliberately unrecognised by most EU leaders.

Unlike the tawdry vision of Lisbon, however, these possibilities depend on the reinforcement and extension of the European social models, not on their subversion in the drive towards an illusion of business supremacy.

## Conclusion: Bolkestein and public service workers

If the Bolkestein Directive had been adopted in anything like its original form, the consequences for public service workers in Britain (and throughout the EU) might have been serious. Essentially, any public service activity with a market aspect would have been open to competition from all Member States (a 'market aspect' here means *either* that the public were charged fees for the service *or* that the delivery of the service was, in part or in whole, outsourced to private companies). The competitive challenge could take several forms: foreign enterprises operating on British territory, perhaps using 'posted labour' which would have been exempt from domestic labour law or transferring some part of the service preparation process back to their home country or elsewhere; the attraction of British consumers into other member countries by the offer of cheaper or less regulated service provision; the supply of services at a distance where this was feasible, *via* telephone or the internet (this could be the case for many types of advice, including the kinds of medical or legal advice which are often supplied as public services). In particular, the original draft directive explicitly targeted the healthcare sector and aimed to open up a market in these services by all three routes.

It would have been difficult or impossible to regulate these new competitor firms, even when they operated in the first way, that is, in Britain itself, because of all the restrictions and prohibitions on the procedures needed for effective regulation – registration, licensing, supervision through named representatives on British territory, obligation to have a British office and so on. Since all of these were to be regarded, in Frits Bolkestein's own words, as bureaucratic protectionism, it would have been very difficult to enforce even those regulations which were in principle compatible with the EU's competition regime. In particular, effective labour market and employment regulation would have been obstructed, perhaps in practice eliminated, by delays: the British authorities would not have been informed about the presence of foreign workers until long after these workers had left Britain.

There can be little doubt that this undermining of regulatory standards was a deliberate feature of the legislation – many big corporations, those governments most committed to Neoliberal strategies and key elements in the Commission are all in favour of a drastic reduction in regulation, including the reduction which will often follow the partial or total privatisation of public services. (In addition, the governments of many new Member States, where incomes are well below EU averages, hoped to penetrate western service markets on the basis of deregulation).

Of course, this competition among service-providing enterprises would have implied competition among their workforces because lower wages and less favourable working conditions would be a key source of competitive advantage in many service sectors. And even when service consumers themselves would not have chosen the externally provided service, they may have had no choice but to accept it because purchasing decisions are often taken not by the consumers but by officials obsessed with cost reductions.

Such would have been the dangers of the directive as originally drafted. The version as amended by the EP is much less of a threat to workers in general and to public service workers in particular. Firstly, it is currently stated that the directive must not change labour law. Thus all employment and labour market regulations valid before the directive remain so; it is especially important that the rules governing 'posted workers' are unchanged.

Secondly, the Parliament's amendments remove some public service sectors from the scope of the directive. These explicitly include healthcare and the situation now seems to be that it is essentially the public utilities such as gas and electricity which remain exposed to the effects of the directive (but not public transport because separate legislation already exists in this case). Of course, most of these utilities have been privatised in Britain. Thirdly, the directive as amended no longer includes a commitment to regulation by a company's country of origin; thus the domestic regulation of service provision in the home country of service consumers is no longer automatically undermined.

But dangers remain for service regulation and for public service workers. Firstly, the directive as amended by the EP will not be the last word. The Commission will try to strengthen the directive as it prepares a new draft. And there will be further legislation – in particular, the Commission may try to weaken the Posted Workers Directive, which it now sees as giving too much protection to national labour market regimes. Secondly, although the EP's version of Bolkestein cannot affect the status of employees, this is not the case for independent workers. Thus service workers in Britain might be subject to competition from enterprises using self-employed or apparently self-employed workers and claiming exemption from British regulations on the basis of Bolkestein. Thirdly, although the EP's version no longer refers to regulation by the country of origin of a service provider, it by no means reinstates the principle of regulation by the country of destination (that is, the home country of the service user). Rather, it promulgates a general 'freedom to supply services' which seems to make all regulatory measures valid only if they do not limit this freedom, that is if they are compatible with freedom of entry and full competition. Doubtless, it will require much litigation to determine the concrete effect of this general right of service provision.

Finally, the EP left almost unchanged the Bolkestein restrictions on specific requirements such as registration, licensing, obligation to have an address in the country of destination and so on. It follows that, although in many sectors it will be impossible for foreign public service providers to compete with domestic ones, where it does prove to be possible, it will be difficult and costly for the British authorities to regulate these competing enterprises. And although there is now no question that those employees of these competitors who are actually present in Britain would be subject to

British law, these restrictions on 'bureaucracy' might well make it harder to enforce the law or to detect infringements.

Thus many dangers remain for public service workers – both in the specific piece of legislation examined here and in the general policy orientation of EU leaderships. The most vigilant scrutiny of forthcoming EU initiatives will be necessary. Even more important will be the reassertion, against the market fundamentalism of the European Commission and against the corporate interests which this fundamentalism serves, of the public interest, of public goods new and old and of the public sphere as such.

## Notes

1. My thanks to Klaus Dräger for his advice, for information on the Bolkestein Directive and for help with documentation. He is not responsible for the views expressed.
2. It is pointed out by Skarpelis-Sperk (2006) that the draft, Bolkestein Directive on services in some places repeats the language of the GATS agreement. She suggests that one aim of the draft was to concentrate competence for European/WTO negotiations on services on the Commission and to minimise the need to consult Member States on service sector concessions.
3. The comparison over time of economic aggregates such as GDP is relatively unproblematic provided one of two conditions holds: the pattern of goods and services is stable or the pattern of relative prices of goods and services is stable. The advent of ICT breaks both conditions simultaneously: there is a huge expansion in the output of computers and related products at the same time as they become very much cheaper. The only unambiguous way to record this outcome is to divide the economy into two sectors and give output data for both. (A similar problem arose when British oil production grew very rapidly at the same time as the price of oil exploded.)
4. This was in fact acknowledged by the High-Level Group which, at the Commission's behest, examined the Lisbon strategy five years later. They wrote: 'The Lisbon strategy is sometimes criticised for being a creature of the heady optimism of the late 1990s about the then trendy knowledge economy, neglecting the importance of the traditional industrial strengths of the European economy...this is a fair criticism' (Kok, 2004, p. 9 with the omission of a quite unnecessary qualifying clause).
5. Bolkestein's prescient warning against the US intervention in Iraq provides argumentation of a much higher level (Bolkestein, 2002).
6. There is in fact a good Neoliberal argument for an approach based on such piecemeal litigation: it would tend to select as targets those barriers to service provision which are most costly and which therefore it could be most remunerative to remove.
7. This expression was a slogan of the British Conservative Party as it returned to office in 1951, but is even more appropriate to the Bolkestein proposals.
8. Article 16, heading 2 of the draft directive: 'The Member State of origin shall be responsible for supervising the provider and the services provided by him, including services provided by him in another Member State.'
9. The general use of the term 'home country control' to describe this state of affairs is completely tendentious. It is the producer who is subject to home

control; correspondingly the consumer is subjected to an external regime – that of another Member State – without perhaps even knowing which Member State it is. 'Home control' might be better used to denote control by the home authorities of the consumer.
10. The rejection of the Bolkestein proposal by the non-profits active in the health-care sector is representative of an almost universal response in European civil society (AIM, 2004).
11. But not ancillary services within healthcare, such as cleaning or catering, which stay within the scope of the amended directive.

# 3
# Welfare Reform as a Response to Structural Crisis

*Geoffrey Wood*

The long period of growth that developed societies experienced from the end of WW2 up until the early 1970s was characterised not only by a specific dominant form of work organisation, but also by a specific mode of regulation – the assembly of institutions that sustained and guided growth (Jessop, 2001: 49). Going beyond economic regulation, post-WW2 Fordism was also characterised by a specific mode of 'societalisation', in other words, sets of institutions and practices governing quasi- and non-economic axis of societal organisation (*ibid.*: 50). The latter included not only specific national training systems and specific state interventions to deal with localised crises, but a specific form of political life emphasising class compromises, and the associated construction of a Welfare State (*ibid.*: 51). Since the economic crisis of the early 1970s, these compromises have come under increasing attack. Strong competition between different national models has precluded the emergence of a single post- or neo-Fordist mode of societalisation. However, liberal market economies have pioneered not only the deregulation of product and labour markets, but also far-reaching cutbacks in the role of the State both in terms of mediating competing class interests, and in terms of the scope and nature of social services offered.

Whilst this process has not been nearly as advanced in more cooperative types of capitalism, there is growing pressure on both the European social model, and cooperative systems in the Far East. At an ideological level, pressures for cutting back on the role of the State have centred on the alleged centrality of the profit motive to the human condition, and practical arguments around efficiency. In practice, the process of 'hollowing out' of the State has been characterised not only by the emergence of new inefficiencies and labour repression, but also by the increasingly important role of quasi-market patronage-centred relationships in governing the outsourcing process (Crouch, 2004).

Against this background, the remainder of this chapter provides a more detailed exploration of the forces and dynamics that underlie the drive to reform public services over the past two decades or so and the way in which they have acted to shape the reforms introduced. It does so by, initially, locating this drive within the economic crises of Fordism. It then moves on to consider the role played by the related rise of 'new public management', and the outcomes associated with the process of 'marketisation' within it; a consideration that encompasses both the cost-effectiveness of public service outsourcing, as well the way in which it has been linked to both dubious, not to say corrupt, decision-making and labour repression. Finally, a concluding section briefly pays attention to how the problematic performance of recent reforms leaves them vulnerable to challenge, particularly in the context of current demographic changes.

## The crisis of Fordism and the weakening of the State

It would be simply incorrect to assume that recent trends towards the weakening of the State, and the prioritisation of individual profit over collective commitments represented the result of a spontaneous shift in public opinion, or, indeed, a dominant 'natural' human instinct. Rather, this represents the product of almost three decades of volatile and unstable growth, in turn the product of intensifying global competition and global overproduction. The latter led to the breakdown of the post-war Social Structure of Accumulation (SSA).

A benign explanation as to the implications of these changes has been provided by a component of the post-Fordist literature that greatly influenced New Labour's policy discourse, centring on 'choice' by stakeholder-citizens, reduced governmental involvement, and diversity in management, regulation and control (Burrows and Loader, 1994; Dean, 1998). In the closing years of *Marxism Today*, the journal advanced the viewpoint that Britain was a rapidly changing and innovative country (Hirst and Zeitlin, 2001: 506). Firms had responded to the crisis of Fordism through the adoption of new manufacturing techniques and organisational forms; Thatcher's success was in part founded on a recognition that the world had changed (*ibid.*). Together with this went the increasing empowerment of employees, and the emergence of a more pluralist society; class solidarities forged around a mass homogenous working class had eroded (*ibid.*: 506). Social relations become more fluid, with a proliferation of individual tastes and needs. Progressives had to recognise these trends and seek to devise non-statist policies relevant to the needs of an altered world (see Andrews, 2004); these arguments were summarised in a 1998 special issue, *New Times*, that, arguably, had great influence on subsequent New Labour policy formulation regarding the provision of public services (see Andrews, 2004; Burrows and Loader, 1994).

There are two basic limitations with this post-Fordist analysis. Firstly, any changes in work and the use of new technology did not provide the basis for a sustained – and sustainable – economic recovery: growth remains unstable and lop-sided. Indeed, Hirst and Zeitlin (2001: 506) argue that British firms seemed determined to re-run 'the basis of macro-economic failures of the 1960s', *inter alia* in a lack of attention to training and skills development, misuse of technology, persistent misunderstanding of competitors' strategies, and excessive short-termism (Hirst and Zeitlin, 2001: 506); in other words, there is little sign of 'new times' at the workplace. Secondly, there has been little sign of a new progressive politics in the community, matching an alleged new pluralism at the workplace: the political discourse remains dominated by two political parties, both now firmly in the neoliberal camp (*ibid.*; Andrews, 2004).

Indeed, the post-war SSA was characterised by far-reaching compromises between employers and labour; its decline led to the restoration of corporate power, rather than pluralist new times, characterised by a sharing of power in the workplace, and the diffusion of a new pluralism into the community (Wolfson, 2003: 257). The reassertion of the dominance of capital over labour led to a reemergence of a crisis of underconsumption, forcing successive waves of cost-cutting, and, hence, a profit-squeeze crisis (Wolfson, 2003: 259; c.f. Harvey, 2003: 149). In turn, this led to a shift in focus to the financial services sector, and to the promoting of shareholder value through successive waves of downsizing and distribution (Lazonick and O'Sullivan, 2000). Nor was this process confined to the private sector. The selling off of State assets provides more opportunities for wealthy investors to make new gains through the buying and selling of publicly traded companies, particularly through further waves of downsizing and the sale of 'surplus' assets (Pollin, 2003: 134). Harvey (2003: 149) argues that the latter process has opened up new fields 'for over-accumulated capital to seize on', releasing new sets of assets at little cost.

Privatisation and the use of private firms to carry out traditional public sector functions has, as Crouch (2003) notes, changed not only the character of public services, but also the underlying notions of citizenship. Traditionally, public services accorded citizens certain basic rights – to education, healthcare, and a range of other social services – on an equal and universal basis (*ibid.*). The new role accorded to private firms recasts the public not as citizens, but as consumers exercising *choice* between a range of service providers through quasi-market relationships (*ibid.*). In practice, not only is real choice often denied to the most marginalised, but shared citizenship is systematically undermined as competing interests groupings vie for access to a diminishing range of resources; shared notions of community centring on basic rights and obligations are displaced by competition, and profits (c.f. Crouch, 2003). Indeed, Harvey (2003: 148) suggests that this process represents a reversion to the early days of capitalism, a new 'enclosing of the commons'.

## Demographic challenges and public sector reforms

In addition to the crisis of Fordism, further factors challenging the Welfare State are the effects of long-term demographic changes. The baby boomers – those born from about 1945 to 1960 – are rapidly ageing, which will place increasing demands on both national social security systems and health provisions, particularly given that life expectancies are increasing (Gunderson, 2003: 318). The declining coverage of private sector pensions is likely to further exacerbate this problem (Neumark, 2003: 305). Whilst some of the pension problems facing older citizens may be deferred through the abolition of retirement ages, this will not resolve pressures on healthcare systems (c.f. Garstka *et al.*, 2005). In contrast to overly optimistic 'third age' accounts that held up the prospect that increasing numbers of the elderly could enjoy a longer retirement period spent in personal recreation and development, it is evident that the issue of ageing populations is one of the central challenges to the Welfare State (Wood *et al.*, 2006).

The baby boomer generation's sheer demographic clout may result in the political discourse shifting towards the concerns of the elderly (Shen and Kleiner, 2001: 27), particularly given the relatively high aspirations of this generation: high expectations of a good retirement and decent health persist, particularly given that the 'baby boomer generation' grew accustomed to increasing standards of living during their formative years (Naegele and Walker, 2004). This might impel the political discourse towards rebuilding, rather than dismantling the Welfare State. However, policies that might help solve the problem – such as mass immigration of skilled workers to broaden the tax base – remain unpopular. In part this reflects a general tendency for members of the middle classes to shift their political beliefs rightward when faced with the prospect of downward social mobility: xenophobia remains the greatest amongst the middle class who have, in objective terms, the most to gain from mass immigration. These fears are exacerbated by the gutter press, who depict immigrants as simply competitors for resources, rather than contributors to future prosperity. A potential future reactionary backlash may be by younger generations who inevitably will have to work longer to access smaller pensions, and who may challenge any expansion of the reallocation of resources to older citizens *via* the Welfare State (Gunderson, 2003). Indeed, right wing accounts have begun to depict the issue of an ageing population simply as that of a burden on the State (Walker, 2005: 818). And it has been argued that the social needs of the elderly at least in part reflect poor lifestyle choices (Peng and Kleiner, 1999: 74). On the one hand, the challenges of an ageing population will inevitably necessitate hard choices as to the State's role in determining the relative allocation of resources between generations. On the other hand, existing government policies have already begun to force this debate to a closure: it is presented as a *fait accompli* that the Welfare State perforce must be diminished, not expanded, with public services in a range of areas being permanently dismantled, and hard policy choices in areas ranging from tax, the rationing of social services, to migration being deferred.

## Outsourcing and efficiency: promises and the erosion of the public ethos

Central to the idea of 'new public management' has been a commitment to the marketisation of public services. In addition to firms gaining new commercial opportunities through privatisation, it was felt that a reorientation towards profits – as adverse to service – would promote greater effectiveness, yet somehow, leave commitments to community and community service intact. These reforms encompassed both the externalisation of public services, and the introduction of private sector managerial styles and values into the remaining areas under State control (Torres and Pina, 2002). It has been suggested that the lack of competition in the public sector has meant that monies are often directed to non-productive areas, where outcomes may be elusive. In contrast, in open competition, firms are likely to focus their attentions on areas where demand is the strongest, and the results were likely to be the most fruitful (Rosenberg, 2005: 295).

Again, Cohen (2001) suggests that in the absence of a market-driven relationship between costs and expenditure, managers will be reluctant to cut costs; outsourcing and outright privatisation will reintroduce the discipline of the market, with a clearer focus on the profit motive encouraging the elimination of inefficient and expensive layers of management, and on a stronger focus on meeting the needs of the public at large (c.f. Gill, 2000: 281).

It has further been argued that non-core tasks could readily be offloaded to specialised providers who have particular expertise in the area, and who are in a position to benefit from large-scale economies of scale (Gill, 2000: 281; c.f. Sauter, 1988: 487). This allows for the public sector to concentrate on core functions, spinning off specialised functions to those with particular expertise in the area (Morgan, 2003: 35). Again, outsourcing may provide a viable alternative to radical and potentially destabilising change in government departments themselves, given that staff in the latter may lack the 'cultural capital' to bring about change on their own, and, hence, may need the external expertise of private firms; in turn, their greater efficiency will bring pressure to bear on remaining public sector staff to improve the quality of their work and service offered (Gill, 2000: 291; Boyne *et al.*, 2004: 193). More ambitious proponents of outsourcing have suggested that the process can be open-ended, with ultimately, even large areas of management being delegated to agencies with specialised expertise in the area (Sisson, 2001: 87). Ideological commitments to removing 'barriers to entrepreneurship' accelerated this process, leading to a reduction in regulatory controls, enabling further reductions in the size and scope of the public sector (Amable, 2003: 116).

The resultant reforms did not only encompass outsourcing, but also the introduction of private sector ways of doing business into the public sector (Ferner, 2002: 317). The latter included an ongoing reexamination of all areas of public sector provision with a view to further privatisation of assets and services and a greater commitment to consumer choice (*ibid.*: 319), encompassing casting the public-at-large simply as 'customers' or 'consumers' of services offered by government. It was commonly held that the immediate needs of customers should be prioritised over long-term fixed investments. This desire to rapidly respond to perceived needs whilst cutting fixed costs would accelerate moves towards outsourcing (Boyne *et al.*, 2004). However, the track record of such reforms remains at best uneven; arguably inadequate attention has been devoted to the actual outcomes for the community at large (*ibid.*: 190).

In many cases, the costs have, in fact, been rather greater than initial estimates, whilst the record of actual service delivery has been uneven. In part, this reflects the extent to which outsourcing places a large range of new responsibilities on the remaining managers (Sanchez-Runder, 2001: 63). The latter includes managing the relationship between different organisations, dealing with the inclusion of additional actors into the relationship between general strategies, and the range of actual management practices and service outcomes; the additional complexities make mismatching more likely (*ibid.:* 63). Leaner staffing policies may result in higher workloads, and greater stress on existing staff, making for higher absenteeism (c.f. Gold, 2003: 210).

Another reason why outsourcing of public sector functions has often proved more expensive is that private sector contractors often engage in 'lowballing', securing government contracts through extremely low initial bids, confronting the client government agencies with 'unexpected' cost increases and time overruns at a later stage (Sauter, 1988: 487). The need to maintain service levels and the limited number of competitors for public service work in a number of areas, in turn, makes it difficult for public agencies to severe ties with poorly performing contractors. Finally, all forms of outsourcing pose a natural tension between cost-cutting and the need to secure short-term profits on the one hand, and on value creation – the enhancement of the quality and nature of the service on a sustainable basis – on the other hand (Morgan, 2003: 38).

Indeed, numerous empirical studies have indeed pointed to the direct relationship between the marketisation of public sector work, and greater costs and poorer levels of service (Sauter, 1988: 488). Marketisation is often poorly planned and directed, and primarily focused on dealing with short-term expediencies, leading to a loss of core skills and expertise and a degradation of accumulated human capital (Lafferty and Roan, 1999: 76). There are often breakdowns in communication between public sector managers and outside contractors, whilst the latter may not have sufficient experience to be fully conversant with the actual range of tasks at hand (Gill, 2000: 281). Hence, there is remarkably little empirical evidence to support frequently made assertions that outsourcing makes for greater efficiency and effectiveness (Boyne *et al.*, 2004: 200).

There is often little monitoring of the skills and organisational commitment of staff deployed by external contractors, forcing the relevant public agency to undertake additional training and supervision, necessitating an expansion of both Human Resources (HR) and line management, even if the overall workforce size is cut (Sauter, 1988: 488). Managers may have little understanding of the HR and other problems that may be experienced by the sub-contractor, problems that can potentially spill over in the remaining parts of the public sector organisation (Morgan, 2003: 41). The contracting out of tasks may thus make coordination harder (Lafferty and Roan, 1999: 82). Hence, outsourcing may not reduce costs, but, in fact, increase them to meet the need for growing numbers of managers (Haque, 2001). This process may be accelerated by the breakdown of government into autonomous agencies, with a great deal of autonomy being delegated to managers, including the ability to adjust pay and service conditions, resulting in a duplication of functions; this encourages latent tendencies towards empire-building, as the concept of a 'unified career bureaucracy' slowly disintegrates (Ferner, 2002: 325).

Hence, as suggested in several other chapters in this volume, the outsourcing and marketisation of public sector functions may simply not make economic sense. Yet, the process of marketisation, and the coterminous erosion of the public service ethos, substituting consumers in the place of citizens with rights and obligations, continues within the majority of mature and emerging markets. To a large part, this reflects the strength of the ideological underpinning of marketisation, reflecting the prevailing agendas of political elites and their corporate allies. Whilst, in the private sector, managers are generally quick to abandon an initiative that does not prove effective or cost-effective, in the public sector ideologies and political expediencies can override basic cost criteria. In other words, a central irony of public sector outsourcing is the fact that the persistence of non-market relations and concerns may drive the process, rather than anonymous 'market forces'. This may indeed, lead to a 'freight train effect that overwhelms common sense', resulting in excessive costs being incurred, with a greater attention being accorded to the realisation of targets than genuinely meeting the needs and concerns of the wider public (Gill, 2000: 289), reflecting broader systemic pressures. This process may be exacerbated by the tendency for costing in the public sector to be based on complex formulas for allocating overheads, making it easy to (by accident or design) blur the costs and benefits of marketisation, even if the coterie of managers gets visibly large and the quality of service diminishes (Gill, 2000: 289). This is particularly so in the case of complex public-private partnership deals, where the genuine costs to the government may be spread over many years, and may not be readily visible.

Finally, it should be reemphasised that the marketisation of the public sphere is characterised by labour coercion; firms benefiting from public sector outsourcing and privatisation have tended to focus their attention on maximising short-term returns through liquidating non-profitable assets, deferring investment and recasting the relationship with stakeholders, encompassing suppliers, the community and employees (c.f. Pollin, 2003). In many cases, the latter has simply involved outright labour repression from worsening the terms and conditions of service to union busting, legal strictures and restraints notwithstanding.

## The public: privatisation and the limitations of the market

There is considerable scope for corruption, or, at least, dubious practice in the award of contracts; politicians are under great pressure to favour specific prospective contractors as payoff for political patronage (Sauter, 1988: 489). Hence, central to the marketisation of the public sector has been the award of concessions to politically well-connected corporations, who are not always the most effective. Government departments may be 'captured' by the firms to whom they hand out contracts; the latter invest heavily in gaining political influence (Krugman, 2004).

In other words, a central irony of the marketisation of the public sector is that those firms that have benefited most are those which have through political influence, sheltered themselves from market forces (*ibid.*). This reflects the fact that not only are certain traditional public sector functions natural monopolies – it is simply not cost-effective to replicate complex infrastructures be it railways or specialised healthcare facilities – but also a product of neoliberal ideologies. As Krugman (2004) notes, if the public sector is held in contempt and seen as of little worth, then permitting powerful firms to repetitively offer a mediocre service in return for lavish subsidies, becomes rather more acceptable. There are numerous instances of firms that have been repetitively granted State concessions despite controversial track records, ranging from Haliburton to Jarvis Rail, yet there seems little pressure to cease such practices. As Crouch (2004) notes, a central feature of the marketisation of the public sector has been the emergence of corporations that are neither State nor purely market, but operate according to personal ties and political linkages; a reversion to premarket relations (Supiot, 2001). Given this, greater 'choice' by the public will inevitably be emasculated to that which is most convenient to inefficient yet politically powerful corporations.

## Legitimising the 'Hollow State'?

As Harvey (2003) notes, privatisation and outsourcing represent the dispersal of accumulated public assets and capabilities into the hands of a limited number of corporations. Yet, this 'predatory' process brings with it its own set of problems. In his classic writings on the subject, Gumplowicz (1889) noted that the institutionalisation process follows on primitive forms of accumulation; institutions legitimise and seek to secure inequalities at whose origins lie primitive – and often violent – acts of expropriation. Yet, a defining feature of neoliberalism has been the paring back of the role of the State in key areas and the associated deregulation of markets; perforce, this makes it very much more difficult to stabilise and legitimise such changes. The latter problem is reflected by the persistent aversion of Western European electorates to endemic attempts by political elites to curtail the remaining features of social democracy. Again, the role of private firms in assuming the functions of the State has often been unstable and erratic; facing pressures to maximise shareholder value in the short term, the relevant firms have often been proved incapable of devoting sufficient attention to building durable relationships with remaining government departments and the consuming public at large. Whilst the conservative media have devoted considerable attention to legitimising the 'hollowing out' of the State, this has proved remarkably ineffective as a result not only of the persistence of alternative voices within the media (c.f. Mann, 2003), but also owing to the visible deterioration in services that has tended to follow both privatisation and outsourcing.

## Conclusion

This chapter has explored the nature of the broad changes in the role and ethos of the public services, which have taken place over the past 30 years, in response to both economic crises and demographic challenges. The post-1970 period remains one of instability and adjustment; government policy shifts remain open-ended and experimental with limited evidence of a coherent new SSA emerging (Wolfson, 2003). Whilst committed to the cutting back of the public domain, and the reallocation of public resources to the private domain, the UK government's policy interventions remain uneven, with little evidence that they have resulted in greater sustainability, resulted in more cost-efficient government, or, indeed, financial gains to all but a small number of insider corporations. This poor track record reopens the possibility for progressive alternatives to the current malaise.

As Fung and Wright (2003: 4) note, progressive defenses of the affirmative State have become weaker in recent years, both in rhetorical force, and in their capacity to mobilise public opinion. Yet, whilst the principle of public ownership of large areas of production has been widely challenged, the central affirmative role of the State has become ever more evident (*ibid.*). This has refocused attention on the specific design of institutions, that makes them unresponsive to grassroots needs and concerns, yet pliable to corporate interests; the challenge is more to seek to identify transformative democratic strategies than a wholesale discarding of a progressive project aimed at equity, social justice and inclusion (Fung and Wright, 2003: 4).

# 4
# Public Sector Employment: Issues of Size and Composition in the UK

*Philip Beaumont, Judy Pate and Moira Fischbacher*

In this chapter we concentrate primarily on what has been happening to public sector employment, in both overall and composition terms, since the New Labour Government came to power in the UK in 1997, arguing that certain aspects of these trends give rise to concern. To do this we initially look at the Conservative legacy and differing views of the stance that the Blair Government has adopted towards the public sector, and then assess both aggregate figures for the UK as a whole, and more detailed ones for Scotland. Scotland serves as a useful comparator with England given that since devolution, the two countries have separate governments and thus differing structural, cultural and accountability characteristics. Of particular relevance is the differing approach the two countries have taken towards private sector practices (for example, competition between health service providers) despite their shared history prior to devolution.

The chapter begins with a preliminary examination of certain alleged tendencies in public sector employment in the UK. Particular attention is paid to overall employment growth (and decline) and to variability in employment growth between services within the sector, with an examination of causal factors. We also consider issues of pay and productivity. While the focus is specific to the UK, given the Blair Government's claim to 'pragmatism' in the reform agenda, the more widespread use of a 'New Public Management' approach means that the themes explored are likely to be of wider interest and relevance.

## The Conservative legacy and the Blair approach: continuity?

Britain in the 1980s and 1990s was the initial 'home' of the notion of 'new' public management. There have been different definitions and measures of this notion (see Table 4.1) but in general the practices of the Conservative Government(s) which attracted most attention and interest in these years were privatisation, attempts to develop policies for market mechanisms, the transfer of various business practices from the private sector, and

**Table 4.1    Key elements of New Public Management**

- A move to 'let managers manage' with the development of hands-on professional management that elevated the role of managers above that of professionals in some parts of the public sector.
- The implementation of explicit standards and measures of performance indicated.
- A move to disaggregate units in the public sector, through privatisation and agencification.
- A shift to greater competition through the use of contracts and public tendering procedures.
- A stress on private sector styles of management and flexibility in hiring and rewarding staff.
- A stress on greater parsimony and discipline in resource use, cutting costs and resisting interest group and public sector union demands for favourable treatment

*Source*: Hood (1991: 4–5) cited in Massey and Pyper (2005: 36–7).

involvement of the private sector in the provision of public services. These practices certainly had an obvious impact on the overall level of public sector employment with jobs in this sector falling (from the early 1980s) for over 15 years in a row (Labour Market Trends, July, 2004: 273).

As the notion of 'New Public Management' spread within Europe (and indeed in other advanced industrialised economies) a number of comparative, cross-European studies were conducted (Ridley, 1996; Pollitt and Summa, 1997; Bach *et al.*, 1999). In essence their major conclusions for the UK under the Conservatives, when placed in a comparative context, were as follows:

1. Change was more dramatic in the UK than elsewhere;
2. Within the UK, change was mainly associated with changes in organisational and administrative arrangements;
3. The most powerful of these organisational and administrative changes was privatisation in the sense of it being responsible for such a large element of the reduction in public sector employment from the early 1980s to the 1990s; and
4. The ideological hostility of the Conservative Government to the notion of a 'large' public sector, combined with characteristics (most notably its highly centralised nature) of the state in the UK, were held to have facilitated this relatively sizeable run down of public sector employment.

Has the election of New Labour changed all this? One relatively early view, which still retains considerable popularity, involved the following observations (Corby and White, 1999: 20):

In 1997 there was a change of government from Conservative to New Labour. To what extent did 1997 represent the end of an era? We argue that it did not: 1997 marked the end of a chapter, not a new book, as the 'plot' has continued. In particular the new government has adopted its predecessor's stance of public expenditure controls, though perhaps influenced more by pragmatism than by ideology.

This 'continuity-pragmatism' based view does, however, have to confront a number of 'awkward' facts of life under New Labour. Specifically, 'employment in the public sector is now 10 per cent higher than in 1998, owing to the creation of an additional 509,000 jobs. The growth in the past five years is a clear break from the trend of the immediately proceeding period' (Labour Market Trends, July 2004: 272–3). Indeed public sector employment as a proportion of total employment is up slightly from 19.5 per cent in 1999 to 20.4 per cent in 2005 (Labour Market Trends, February 2006: 531).

To help explain these trends some commentators have emphasised elements of change, as well as those of continuity, in the approach of New Labour to the public sector (Boyne *et al.*, 2001: 1–4); the abolition of Compulsory Competitive Tendering (CCT) in local government and more emphasis on joined-up services *via* the establishment of network-type arrangements are often cited as elements of change. The issues of continuity and change are certainly not viewed as the only elements in New Labour's approach to the public sector. For instance, one recent review has identified five elements that differing commentators have stressed in seeking to fully understand the approach of the Blair Government towards the public sector (Perri and Peck, 2004: 84): inconsistency and incoherencies; ideology (the early so-called 'third way'); managerialism; continuity; and centralism. Our own view is essentially very similar to that of Massey and Pyper (2005: 59) which in essence has three tenets:

1. The key features of New Public Management (see Table 4.1) have carried over between the Conservative and New Labour administrations
2. However, 'in government, the Labour Party has attempted to differentiate its approach from that of the previous Conservative governments, and effectively give its managerialism a softer, friendlier and more accommodating image. Hence the emphasis on constitutional and political reforms rather than mere market reforms as the route to enhance citizenship' (Massey and Pyper, 2005: 59).
3. There are some costs or negative consequences to the new public management approach. According to Massey and Pyper among these are '…its tendency to spawn its own bureaucracies, the destruction of professionalism in certain parts of the public sector, the toleration of non-consultative and domineering managerial styles, lower morale in

workforces, the devaluation of certain types of accountability and denigration of the traditional public service ethic' (*ibid.*: 59).

So far in this section we have briefly outlined some of the different perspectives or lenses that commentators have adopted in seeking to understand the Blair Government approach to the public sector, and ultimately the outcomes achieved. There are, however, two relatively critical perspectives on the approach adopted. Firstly, the argument that 'money is being thrown at the problem' *via* public expenditure increases but that limited, real substantive and sustainable reform and improvement of service delivery has come about. This criticism is backed up by the growing body of comparative, public sector research which has variously documented, particularly in relation to healthcare, how surprisingly little actual change has resulted from even large scale, legislative-based change programmes (Le Grand, 1999; Hacker, 2004).

The second critical perspective involves the contention that some of the Blair change initiatives may have been essentially dysfunctional or counter-productive in nature. The use of performance targets, measurement system and league tables have been particularly singled out for criticism in this regard (Bunting, 2005). The adoption of these measures that are ostensibly intended to release resources to the front line (Gershon, 2004) has instead become the focus of the media as a source of the relative growth of indirect labour ('bureaucrats' to manage the systems). Underlying this line of criticism are certain questions (who exactly are indirect labour?) and implicit assumptions (indirect labour is less productive than direct labour and contributes little to end-user delivery and satisfaction) which have tended to be essentially skated over. This being said, 'if one regards the central problem of public administration as that of creating a formal institutional system that aligns agent interests with those of the principals' (Fukuyama, 2004: 79) then both the approach adopted and the resulting line of criticism are likely to be of relevance and importance beyond the UK. In developing these arguments, the following sections pursue some of these criticisms and assumptions in more detail.

## Concentrated growth: The NHS and education

In the previous section we noted the fact that total public sector employment has increased by some 10 per cent in the 1998–2003 period, whereas it declined over the prior 15 year period. It is notable, however, that under New Labour, there is a close correlation between this increased public expenditure and employment, but with variability across services within the sector. Any and all such aggregate statistics for public sector employment in the UK do, however, need to be seen in the context of ongoing attempts to improve the underlying quality of such figures. These ongoing

**Table 4.2   Public sector employment, health and education 1995–2003**

| Year | NHS (in thousands) | Education (in thousands) | Total public sector jobs (in thousands) |
|------|------|------|------|
| 1995 | 1182 | 1188 | 5211 |
| 1996 | 1186 | 1191 | 5068 |
| 1997 | 1203 | 1193 | 4958 |
| 1998 | 1201 | 1204 | 4945 |
| 1999 | 1222 | 1322 | 5094 |
| 2000 | 1251 | 1301 | 5111 |
| 2001 | 1286 | 1351 | 5203 |
| 2002 | 1356 | 1362 | 5292 |
| 2003 | 1419 | 1450 | 5454 |

*Source*: Labour Market Trends, July 2004: 272.

initiatives have been driven by a number of recent Government Reviews calling for better data, which have reflected concerns that estimates have derived from a variety of sources often involving different definitions, reference dates and geographical coverage (Labour Market Trends, April 2005: 139–40).

As the content of Table 4.2 indicates, above average employment growth is very much a feature of Education and Health, which have received sizeable public sector expenditure increases under New Labour.

In essence, employment increased by some 22 per cent in the NHS between 1998 and 2004, with education growing by some 16 per cent, both well above the average (10 per cent) for the public sector as a whole in these years. At present education and health account for some 60 per cent of total public sector employment, a figure substantially above that (40 per cent) of some 20 years ago (Labour Market Trends, July 2004: 271).

The above average growth in education and health has been central to '...one of the hottest political topics of the moment, i.e. how many of these jobs are for front-line professionals (doctors, nurses, teachers... etc) and how many are back-office managerial and administrative staff' (Philpott, May 2005: 32). Furthermore, Philpott suggests that the resulting political debate has been rather 'simplistic' in nature, and the comprehensive evidence is in relatively short supply. However, his own 'rough calculation' is that front-line professionals accounted for some 25 per cent of the net increase in public sector employment between 1998 and 2004, with a similar figure involving 'back-office managers and administrators' and the remaining 50 per cent being for intermediate staff (Philpott, May 2005: 33).

In Table 4.3 on page 64 we set out some figures for the NHS in Scotland which allow us to make a preliminary examination of this issue.

Staff numbers within the NHS in Scotland have increased overall by 10 per cent between 1998–2004. The scale of staff increases, however, varies

**Table 4.3   NHS Scotland, some selected staff categories 1994–2004**

| Year | All staff | All medical staff | Nursing/ midwifery staff | Administrative, clerical and senior management | |
|---|---|---|---|---|---|
| | | | | Numbers | % support staff |
| 1994 | 136,927 | 10,848 | 63,488 | 44,157 | 32 |
| 1995 | 137,321 | 11,108 | 63,273 | 43,622 | 32 |
| 1996 | 135,666 | 11,390 | 62,477 | 41,873 | 31 |
| 1997 | 134,835 | 11,763 | 61,961 | 40,716 | 30 |
| 1998 | 134,248 | 11,899 | 61,374 | 40,161 | 30 |
| 1999 | 135,216 | 12,135 | 61,644 | 39,891 | 30 |
| 2000 | 135,589 | 12,183 | 61,579 | 39,985 | 29 |
| 2001 | 137,720 | 12,566 | 62,379 | 39,979 | 29 |
| 2002 | 142,446 | 13,163 | 63,356 | 41,975 | 29 |
| 2003 | 147,512 | 13,432 | 64,317 | 44,534 | 30 |
| 2004 | 149,896 | 13,704 | 64,855 | 45,447 | 30 |

*Source*: ISD Scotland.

significantly among types of job. With regards to clinical personnel, the numbers of medical staff have increased by 13 per cent per cent during the time period as compared to only a 5 per cent increase for nursing/midwifery staff. Administrative employees and senior management, in comparison, have increased in line with medical staff trends at 12 per cent. In short, there is no overwhelmingly clear cut evidence for the proposition that indirect staff numbers have grown disproportionately. Overall growth in NHS employment in England and Wales during a similar time period (since 1997) is higher than in Scotland and shows more marked differences between occupational groups (*Economist*, 2006). The total increase of 29 per cent includes a growth rate of 49 per cent for hospital consultants and 78 per cent for managers. Growth in other disciplines (scientific, therapeutic, technical nursing and general practice) although smaller in relation to hospital consultants and managers, are nonetheless sizeable – 'That increase of 29 per cent was almost matched by the increase in hospital and community nurses, whose ranks swelled by over 80,000' (*ibid.*: 32).

## Declining employment numbers: the case of social services

In marked contrast to the position of education and health, there are parts of the public sector where declines in employment have occurred. This is illustrated by the contents of Table 4.4.

Service specific factors may be the major cause of decline in these particular cases. For instance the fall in armed service numbers is clearly associated with the end of the cold war, while the fall in local authority construction numbers is due to the policy initiatives under the

**Table 4.4   Declining areas of employment in the public sector 1995–2003**

| Year | HM forces (in thousands) | Other Central Government[1] (in thousands) | Local Government social services (in thousands) | Local Government construction (in thousands) |
|---|---|---|---|---|
| 1995 | 230 | 708 | 412 | 83 |
| 1996 | 221 | 612 | 406 | 76 |
| 1997 | 210 | 582 | 403 | 65 |
| 1998 | 210 | 581 | 395 | 61 |
| 1999 | 208 | 584 | 388 | 59 |
| 2000 | 207 | 586 | 386 | 59 |
| 2001 | 204 | 596 | 377 | 57 |
| 2002 | 204 | 606 | 367 | 47 |
| 2003 | 206 | 628 | 351 | 45 |

*Source*: Labour Market Trends, July 2004: 272.

Conservative and New Labour Governments to increasingly 'buy in' private sector services as an alternative to directly employed construction employees.

The decline in local authority social services is arguably a more complex matter, and trends in aspects such as recruitment and retention of labour have received relatively short shrift in many discussions of changes in public sector employment, where the emphasis is so frequently centred on the role of government policies of the day. A recent review of the 'Social Care Labour Market' in Scotland is a useful document in this regard (February, 2005). It initially notes that the social care sector includes private, voluntary and public employment. Between 1994 and 2003 employment in social care increased by some 23 per cent (96,000 in 1994 to 118,000 in 2003), with the independent sector (private and voluntary combined) growing by 76 per cent in the period 1994–2003, and more recently accounting for more than half of social care employment. This has been achieved through recruitment in particular occupational disciplines – home carers, social work helpers, residential care home staff, occupational therapists and physiotherapists.

The report notes that over the period 1994–2003 the level of employment within the public sector has remained fairly stable compared to the independent sector (Social Care Labour Market, 2005: 5), although due to arrangements under Transfer of Undertakings (Protection of Employment Regulation) (TUPE), some staff have moved within the public sector from employment within social services (local authority) organisations to the NHS. Moreover, there has been a turnaround in employment levels between 1995 and 2002 following on from a pre-1999 downward trend (*ibid.*: 60). This clearly indicates an interesting comparison to the wider overall UK position (see Table 4.4) which may result from a combination of different statutory requirements, different systems of service provision, economies of scale and rural factors.

The report went on to note that in local authority social work in Scotland 'it is evident that from 1999 there have been rising whole time equivalent staffing levels. Vacancy figures are available from 2000 and there has been a growing gap between actual staffing levels and numbers of posts. Evidently employment levels have been expanding in local authorities but demand has been faster than supply which has been reflected in vacancy rates' (*ibid.*: 18). The contents of Table 4.5 below provide an indication of vacancies as a percentage of posts in social work in Scottish local authorities in January 2005.

The inter-related issues of staff turnover, recruitment and retention in social work have since contributed directly to Scotland-wide initiatives. These initiatives seek to improve the image of social work and support of front-line staff. Individual local authorities have simultaneously sought to improve terms and conditions of employment and to introduce work-family balance programmes.

## Pay and productivity

Trends in pay are also of concern, given the growing preoccupation with productivity. A recent issue of Labour Market Trends (February 2006: 51) reported that UK public sector *median* gross weekly earnings for full time employees in 2005 were £476 compared to £412 in the private sector, with the comparable *mean* figures being £531 in the public sector, and £514 in the private sector. Any observed average wage differentiated in favour of the public sector has always made the government of the day 'nervous' because of the predictably critical comments in the media from employer representative forums such as Confederation of British Industry (CBI). Recent experience under the New Labour Government has not been exceptional in this regard.

In many ways the interest in the average public-private sector wage level, and changes in relative growth, is an odd preoccupation given that the

**Table 4.5   Social work departments in Scottish local authorities, vacancies as a percentage of posts, January 2005**

Scotland (as a whole) 11 per cent

The unfilled vacancy rate ranged between a high of 38 per cent and a low of 0 per cent

There was a total of 32 local authorities with a quarter of these having unfilled vacancy rates of more than 20 per cent

*Source*: Annual Staff of Scottish Local Authority Social Work Service Census, 2005.

occupational mix, and education (human capital) levels, of the two sectors are so different in nature. Indeed this is very much the view of Income Data Services, an independent and experienced commentator on pay levels and movements in the UK. In a recent Pay Report (2005) they noted that the New Labour Government has become, since 2003 in particular, increasingly uncomfortable with signs of relative growth in public sector average earnings levels. However according to their analysis this growth has not been due to higher basic pay increases, but rather has stemmed from a combination of extra payments and reformed salary structures to deal with recruitment-retention problems, extra money due to the cost of 'pay modernisation' (new grading structures), and the transfer ('contracting out') of lower paid jobs from the public to the private sector. The contents of Table 4.6 below list the key issues that Incomes Data Services viewed as central to the public sector pay round in 2005, many of which were expected to be prominent in future pay rounds.

A second long-standing question is that of just how productive are public sector employees? The answer to this all-important question has never been straight forward because of the difficulty of measuring the output of the public sector, much of which does not have a market price. Since 1998 the Office for National Statistics has consciously moved away from the historical indirect approach of measuring public sector output by reference to the cost of employing people to a direct one. This involves calculating productivity by dividing the percentage change in real government output by the percentage change in real government input; such calculations now cover nearly two-thirds of the public sector.

These calculations for the years 1995–2001 (Philpott, May 2005: 35) indicate falling public sector productivity in these years. However such calculations are still not without their limitations and criticisms, much of which involves difficulties in adequately accounting for quality improvements in public sector outputs. Such concerns have been articulated in a number of recent independent reviews commissioned by the Government, and the Office for National Statistics has therefore pilot tested various quality adjustment measures in health and education. For example, a recent study

**Table 4.6   Key issues in the public sector pay round for 2005**

---

- Higher earnings growth from the cost of assimilation to new grade structures
- Low basic increases sought by the Treasury
- Long-term agreements prevail
- Further growth of competency pay
- Focus on quicker progression through ranges
- Conflict over pensions
- Equal pay issues central to change

---

*Source*: IDS Pay Report, 935, August 2005.

(*Economic Trends*, 2006: 13–37) reported that education sector productivity has been falling since 1995, although less markedly since 2002. Herein lies an inherent difficulty in measuring productivity because, for example, whilst an increased pupil-teacher ratio might be indicative of a greater number of pupils being taught per teacher (and thus a more productive education system), it might similarly be connoted with a decline in quality, as a low teacher-pupil ratio is indicative of increased contact and thus better quality education. Thus, efforts to take account of quality changes have resulted in revised estimates that involve a range: productivity growth could have averaged around +2 per cent in a year since 1998 (highest estimate) or have fallen by an average of –2 per cent a year.

Directly relevant to productivity levels are the levels of sickness absence, recruitment and retention. The Chartered Institute of Personal and Development (CIPD) Annual Survey on absence management for 2005 reported an average level of sickness absence of 3.7 per cent, or 8.4 days per employee per year with public sector figures the highest at 4.5 per cent or 10.3 days per employee per year. Table 4.7 below lists the role of 'stress' as the source of sickness absence for various categories of staff absence in the public sector compared to the overall survey figures.

These figures are potentially a manifestation of a wider problem of poor morale which in turn, has the capacity to undermine future recruitment and retention. Although the CIPD survey figures do not on the face of it identify a particular problem, there are data within the report that suggest that the image of the sector fares less well and that in the longer term, recruitment and retention within particular occupations may become more difficult. The figures show, for example that 83 per cent of public sector organisations reported recruitment difficulties for one or more category of vacancy compared to 85 per cent for the survey as a whole and 69 per cent of public sector organisations reported that they had occupational retention difficulties compared to 73 per cent for the survey as a whole. However, the 'image of the sector/occupation' was rather more of a

Table 4.7   **Stress as a cause of sickness absence, various categories of staff absence, public sector compared to all respondents, 2005**

|  | Public sector (%) | All respondents (%) |
| --- | --- | --- |
| Short-term absence, manual employees | 59 | 42 |
| Short-term absence, non-managerial employees | 66 | 56 |
| Long-term absence, manual employees | 17 | 13 |
| Long-term absence, non-managerial employees | 49 | 36 |

*Source*: CIPD, 2005a.

problem as a reason for recruitment difficulties in the public sector (24 per cent) than for the survey as a whole (16 per cent) and retention difficulties for managers/professionals was rather more of a problem for the public sector (33 per cent) than for the survey as a whole (26 per cent) (CIPD, 2005b).

Further discussion of the productivity figures and the relative contribution of sickness/absence are beyond the scope of this chapter except to note that earlier influences of the New Public Management ethos such as the increase in targets, bureaucracy and the reduced level of professional control are thought to contribute to poor morale/increased sickness absence. This was captured in a quote in the *Daily Telegraph* (July 8th 2006) where Mark Serwotka, Public and Commercial Services union (PCS) general secretary was reported to have said, 'Our members are being forced to meet unreasonable targets as their work is de-skilled and they are reduced to nothing more than robots'. As Bunting (2005) also stresses, these factors must be considered in the round.

## Conclusion and implications

The above analysis of public sector employment trends suggests the continuing influence of the New Public Management approach, but also some variation in the way in which practices are manifested. Whereas the Conservative Government reduced employment, the Labour Government has increased employment, thereby reversing a 15 year downward trend. On the face of it, this is to some extent a reflection of the Conservative's promotion of privatisation where certain types of jobs were privatised (cleaning, catering, some logistics etc), *versus* Labour's traditional stance towards retaining services within the public sector. However, current moves by the Labour Government have greater resonance with privatisation than in the past: witness recent media coverage of proposals to outsource all NHS purchasing to a US firm (*The Times*, 26th July, 2006) and it would seem from the data that increases in employment in some services have the capacity to mask losses in others.

The analysis of levels of employment shows variability both between services (for example, health, education, social care and defence) and within services in terms of different growth rates across occupational groups. This employment pattern gives rise to the question of whether one might helpfully continue to refer to the 'public' sector. As variability increases across public services, and as local pay bargaining takes hold within health and education (for example), generalisations in employment terms to 'the public sector' become somewhat inappropriate and unhelpful. At the same time, there is a growing government discomfort over perceptions of its spending approach and the apparent decline in the quality of public services. Employment is increasing but efforts to contain public spending continue and as such, there is, and will continue to be, greater scrutiny of service efficiency, service quality and overall productivity.

Some of these dimensions (particularly those relating to productivity) are difficult to address from an evidence-based point of view. Whilst the UK does have better data than some other economies, there remains a need for more accurate, comprehensive and consistent measures of change in public sector employee *attitudes* and *behaviour* over a relatively long period of time (pre and post New Public Management) and few research studies of this nature have been undertaken. Future research should consider issues such as organisational identification given that it has been found to be 'positively associated with performance and organizational citizenship behaviours, and negatively associated with turnover intentions and actual turnover' (Kreiner and Ashforth, 2004). Sickness absence in the public sector is another pertinent issue for future research. Current practice amongst some organisations is to attempt to address this issue by way of placing an increasing emphasis on more rigorous return to work interviews. Other organisations have sought to provide a more supportive work environment *via* the introduction of employee well-being programmes (Dibben *et al.*, 2001). Many experienced observers consider, however, that it is the combination of these two approaches that is most likely to yield a reduction in the sickness absence figures. This contention merits detailed, longitudinal examination.

In addition to an agenda that concerns the quality and nature of research data, researchers and policy makers need to consider the direction of future public sector employment research in order to take account of a number of underlying considerations. These include the causes and effects of a decline in morale and a decrease in the level of trust in senior management and the impact on productivity, recruitment and retention. There are also growing concerns about the cost of public sector pensions, poor pay relative to the cost of living in some parts of the UK, assaults on front-line public sector workers from members of the public and staff bullying. Finally, and somewhat imminently, is the problem of what Bunting (2005: 131) refers to as the 'demographic timebomb ticking away under the public sector' where,

> Twenty-seven per cent of public sector workers are now over fifty. Their fast-approaching retirement within the next decade will coincide with rising expectations from the electorate for a better standard of service.
>
> (Bunting, 2005: 131)

The implications of this 'time bomb' can be understood in relation to both a loss of knowledge and a loss of expertise.

These imminent challenges need to be understood and addressed in policy terms within the context of the direction of public sector employment that is framed by the New Public Management philosophy outlined at the start of this chapter and by concomitant new forms of organisation and governance. Collectively, they represent an interesting research agenda and an essential policy and practitioner agenda that will underpin future trends in public sector employment and productivity, not to mention the quality of public services.

## Acknowledgements

We would like to thank John Philpott, Chief Economist, CIPD London, for his helpful comments on and input to this chapter.

## Note

1   HM Forces, the NHS, and other central Government are the major categories of Central Government Employment

# Part II

# The Consequences of 'Modernisation' for Public Service Workers

# 5
# A Declining Public Service Ethos?

*Catherine Needham*

Whilst the boundary between public and private services in the UK becomes ever more porous, the notion of a distinctive public service ethos remains surprisingly popular. When the Public Administration Select Committee (PASC) launched a programme of inquiry into the government's public service reforms in 2001, it began with ethos. Its report published in 2002, concluded, 'The public service ethos should not be seen as an echo from the past, but as an indispensable ingredient of any public service deserving of the name' (PASC, 2002: 83). In speeches in June 2006, both the Prime Minister Tony Blair and the Leader of the Opposition David Cameron premised public service reform on retaining the public service ethos (Blair, 2006; Cameron, 2006). From Cabinet ministers, MPs and civil servants to trade union leaders and consumer representatives, public service reformers frequently insist on the importance of a public service ethos (Barber, 2003; Brown, 2004; Bichard, 2006; Hutton, 2005; Mayo, 2006; Prentis, 2004; Reid, 2004; Wright, 2003).

This ethic of public service seems to be one of the survivors of the years of public service upheaval under Thatcher, Major and Blair. Yet whilst there may be a consensus, outside of public choice theories at least, about the importance of a public service ethos, there are divergent views about what the term means, and what role it should play in the future of public services. In particular there are tensions between those that see the ethos as an essential and enduring feature of public services, those that see it as a positive but declining aspect of the traditional Welfare State, and those that view the public service ethos as something that needs to be drummed into unresponsive bureaucrats.

Understanding the way that the public service ethos is positioned in contemporary public service reforms is vital to making sense of the shifting priorities of reformers. The public service ethos has traditionally played a role in ensuring the probity and impartiality of civil servants, but it also encompasses a commitment to serve people whose weak market power left them reliant on the State. The discussion here begins by considering various definitions of the public service ethos, and the ways in which defenders and critics of the ethos bring it into discussion in order to support their case. Exploring the meaning of the public service ethos and some of the contexts in which it is invoked reveals its elasticity as a term. This chapter goes on to contrast traditional notions of ethos, associated with the public sector and norms of propriety, with newer notions associated with customer care and value for money. Finally, the discussion explores targets and choice – both key strands of Labour's public service reforms – in the context of ethos, arguing that both approaches limit bureaucratic discretion and deny the importance of ethos.

## What is a public service ethos?

The need for a public service ethos rests, as Rohr points out, on the exercise of discretionary power by bureaucrats, and the need to ensure that this discretion is used to advance public interest rather than personal gain (Rohr, 1989). The distinctive features of public services – such as limited exit powers for service users and oversight of bureaucrats by non-expert politicians – create a need for *intrinsic* motivations to ensure that bureaucrats act in the public interest (Le Grand, 2003: 5). These differ from *extrinsic* motivations such as material reward or fear of sanctions.

An ethos is defined by the PASC as 'a principled framework for action, something that describes the general character of an organisation, but which, and more importantly, should also motivate those who belong to it' (PASC, 2002: 3). Pratchett and Wingfield follow March and Olsen (1989) by seeing an ethos as providing a 'logic of appropriateness' for those working in public services (1996: 652). The content of the public service ethos is usually provided in list form. The PASC Report provides the following: impartiality, accountability, trust, equity, probity, 'service' (PASC, 2002: 12). Similar lists can be found elsewhere (Nolan, 1995; Pratchett and Wingfield, 1996; Farnham and Horton, 1996: 20; Plant, 2003). Such lists place emphasis on the normative features of the ethos, although Perry and Wise and others have argued that there will also be rational and affective aspects to ethos (Perry and Wise, 1990; Brewer *et al.*, 2000). Rational motivations are those that advance an individual's self-interest, such as the self-esteem that comes from working in the public interest. Affective motivations are about an individual's emotional response to an organisation, including altruism and empathy.

What is often ambiguous in definitions of the public service ethos is whether it is a description of public servants' behaviour or an aspiration. As the PASC Report points out, '[I]t is not clear whether [the public service ethos] is seen as an existing attribute of public services that deserves celebration, or as a desirable attribute of reformed public services that is a goal for achievement (or a mixture of both)' (PASC, 2002: 3). The report concluded that the public service ethos was 'a benchmark, against which public service workers and institutions should continuously strive to measure themselves.'

Translating this benchmark into a guide to behaviour may be difficult. The problem of adapting lists of attributes into actions has led some to describe the concept of ethos as 'nebulous' (Corby, 2000, in Hebson *et al.*, 2003). Pratchett and Wingfield's survey of local government officers in the early 1990s found support for certain key values – such as accountability, impartiality, loyalty and public interest – but considerable divergence in the practical interpretation of these values (Pratchett and Wingfield, 1996). The 2002 PASC Report recognised that a public service ethos was not self-sustaining but needed to be 'nourished and cultivated', calling for a Public Service Code to be adopted by all organisations providing public services (PASC, 2002: Summary).

## Four approaches to the public service ethos

The public service ethos is a useful lens through which to consider recent public service reforms because of its varied deployment by different stakeholders. Four uses of the public service ethos can be picked out. First, it is used by politicians to signal support for public service workers; second, it is used by trade unionists and those working in public service to emphasise the distinctiveness of public services over private ones; third, it is used by public service reformers as the hook on which to hang new customer-oriented approaches to service delivery; fourth, it is evoked by critics of public services as emblematic of what is wrong with existing service delivery. These perspectives are explored in turn.

In the first context, the public service ethos is used to signal a basic sympathy and understanding for public service workers. Its use in this way by opposition parties can be seen in a 1991 article in *Public Administration* by the then Labour Shadow Chancellor John Smith. The article was entitled 'The Public Service Ethos', and in it he wrote, 'After a decade in which public servants (be they teachers, nurses, health workers, carers, local government employees or civil servants) have been hounded and pilloried it is time for a new commitment to the value, and values, of public service' (Smith, 1991: 517). In June 2006, David Cameron gave a speech in much the same vein – and in an apparent *volte face* to Thatcherist Conservative Party thinking – to a National Consumer Council seminar. Again entitled 'The Public Service Ethos', Cameron used it to make a similar point: 'Instead of using public servants as scapegoats we should acknowledge their successes. Instead of constantly beating up on the public sector and telling it to be more like the private sector, let's be more reasonable and constructive' (Cameron, 2006).

This tactical use of the public service ethos is not restricted to opposition politicians. Although Tony Blair courted controversy in 1999, telling a meeting of venture capitalists: 'You try getting change in the public sector and public services – I bear the scars on my back after two years in government' (Watt, 1999), ministers came to talk more emolliently about the value of the public service ethos in Labour's second term. Blair told a BBC interviewer that despite fundamental restructuring, 'The essential value and ethos of the public service should remain' (Blair, 2002). The then Health Secretary John Reid observed in an interview, 'The ethos of the NHS remains the glue of the service'. He defined this ethos as 'a commitment, in which there are millions of individuals in this country, to help their fellow citizens...to contribute to the public good' (Hall, 2003). Charles Clarke, then Education Secretary, wrote the foreword to a 2002 think-tank pamphlet on ethos. He noted: 'The ethos of public service is as intrinsic to public service as the practice itself, helping to create and manage the expectations and aspirations of all stakeholders' (Aldridge and Stoker, 2002). In a speech to the Labour Party conference in 2004, Chancellor Gordon Brown spoke of the importance of 'the ethic of public service', and described public service as 'a calling, not a career' (Brown, 2004).

This deployment of the public service ethos appears designed to help ministers to neutralise fears about the direction of public service reform. It has been evoked more as Labour's public service restructuring has become more radical. Its generalised goodwill offsets attacks against specific aspects of the public service, as for example in May 2006 when John Reid described elements of the Home Office as 'dysfunctional' and 'not fit for purpose' following the failure to make provision for deporting foreign criminals (Johnston, 2006).

The second category of comments about the public service ethos are also a response to public service upheaval. However, here the ethos is used as a talisman against radical change, rather than a diversionary tactic. Union leaders in particular have evoked the public service ethos to resist the involvement of profit-making businesses in public service provision. Brendan Barber, General Secretary of the Trades Union Congress (TUC), wrote in a newspaper article: 'The great thing about the public service ethos is that it reflects our full humanity. It recognises that we can be motivated by higher values than simply the pursuit of profit' (Barber, 2003). Similarly, in giving evidence to the PASC, the General, Municipal, Boilermakers and Allied Trade Union (GMB) trade union emphasised the importance of ethos in providing non-pecuniary incentives to staff: 'It is public service ethos which motivates low paid GMB members such as care assistants and hospital ancillary workers to continue with stressful jobs in often poor conditions when they could be earning more at the local supermarket' (PASC, 2002: 9).

Dave Prentis, General Secretary of Unison, wrote to the *Guardian* in September 2004, rejecting claims by the Confederation of British Industry (CBI) that private companies could embody the public service ethos:

The CBI's John Williams muddies the waters when he says private-sector staff show just as much commitment as staff in the public sector... This is not about staff or their commitment but the behaviour of private companies, which ultimately have a duty to put the interests of shareholders before those of the public. This means that decisions to walk away from unprofitable contracts, despite the chaos left behind, are all too common. We see private care homes sold off because of rising property prices with no thought for the elderly residents left in limbo. That's what distinguishes the private from the public sector ethos, not the commitment of individual staff.

(Prentis, 2004)

Here then the ethos is evoked as a distinctively public sector concept, which is incompatible with profit-making and is at risk from those private interests that might have an interest in running public services.

The third approach to the public service ethos uses it as an elastic rather than fixed concept, which needs to be strengthened by an injection of the private sector service ethic. As John Reid put it in the *Guardian* in November 2004: 'So to the traditional ethos of public service we need to add another element of customer care – organising public services around the convenience of the public – if we are truly to meet modern expectations' (Reid, 2004). John Hutton, then pensions minister, said in a speech to the Social Market Foundation in 2005: 'Yet making the goal of customer satisfaction fundamental to the ethos of public services is essential if we are to succeed in moving from the paternalistic statism of the past to the progressive, individual empowerment of the future' (Hutton, 2005). The PASC Report on ethos set out the standard for the public service ethos as follows: 'Aim to deliver public standards that match in quality the best private equivalents, including standards of customer care' (PASC, 2002: Summary). Here then ethos involves a new 'synthesis' between the traditional ethos and private sector models of customer service (Brereton and Temple, 1999).

The fourth account of the public service ethos shares this interest in customer care but argues that the ethos in practice is a negative and obstructive force. Ed Mayo, Chief Executive of the National Consumer Council reported public dissatisfaction with public services, 'If there is a public service ethos, one person said to us, it is that they are doing you a favour' (Mayo, 2006). Julian Le Grand similarly points to public dissatisfaction with public service:

It is worth noting that the view that the public services are staffed by helpful, welcoming knights is not one necessarily held by the public. When asked by MORI what words they think applied to public services in Britain today, the highest ranked adjectives were (in descending order) bureaucratic, infuriating, faceless, hardworking (a positive note there), unresponsive and unaccountable. The lowest ranked were friendly, efficient, honest and open.

(Le Grand, 2006)

In interviews with local government officers Pratchett and Wingfield found that a quarter of their respondents characterised the public service ethos 'as being a largely negative concept that encouraged inefficiency and obstructive bureaucratic behaviour, and in some instances, even corrupt activities' (1996: 644).

For this last set of authors then the public service ethos has negative associations. Together, these four rhetorical positionings of the public service ethos highlight the elasticity of the term and also its limitations as an analytical tool. In public services, it has been used to describe all the things that may be positive about service providers – impartial, hardworking, caring – but also some of the things that are negative – bureaucratic, unresponsive, faceless. This ambiguity is acknowledged by the PASC Report which notes, 'Government in one voice suggests that the existing ethos of the public services represents a blockage to reform, while in the other voice it says that this ethos represents an asset to be built on' (PASC, 2002: 37).

## Public service ethos: old and new

What is not at issue in any of these accounts is the need for public service workers to be honest, impartial providers of a high quality service. Ministers, as the quotes above suggest, are committed to establishing a public service ethos that syntheses traditional concerns of ethos with newer notions of customer care. Two questions are raised by this approach. The first, dealt with in this section, is how far these aspects can be synthesised. The second, discussed in the next section, is how the public service ethos fits with other aspects of New Labour's reform agenda, particularly performance targets and user choice.

A common feature of literature on the public service ethos has been the distinction between older concerns with probity and equity, and newer priorities such as value for money and customer service (Brereton and Temple, 1999; PASC, 2002; Aldridge and Stoker, 2002). The former is usually traced back to the 1854 Northcote-Trevelyan Report which recommended the use of permanent tenure and fixed salaries to inculcate an ethos of honesty and fairness among public servants (Hood, 1991: 12–13). The concern for value for money and customer care is linked to the new public management-type reforms adopted since the 1980s (Hood, 1991; Brereton and Temple, 1999). Whilst some argue that the public service ethos is an elastic concept which can easily be stretched to encompass these new aspects, others argue that the two cannot be combined. These positions are examined in turn.

The case for synthesis is made most cogently by Brereton and Temple (1999). They argue that 'the thesis, the public sector ethos, has been confronted by its antithesis in developments such as new public management', but refute any claim that the resulting synthesis has been negative (1999: 470). They argue that the content of ethos is being successfully modified to incorporate some of the values that are explicitly attributed to the private sector: 'Public and private actors are now developing strategic policy together in all our regions; such cooperation is forging a new public *service* ethos rooted both in public notions of, for example, honesty, impartiality and community service and private notions of, for example, competition and customer care' (Brereton and Temple, 1999: 466 – emphasis in the original).

In this model of what Brereton and Temple call the 'pseudo market', private sector standards of customer care become the model for public service (Brereton and Temple, 1999: 471). Rather than being dependent on the expertise of the public sector professional it becomes a relationship of responsiveness to the user as customer. This is a 'pseudo market' in the sense that it simulates private sector levels of responsiveness to the customer without introducing the market disciplines that create incentives for such responsiveness in the private sector (Brereton and Temple, 1999: 471). In this account the split between old and new components of a public service ethos becomes largely artificial. Indeed as the PASC Report points out, even Northcote and Trevelyan were concerned to improve civil service performance as well as to end cronyism and patronage (PASC, 2002: 68).

A key feature of this newly synthesised ethos is that it rejects the language of public *sector* ethos in favour of public *service* ethos (Brereton and Temple, 1999: 466; PASC, 2002: 23–4; Aldridge and Stoker, 2002; Wright, 2003). The ethos is distinctively public not because of who provides the service, but simply because it is associated with a public service, be it health, education, housing, welfare, etc. Such a shift facilitates the stretching of the ethos to encompass non-state providers of these services. As the PASC Report notes, '[A] public service ethos can exist whether a particular service is delivered by a public or private agency' (PASC, 2002: 29). Thus private and voluntary providers of public services can adopt this ethos just as effectively as core civil servants. Indeed, their extra flexibility and entrepreneurialism may allow them to do so more effectively than rule-bound civil servants.

However, a case can also be made against synthesis of traditional, process-oriented conceptions of ethos and newer, results-oriented conceptions. For those authors that emphasise the shortcomings of public service provision, the traditional public service ethos is part of the problem rather than the solution (Le Grand, 2006; Mayo, 2006). Indeed, from this perspective, it can be argued that the traditional public service ethos kept issues of service quality off the agenda, diverting attention onto issues of honesty and impartiality. Certainly service quality was (at best) implicit in traditional notions of ethos (Brereton and Temple, 1999, pp. 457, 466; PASC, 2002: 23–4; Aldridge and Stoker, 2002; Wright, 2003). Reports on improving civil service performance reaffirmed the principles of Northcote-Trevelyan, rather than admitting any shortcomings of the public service ethos (Fulton, 1968; Cabinet Office, 1994). The ethos of public servants periodically resurfaced as an issue when standards of integrity appeared to be slipping, such as during the Ponting case in 1984–5 and following the multiple 'sleaze' allegations in the mid-1990s (Chapman, 1993: 166–7; Greenaway, 1995: 368; Nolan, 1995; Doig and Wilson, 1998). However, generally the response to such problems was simply to restate the Northcote-Trevelyan tradition, as the 1995 Nolan Report did by evoking the 'generally accepted principles which have been in place since the mid-nineteenth century' (Nolan, 1995: 43).

In this negative account of the traditional public service ethos there are echoes of the public choice critique of bureaucracy, which stressed the need for external incentives and sanctions to curb internal tendencies towards profligacy (Downs, 1956; Niskanen, 1971; Dunleavy, 1991). In the public choice account, bureaucracies do embody a distinctive set of values, but these are oriented towards increasing the size or prestige of their bureaus rather than delivering higher quality services for clients. Similarly, consumer representatives continue to highlight ways in which public service providers rely on professional norms of service rather than actually listening to their users (Policy Commission on Public Services, 2004).

The scope to synthesise older and newer notions of the public service ethos has also been denied by those authors that emphasise the value of the traditional ethos. Here, the New Public Management-type reforms are seen as having a corrosive impact on traditional values (Greenaway, 1995; Haque, 1996; Doig and Wilson, 1998). As Hood puts it, the New Public Management reforms 'to some degree removed devices instituted to ensure honesty and neutrality in the public service in the past (fixed salaries, rules of procedure, permanence of tenure, restraints on the power of line management, clear lines of division between public and private sectors)' (Hood, 1991: 16). Doig and Wilson point to the damaging impact of the Thatcherite Reforms on standards in public life, arguing that a new enterprise culture had replaced public values with commercial ones and led to a culture of 'sleaze' (Doig and Wilson, 1998). Similarly, Greenaway argues that 'the informal codes of culture, conduct, education and socialisation' have been eroded by the institutional fragmentation of the Thatcher-Major era (1995: 373). In this account, the mechanisms that establish probity and fairness run counter to, and are damaged by, the mechanisms that foster value for money and customer care. Flynn highlights the corrosive effects of market mechanisms on shared values and commitments in the public sector (Flynn *et al.*, 1996). Hebson *et al.* in a review of ethos in public-private partnership arrangements found that new values associated with consumer sovereignty eroded the transparency of rules and clear demarcation between task and person associated with the traditional public sector ethos (Hebson *et al.*, 2003: 485).

It is certainly the case that different assumptions underpin the traditional and newer components of the public service ethos. The concept of accountability, for example, is employed differently in the two approaches. Pratchett notes that New Public Management-type reforms mean that public servants 'are all now encouraged to see accountability as a concept linked to discrete and easily measurable performance criteria, rather than to broader principles of democratic accountability' (1999: 367-8). While traditional approaches emphasise accountability to political leaderships, customer care approaches valorise the immediate responsiveness of providers to users. In the customer care model, political forms of accountability can be discredited as unresponsive and ineffective. The point is illustrated by a comment from the Conservative Public Services Minister William Waldegrave in 1994, rejecting arguments for constitutional protection for social rights: 'Would a Bill of Rights provide compensation for commuters stranded on a wet railway platform? Of course not' (Waldegrave, 1994: 85).

The public-private relationship is also configured differently in the older and newer variants of the public service ethos. Brereton and Temple point out that the traditional notion of a public servant as honest and impartial was developed in contrast to a venal and profit-driven private sector, whereas the customer care component of ethos assumes 'a meeting of public and private ethics' (1999: 458; 436). The criteria of service quality also change, becoming 'defined by the client/customer and not by the producer/professional' (Brereton and Temple, 1999: 471). The customer orientation transfers the ethical considerations of public service from process to end product. '[E]thical considerations are now couched in terms of optimum outcome for customers rather than the motives of the actors engaged in service provision' (Hebson *et al.*, 2003). It is a shift from deontological assumptions that ethical actions rest on motivations to a teleological concern with the consequences of such actions (Pratchett, 1999: 371). Mechanisms such as customer satisfaction surveys become the key measures of success for public service providers.

In this outcome-oriented model of ethos, concerns about who provides the service can be set aside as distracting details. As Blair puts it in a speech on public service reform, 'The point, very simply, is this: the user comes first; if the service they are offered is failing, they should be able to change provider; and if partnership with other sectors can improve a service, the public sector should be able to do it' (Blair, 2001). This 'user comes first approach' delegitimises concerns about other aspects of service provision such as treatment of the workforce. John Reid dismissed a journalist enquiring into the employment status of contracted out staff in the health service: 'I'm sorry to be rude but do you ever ask questions about patients? Like every other journalist...you have asked every single question about conditions of employment, about the doctors, about the cleaners, about the porters...no bastard mentioned the patients' (Hall, 2003).

The Public Administration Select Committee Report on ethos called for an end to rigid distinctions between the public, private and voluntary sectors. It argued that 'stereotypes' were unhelpful, and that it was important to avoid thinking that 'the motivations of private sector workers are inferior to those of public sector workers. Private companies are increasingly expected to demonstrate social responsibility and to take account of the world beyond the balance sheet' (PASC, 2002: 41). The committee recognised that the profit motive could put the public service ethos, 'under strain', but argued that private and voluntary sector organisations could uphold the public service ethos if it was 'soundly build into the contracting process' (PASC, 2002: 33).

The difficulty of building an ethos into a legalistic contracting process may not be overcome so easily, however. Hebson *et al.* present data from public service workers outsourced in public-private partnerships (PPPs), highlighting the difficulties they have in sustaining a public service ethos in the new environment. They note, '[T]he contractual relations of PPPs have changed norms of accountability and bureaucratic behaviour among managers. For workers, while certain values appear resilient, the cost cutting and work intensification associated with PPPs present a significant threat to the long-term survival of the traditional public service ethos' (Hebson *et al.*, 2003: 482). In a review of the role of third sector organisations in providing employment services, Davies concludes: 'Voluntary organisations and, even more so, profit-oriented companies are poor vehicles for core functions of the State. A transfer of such functions from the State raises vital issues of accountability. It also has the potential to damage those voluntary organisations that rely on an independence from the State' (Davies, 2006: 51). Voluntary bodies may lose their distinctive independence and critical stance without acquiring the transparency and accountability embedded in the public service ethos.

Certainly it is not clear that a customer care approach offers a common guide to behaviour which can be applied consistently across organisational settings, or is any less 'nebulous' than traditional accounts of ethos. Data gathered by the author, drawing on interviews and documents from case studies in central and local government, suggest that there is broad endorsement of customer terminology but inconsistency in its interpretation (Needham, 2006). Treating users as customers appears to combine different variations of the following: user choice, payment for services, improved access, personalisation and courteous provision. It is too early therefore to suggest that a new 'logic of appropriateness' has developed among public, private and voluntary providers of public services, based on a common ethos of customer service.

## Targets, choice and ethos

To understand the future development of the public service ethos it is necessary to position it within the context of New Labour's reform programme for public services. It is common to tell the story of New Labour's public service reforms in terms of a first-term emphasis on performance targets and a second- and third-term focus on user choice (Mather, 2003; Hindmoor, 2005). Blair himself gives this account of Labour's changing priorities:

> In respect of public service reform, the first term was about introducing proper means of inspection and accountability for public services and about intervention where there was failure. Inevitably, it was driven from the centre… But it only takes us so far. Now there is a sustained programme of investment, with public spending rising as a percentage of GDP every year…I want to focus on health and education. Here, reform means putting power in the hands of the parent or patient so that the system works for them not for itself.
>
> (Blair, 2003)

Although the transition is less neatly periodised in practice, and differs between services, this simplification does highlight the key trends of New Labour's reforms. New Labour moved quickly on coming into office to establish a Best Value regime in local government, and to establish Public Service Agreements at the national level. An infrastructure of audit and inspection centred at local level around the Audit Commission, and at national level around the Treasury and the National Audit Office. For those working in public services, the target regimes clarified priorities and created penalties for underperformance.

In Labour's second term, largely in response to a recognition that targets plus investment had not delivered the expected improvements, the government moved to expand user choice (Le Grand, 2006). Patients were to be given a choice of hospital; parents were to be given different types of school to choose from; users of social care services would have more freedom to buy in their own choice of support packages. Thus whilst Brereton and Temple, writing in 1999, describe the customer care approach as a 'pseudo market', seeking to replicate market responsiveness *as though* customers had an exit right, under New Labour public services are moving closer to a fully market model. Here exit replaces internalised norms of service as the stimulus for service improvement. Providers must offer good customer care or risk losing their patients/pupils/clients and the money that comes with them.

Both targets and choice are designed, in different ways, to solve the problem of bureaucratic discretion. As Blair's adviser on public services, Julian Le Grand, makes clear in the context of the NHS:

> In the unreformed NHS patients had little choice over where, when and how they were treated; in the unreformed education system parents had little choice of school. This was bad in and of itself, because it disempowered both patients and parents. But, even more importantly, it was destructive because the absence of choice also meant an absence of incentives for providers to improve.

He argues in favour of the expansion of markets in public services to create new incentives for improvement:

> If a provider has a monopoly on the supply of a service, it can ignore the complaints of its users with relative impunity. Only if it knows that ultimately the dissatisfied can exit – can go elsewhere – does it really have an incentive to improve.
>
> (Le Grand, 2006)

Here then is a denial of the value of intrinsic motivations in improving services, and an account of the rationale behind New Labour's reforms. Yet this account raises questions about what is left for a public service ethos to do. The incentives are deliberately structured to leave as little room as possible for ethical motivations. Workers are still required to be honest and committed to their work, of course, but this requirement applies across all organisations, and has no distinctive public content. For all that ministers have continued to assert the importance of the public service ethos it is hard to see that they would argue with the following statement, made to the Public Administration Select Committee by the law firm Nabarro Nathanson: 'Public service ethos is not different or superior to the private or voluntary sector ethos' and there is 'an implied arrogance' in suggesting otherwise (PASC, 2002: 16). If this claim is endorsed, the existence of a distinctive ethos of public service becomes redundant.

There are some signs that the government is taking an interest in ways to engage and motivate public service workers that are not target- or market-based. 'Localism' is on the agenda, and ministers have started to talk about the need for a 'double devolution' of power down to town halls and out into communities, suggesting more scope for frontline innovation (Miliband, 2006). This builds on the Gershon-led agenda to get more resources to the frontlines (Gershon, 2004). In May 2006 the Cabinet Office and TUC launched a Drive for Change initiative to ensure that public service employers listen to and include the workforce in reform and change (Cabinet Office/TUC, 2006). However, these initiatives are separated out from core programmes for public service improvement, and show little sign of reversing the presumption that only extrinsic carrots and sticks will make health, education, housing, social care services, etc, better. The double devolution agenda can be construed as a new rationale for widening private and voluntary sector involvement in service delivery, rather than a sign of trust in existing public service workers. In this interpretation, talk of greater workforce involvement becomes yet another rhetorical flourish: an effort by ministers to convince public service workers that they still believe in the distinctive values of public service even whilst all other indicators point in the opposite direction.

## Conclusion

The public service ethos appears, on one level, to be the great survivor of years of public service restructuring under the Conservative and Labour Governments since 1979. It continues to be invoked in speeches from senior members of government and opposition parties, all of whom attest to its central place in the future of public services. However looking in more detail at how the public service ethos is invoked in debate reveals a much more fragile picture. Politicians use it to gain leverage over opponents: 'only *we* truly understand and can protect public services!'. Unions and public service workers invoke it as a barrier in the defence against privatisation. Reformers exploit its elasticity to stretch the ethos towards notions of customer care and value for money, which can as easily be provided by the private and voluntary sectors as the State. Critics of public services point to the ethos as the root cause of public sector rigidity and poor delivery. Thus the ethos serves an important symbolic role for those who seek to resist the marketisation of public service, as well as for those that seek to advance it.

Beyond this symbolic role, the public service ethos has been hollowed out by attacks on its distinctiveness and threats to its purpose. The notion of a public sector ethos is junked in favour of a more elastic and catch-all public service ethos, which links traditional notions of probity to models of customer care. Although dismissed as nothing but an updating of the concept, what is happening here is a redesigning of the content set of the ethos itself – marking a move from a set of procedural requirements that could only be met within the public sector, to a customer care approach in which the public sector has to play catch-up with other providers. Target and choice regimes in public service delivery are designed to minimise reliance on an intrinsic ethos of public service, replacing ethos with extrinsic motivations of audit and exit.

The hopes of reformers – that the public service ethos will live on as a synthesis of traditional and modern values – look optimistic if not disingenuous. Services provided under contract, or under the terms of performance management systems dismantle traditional cultures of ethos, whilst relying on extrinsic motivations to take their place. Between the carrot of performance-related pay and the stick of inspection regimes, it is no longer clear that public servants need to have any kind of ethos other than the sort of generalised commitment that any job requires. As market opportunities are expanded in the public sector, and the government increasingly relies on user exit to incentivise service providers, the public service ethos is not expanded but restricted. It may be inaccurate and naïve to believe that there ever existed what Brereton and Temple call 'a lost code of public ethics' (1999: 472), but there needs to be a more honest account of the rejection of an ethical basis for public service provision and an acknowledgement of what is being lost in the name of customer care.

# 6
# Equality and Modernisation

*Susan Corby*

'Modernising' is a slippery word, as can be seen elsewhere in this book. It can take on different meanings in different contexts and can be equated with values, as well as policies and strategies. Underpinning the term 'modernisation', however, is the attempt to ensure that service delivery is sensitive to users' needs and responds to their expectations. To achieve this, the government is of the view that service deliverers need to reflect the diversity of service users, for instance in respect of gender, ethnicity and disability, in order to understand and relate to users' requirements. Thus equality is an integral part of improving public services (Cabinet Office, 1999).

Against the above background, the contention of this chapter is that the State, as employer, has, since the election of New Labour in 1997, been putting equality and diversity issues at or near the top of the public sector agenda under the umbrella of its public service modernisation programmes and accompanying its rhetoric with both legislation and voluntary measures. In spite of this, however, there are barriers to progress, some of which stem from the government's own policies and practices in other contexts. So although progress on equality has been made, there are impediments which can be summarised as two steps forward, one step back.

The plan of this chapter is as follows. Initially, the post-war developments in relation to diversity and equality prior to the election of New Labour are traced. Subsequently, the approach of the Labour administration from 1997 up to the time of writing is examined through an exploration of what it has done in terms of creating a linkage between equality and public sector modernisation, introducing new legal duties on public bodies and encouraging voluntary action to improve the 'equality performance' of the public sector relative to the private sector and promoting the incorporation of equality issues into public sector procurement processes. Finally, attention is paid to the barriers to progress which still exist – the cost implications of equal pay, organisational restructuring in the public sector and the culture of the uniformed public services – and some concluding observations are made.

## Before New Labour

### 1945–79: developments on equality

Public services as we know them today were shaped in the two decades after the Second World War, with the extension of the Welfare State, including the establishment of the National Health Service (NHS) and the expansion of education through the growth of the university sector, the establishment of polytechnics and the raising of the school leaving age (Colling, 1997).

Essentially, moves to equality occurred in the public services before they occurred in the private sector. For instance the government accepted the principle of equal pay in the civil service and, shortly afterwards in other areas of public service employment, including education and local government i.e. well before the Equal Pay Act of 1970 (Deakin and Morris, 2005). Furthermore, five years before the Sex Discrimination Act 1975, the civil service, concerned about the loss of experienced female civil servants, set up a committee to propose measures to enable women to combine a civil service career with family responsibilities. The committee's recommendations, which were virtually unprecedented, included the provision of part-time work, increased maternity leave and the establishment of workplace nurseries (Civil Service Department, 1971).

As to local government, from the late 1970s to 1987 over 200 local authorities adopted equal opportunities policies, some of which had far-reaching aims, while unions and management jointly revised pay structures for local authority manual grades to take into account 'equal pay for work of equal value' principles (Coyle, 1989). In addition, the Race Relations Act 1976 imposed an obligation on local authorities to promote racial equality in carrying out their functions and certain local authorities also took positive action to employ disabled people (Leach, 1989).

The Greater London Council (GLC) was at the forefront of the drive to implement equality policies (Coyle, 1989). In particular, in 1983 the GLC and its sister organisation, the Inner London Education Authority, made compliance with equal opportunity procedures and practices a condition of securing a contract to provide goods and services and established a unit to review the equality practices of contractors seeking retention on an approved list. This so-called contract compliance was copied by 19 other local authorities, resulting in significant numbers of private sector companies changing their employment policies and practices (Institute of Personnel Management, 1987).

### 1979–97: retrenchment under Conservative governments

The equality initiatives outlined above were concentrated in central and local government, rather than elsewhere in the public services, and were curtailed by the Conservative Government led by Mrs Thatcher in the late 1980s. Thus the Local Government Act 1988 outlawed contract compliance with regard to sex and disability and circumscribed it in respect of race (Godwin, 2004), while rate-capping in 1987 resulted in equal opportunities initiatives being reduced because of budgetary constraints (Corby, 1994; Leach, 1989).

Furthermore, local authorities were required by the Local Government Act 1988 to put certain services out to tender with negative effects on equality. Women, especially part-time women, suffered a decline in take-home pay or were more likely to lose their jobs compared to their male colleagues and the number of disabled workers employed decreased (see Escott and Whitfield, 1995 for a full discussion). Similarly, ministerial pressure to contract out ancillary services in the NHS impacted adversely on women (Kelliher, 1996).

There were some equality initiatives under the Conservative Government led by John Major in the 1990s. For instance, in 1991 the then Health Secretary adopted certain steps to secure the advance of women in the NHS by the year 2000 under the nationwide. Opportunity 2000 Programme, spearheaded by Business in the Community (Corby, 1995). Similarly, from the 1990s, certain targets and action programmes were drawn up to aid the advancement up the civil service hierarchy of women, ethnic minorities and disabled people. Such actions, and any resulting progress, however, were limited (Cabinet Office, 1998).

## New Labour

### Equality and the modernisation agenda

When the Labour Government came to power in 1997, it sought to 'modernise' public services and made equality an integral part of its modernisation agenda. Thus in its seminal document, *Modernising Government*, it said:

> [The public service] is committed to achieving equality of opportunity. But we must accelerate progress on diversity if this country is to get the public service it needs for the new millennium.
>
> The public service must be a part of, and not apart from, the society it serves. It should reflect the full diversity of society. At present it does not. Women, people from ethnic minority groups and people with disabilities are seriously under-represented in the more senior parts of the public service.
>
> Addressing this is a top priority. The Government wants a public service which values the differences that people bring to it (Cabinet Office, 1999: 59).

This intertwining of equality, public service modernisation and users' needs was reflected in other official pronouncements. Thus the Department of Health said:

> NHS staff are a precious resource. They are what make the NHS tick. A modern NHS must offer staff a better deal in their working lives... Improving the working lives of staff contributes directly to patient care through improved recruitment and retention – and because patients want to be treated by well-motivated, fairly rewarded staff (Department of Health, 2000a: 50 and 53).

Similarly it has also been said:

> In modernising services and employment, the Government is committed to inclusiveness... Securing and developing a workforce that reflects and understands the diversity of the population is fundamental to serving the needs of all, and such diversity helps to reassure users that they will be more likely to get the service they need (NHS Executive, 2000a: 7).

Numerous, similar quotations can be found essentially arguing that the diversity of staff goes hand in hand with better patient care (Department of Health, 2003). Moreover, the National Audit Office observed:

> ... government bodies that reported doing very well in meeting the needs of the gender and race strands through service delivery also tended to report doing well in terms of the gender and racial compositions of their workforces (National Audit Office, 2004: 50).

In short, as can be seen from the above quotations, the government has propelled equality issues up the agenda, using mainly business case arguments as its rationale and, albeit to a lesser extent, social justice arguments.

**Public duties**

The government is translating its rhetoric into reality first and foremost by using its powers as lawmaker. Under the Race Relations (Amendment) Act 2000, effective in May 2002, it imposed general duties to make the promotion of racial equality central to the work of public bodies. In addition there are specific duties: listed public bodies are required to publish a race equality scheme which has to be reviewed every three years and are bound by specific duties on employment. These require the collection of ethnic monitoring data on such matters as staff in post, applications and selection for employment, training and promotion and those involved in grievance and disciplinary procedures; then the analysis of the collected data; and finally the taking of whatever steps are needed to remove any barriers and promote equality of opportunity (Commission for Racial Equality, 2002).

Where there is not compliance with these specific duties, the Commission for Racial Equality (CRE) can issue a non-compliance order and follow this up by seeking an enforceable court order. In 2004, the CRE warned 52 public authorities that they were not in compliance. Since then most have put their house in order and the CRE 'has not instigated any court actions' (Incomes Data Services, 2005a: 2).

Duties on public bodies, however, are not limited to racial equality. The Disability Discrimination Act 2005 imposes duties on public authorities to promote equality of opportunity for disabled people, similar to the duties on race. Thus there are general and specific duties central to which is the drawing up of a Disability Equality Scheme, and certain employment duties including the carrying out of an impact assessment of policies, procedures and practices. These public sector duty provisions are to be implemented in December 2006 and the enforcement mechanisms of the Disability Rights Commission are analogous to those of the CRE.

The government plans a similar duty for gender in 2007, by, for instance, requiring public authorities to carry out gender impact assessments and to have policies on promoting equal pay (Women and Equality Unit, 2005). Meanwhile, the Scottish Parliament, the Greater London Authority, the Welsh Assembly and public authorities in Northern Ireland have specific duties across various equality strands, including sexual orientation, age and religion, as well as gender, race and disability (Barnard and Hepple, 2000; O'Cinneide, 2003a).

These duties on public bodies move beyond the fault-based model of discrimination law with its reliance on individuals making complaints in an adversarial legal system, and remedies designed to compensate the individual after the event. Thus the duty bearer, even though not responsible for creating discrimination, becomes responsible for eliminating structures, policies and practices that are found to have an adverse impact on the protected group (Fredman, 2002). The objective is to make 'equality a central goal of [public bodies'] day-to-day activities' (O'Cinneide, 2005: 228).

These duties also have the potential to be a powerful tool to ensure that equality issues are brought to the forefront of public authorities' concerns. A note of caution at this juncture, however, must be sounded. First, these duties only impose an obligation on public bodies to give 'due regard' to equality, i.e. to balance the importance of equality against other considerations, 'thus incorporating the requirements of relevance and proportionality' (O'Cinneide, 2005: 229). Second, there is a danger that at least some authorities will focus on process compliance and pay scant attention to outcomes.

Third, while the duties are proving a powerful lever for change in Northern Ireland, the Greater London Authority (GLA), the Scottish

Parliament and the Welsh Assembly, there has been considerable political support in those places, so their value 'will only be tested when they are applied in less favourable political waters' (O'Cinneide, 2005: 232). Fourth, the enforcement mechanisms (except in respect of the duties in Northern Ireland) are weak (O'Cinneide, 2003a). Accordingly, public duties' 'ultimate utility remains to be determined' (O'Cinneide, 2003b: 93).

## Voluntary measures

The government has attempted to translate its rhetoric into reality by voluntary measures, as well as by the legal measures outlined above. This is illustrated, initially, by examining the actions it has taken in relation to the three largest public services: first, the civil service, where over half a million people work; second, the NHS where one-and-a-half million people work; and third, local government where nearly three million work (Hicks and Lindsay, 2005). Then attention turns to a consideration of the public sector as a whole and how developments in it compare with those in the private sector.

In short, the government has adopted a number of measures to enhance diversity in the civil service. For instance, shortly after Labour came to power, the Cabinet Office introduced a single overarching programme for action to replace separate programmes in respect of gender, race and disability and set targets for 2004 to address under-representation at the most senior levels to provide a visible signal of change.

In 2004 most of these targets were met (Cabinet Office, 2004; Equal Opportunities Review, 2004b), so new and more challenging equality targets were set for 2008, together with a 10-point plan to achieve the targets. These include the establishment of so-called Diversity Champions in departments and a Diversity Champions Network; the appointment of a new senior diversity advisor based in the Cabinet Office; regular equality audits of performance appraisal outcomes; mainstreaming equality; and positive action measures including outreach recruitment, requiring departments to run developmental schemes for under-represented groups and a Civil Service Bursary Scheme for disabled staff with potential to reach the senior civil service (Cabinet Office, 2005a).

The government has also been at the forefront of taking action on equal pay. From 2001, it committed departments to carrying out equal pay reviews, which uncovered gender pay gaps in virtually all civil service departments and agencies. Following on from this, in 2003 it published a summary of civil service equal pay action plans, setting out the key steps already taken. These included shortening incremental scales and introducing transparent pay progression systems (Equal Opportunities Review, 2004a).

In the NHS too, a variety of voluntary initiatives have been taken to foster equality and diversity as part of NHS modernisation plans. These include those embodied in *Working Together* issued in 1998 which set strategies and objectives to ensure that equality of opportunity 'is integrated into everything the NHS does' (NHS Executive, 1998: 9) and *The Vital Connection* (NHS Executive, 2000b). This last document asked NHS employers, for instance, to implement flexible working arrangements, to monitor the diversity of their workforce, to work towards nationally set equality targets for ethnic minority and female representation in executive posts at board level and to be able to demonstrate a year-on-year reduction in the level of harassment at work. The priorities and targets set by *The Vital Connection* were then reinforced in a further initiative: *Improving Working Lives* (Department of Health, 2000b).

The NHS Executive (2000b) also issued *Positively Diverse*, which reported on the equality audits carried out by 37 NHS organisations. This led to the production of a number of *Positively Diverse* materials , including a 'quick guide', which set out a strategy for NHS employers to adopt and to tailor to their circumstances. This strategy requires a participant employer to:

- find out where it is,
- decide where it wants to go,
- design how it is going to get there,
- set specific standards so it will know when it has arrived.

There are lead sites and a sharing of successful initiatives, such as the establishment of black and ethnic minority networks, and training for managers on how to prevent harassment (NHS Employers, 2005).

As to equal pay, the NHS introduced a new pay system *Agenda for Change*, with effect from October 2004, on the grounds that it considers that 'there is a clear link between a modern pay system for staff, which rewards them for what they do, and better and more flexible services for patients' (Department of Health, 1999: 13). This new pay system, which covers all NHS staff except doctors and dentists and the most senior managers, is posited on equal pay for work of equal value principles, with a single pay spine replacing the different pay arrangements for the NHS's many job 'families' (Department of Health, 1999).

As to local government, the main impetus for equality resides within the government's Best Value (BV) initiative. This essentially is because in 2002 the Employers' Organisation, together with the three statutory equality Commissions, developed an *equality standard* with five levels. These range from level 1 (the adoption of a comprehensive equality policy including commitments to develop equality objectives and targets, to consult staff and to carry out equality impact assessments) to the exemplary level 5 (achieved targets, reviewed them and set new targets). In 2003/04 the level reached under the *equality standard* was included in the BV performance indicators, which provide information on how local authorities are performing. Although no local authority had achieved level 5 and just over a quarter had not implemented the standard at all, half had achieved level 1 (Incomes Data Services, 2005b).

Local government, however, has been more dilatory on the equal pay front. The 1997 Single Status pay agreement was designed to address concerns about equal value, principally by requiring job assessment to be based on an analytical job evaluation scheme. The agreement is a framework one and local authorities are free to choose either the National Joint Council bespoke job evaluation scheme, or some other scheme. Also local authorities are free to design their own grading systems, though they must be fair and non-discriminatory.

Notwithstanding this flexibility, many local authorities have been slow to implement a new pay structure, fearing the complexity of the process and the costs of implementation. Indeed, only 25 had done so by 2003 (Local Government Commission on Pay 2003). In fact, although equal pay reviews are part of level 2 of the *equality standard* and the 2004 pay agreement provides for new local pay structures by April 2006, local government only started to focus on equal pay when equal pay claims were launched by employees – see below.

## Public/private sector comparisons

This chapter, having looked at the *initiatives* being taken in the three largest public services, now looks at *outcomes* in the public sector overall, taking a relative approach and comparing the public sector with the private sector. In short, the public sector has more equality provisions in place than the private sector and this comes over loud and clear in research[1] carried out by this author with colleagues, which drew on questionnaire responses from 454 employers in south-east England, as well as interviews in 40 organisations (Corby *et al.*, 2005).

This research found that although equal opportunity policies were widespread in both the public and private sectors, where organisations had such policies, the public sector was much more likely to communicate them by ongoing training than either private services or private manufacturing, as Figure 6.1 below shows.

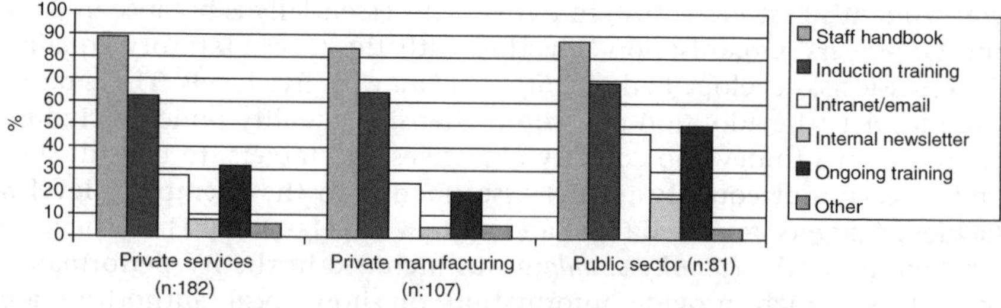


*Figure 6.1*   Communication of equal opportunities/diversity policies

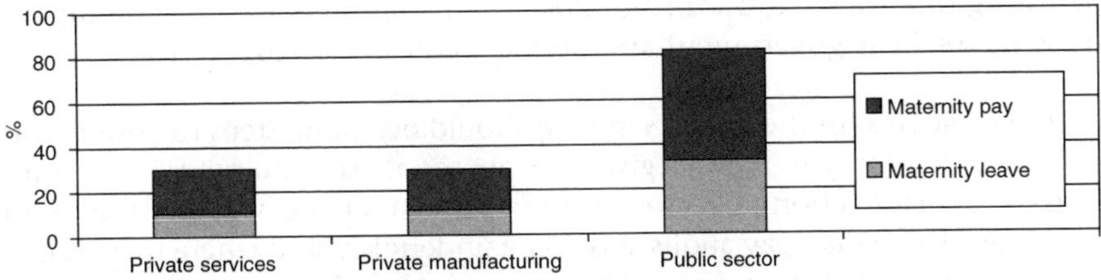



*Figure 6.2*  Provision of maternity leave/pay above the statutory minima

Similarly, whereas over one-third of public sector organisations monitored the gender profile of their workforce, just over one in ten private sector organisations did so. Moreover, the public sector was more likely than private services and private manufacturing to provide line managers with formal training on gender issues and to provide maternity leave and pay above the statutory minima: see Figure 6.2.

These findings, suggesting that the public sector takes more action to foster equality than the private sector, are also echoed in other research. Research by Woodhams and Corby (2006), based on questionnaire responses by 339 organisations in 2003, found that public sector organisations were more likely to employ a higher percentage of disabled people than private sector organisations.

In a similar vein, according to the Workplace Employment Relations Survey 2004, public sector workplaces were more likely than private sector workplaces to monitor recruitment, selection and promotion by gender, ethnicity, disability and age and to review their equality policies (Kersley *et al.*, 2006). Also, public sector workplaces were far more likely than their counterparts in the private sector to have special procedures to attract applications from women, ethnic minorities and disabled people and to provide paternity leave on full pay, rather than the statutory minimum (Kersley *et al.*, 2006) .

Furthermore, a telephone survey of 2,504 women carried out in 2005 found that mothers working in the public sector were more likely than their private sector equivalents to receive occupational maternity pay (37 per cent compared to 19 per cent) and to return to work after maternity leave; while fathers employed in the public sector were more likely than their private sector equivalents to take paternity leave (Smeaton and Marsh, 2006).

Bewley (2006), using Office of National Statistics figures, found that the gender pay gap was smaller in the public sector than the private sector. Moreover, research undertaken for the Equal Opportunities Commission in 2004 found that public sector organisations were almost twice as likely as private sector ones to have conducted an equal pay review (EPR) or to be planning one (Brett and Milsom, 2004). This figure is likely to be higher now: in 2005 the government and public sector unions agreed that:

> All employers [in the public services] should be taking steps to ensure that they are complying with legislation on equal pay and where necessary have in place action plans to close any unjustifiable pay gaps. In order to achieve this, equal pay audits should be undertaken and where there is evidence of inequality in pay and conditions of employment, action should be taken to eliminate discrimination (Public Services Forum, 2005: 1).

## Procurement

An integral part of the modernisation agenda is an emphasis on end results and standards of public service and the need to have open competition to identify the best supplier, whether from the public or private sector (Cabinet Office, 1999). This has led to public authorities in Britain spending billions of pounds every year on contracts with private and voluntary organisations for goods, works and services (Commission for Racial Equality, 2003a) and increasingly, diversity and equalities issues have come to influence the procurement process (Godwin, 2004).

The legal duty to promote race equality under the Race Relations (Amendment) Act 2000, as discussed above, applies to procurement. This is because where a public authority's function is carried out by an external supplier, that public authority remains responsible for meeting the duty and must build relevant race equality considerations into the procurement process. Again it is argued that this leads to higher quality services. As the CRE has said:

> For public authorities, integrating race equality into the procurement process can improve the quality of their services making these more appropriate and more responsive to the needs of different communities. It can also improve the overall value for money of the goods, works, or services they purchase (Commission for Racial Equality, 2003a: 8).

The previously mentioned public duties in regard to disability and gender will similarly apply to procurement activities when the relevant legislation takes effect, but already the Office of the Deputy Prime Minister[2] (ODPM) has made it clear that all the various equality strands should be considered at each stage of the local government procurement process. Moreover, the ODPM has said that best value for money in procurement does not mean lowest initial cost; it means selecting the bid that offers the optimum combination of whole life costs and benefits (ODPM, 2003). This approach is reflected in the draft procurement strategy of the Olympic Development Authority, which states that supplier diversity will be a key criterion in assessing tenders to build the UK's Olympic Park (Ewing, 2006).

One organisation that is in the forefront of the promotion of equality in the tendering process is the GLA, which is a £30 million organisation and which already has a statutory duty to promote equality generally, i.e. in relation to gender, disability, sexual orientation, age and religion as well as race (O'Cinneide, 2003a). The GLA's procurement objectives include the purchase of goods and services from suppliers who have a commitment to equality of opportunities for their workforce and their customers. It says:

> The Authority will encourage applications for inclusion in its tendering processes from all of London's diverse communities. It will endeavour to appoint contractors who are committed to promoting equality of opportunity in their own employment practices and service delivery methods.... Monitoring will take place on the diversity of businesses securing GLA contracts and fair employment provisions will be required in all GLA contracts (Greater London Authority, n.d.: 5).

Of course many public authorities are not as progressive as the GLA and at this juncture progress is patchy. For instance, in 2004, the procurement strategies of barely half of all local authorities recommended the inclusion of equality and diversity issues as a criterion for supplier selection on all contracts (Hughes, 2005).

Nevertheless, public procurement provides 'a significant lever for change' in the private sector, especially with the forthcoming legislative changes to extend the duty upon public bodies to other equality strands (Godwin, 2004: 8). This is supported by the research undertaken by the author with colleagues in south-east England. For instance, a Human Resource (HR) manager in one manufacturing company who was interviewed said:

> So when it comes to tenders [from public sector bodies] we're being asked questions in terms of, you know, what monitoring do we do, what processes have we got in place to deal with sort of racial issues or equality issues.

She then explained that such external pressures gave her a much better case to go to her boss to say that she needed time and space to devote to equality issues and that such a business argument would be more likely to convince her boss than if she just went to him with social justice arguments (Corby *et al.*, 2005: 23).

It is worth noting that pressure from public authorities does not just relate to procurement. In this same research, an HR manager of a restaurant chain which had modern apprentices said:

> We had an ALI [Adult Learning Inspectorate]. We'd never had one of those before and it was a very, very steep learning curve for us because

they picked up on the fact that we don't monitor the workforce. We don't do this. We don't do that and we've started to do it (Corby *et al.*, 2005: 23).

## Barriers to progress

While undoubtedly the government has made equality and diversity an integral part of its modernisation agenda, significant barriers to progress remain. Two of these barriers can be put firmly at the government's door: a failure to fund gender pay equality fully and the restructuring of public services. Accordingly we deal with these two barriers first. The third barrier, a barrier of long-standing, is the culture of the uniformed public services which, despite efforts to the contrary, remains largely impervious to measures to promote equality.

## The costs of equal pay

Many public sector pay systems have not been gender equality compliant, but it is costly for the public sector to develop and implement new pay systems. This is because the public sector is female intensive. In 2004, 65 per cent of public sector workers were women, compared with 41 per cent of private sector workers (Heap, 2005) and new equality proof pay systems often mean increasing the pay of women as compared to men to compensate for past pay gender inequalities. Moreover, the public sector is labour intensive: labour comprises over two-thirds of its variable costs (Corby and White, 1999). Thus, cost can be a major barrier to progress on gender pay equality.

In some public services, however, where new pay systems have been developed and implemented on equal value principles the government has provided new money. For instance, it found some additional funding for the implementation of *Agenda for Change*, the new pay system for the NHS (Brodie, 2006) and it is providing limited additional funding for the implementation of new pay structures in higher education institutions (HEIs) (Egan, 2003).

It has not, however, provided additional funding for the Single Spine Agreement (SSA) concluded between local authority employers and unions nationally. The SSA dates back to 1997 but even after six years, the vast majority of local authorities, as previously noted, had not implemented it, citing the (actual, assumed or feared) costs as a major reason for delay (Local Government Commission on Pay, 2003). Indeed, after eight years, it was estimated that only 25 per cent of local government staff had transferred on to the SSA (Cole, 2006).

This dilatoriness, however, has left local authorities open to equal pay claims. Largely this is because predominantly female groups of employees, such as home helps, although being put on the same job evaluated grade in

1986 as mainly male groups of employees, such as gardeners, street lighting attendants and refuse collectors, have received less take-home pay because they do not receive bonus payments, unlike their male comparators, and these bonuses can be as much as 80 per cent of basic pay. No win/no fee lawyers have started to represent such women and some local authorities have agreed settlements (Brodie, 2006).

Such settlements have been large both because of the numbers of employees involved and because, after a ruling from the European Court of Justice, equal pay compensation can go back six years (five years in Scotland). Already local government employers in north-east England have paid out over £100 million in equal pay settlements (Brodie, 2006). In Scotland there are estimates that such settlements will cost over £500 million (Diversity at Work, 2006b).

Although the government is allowing some English local authorities to increase their borrowing or to use capital receipts to fund their liabilities, it is not providing any additional funding (Diversity at Work, 2004). Local authorities, therefore, argue that they may have to cut jobs and services to meet their equal pay obligations as the government is threatening to cap excessive council tax rises (Brodie, 2006).

There have been other equal pay claims elsewhere in the public sector. At North Cumbria Acute Hospitals NHS Trust, where equal value cases resulted in the employer having liabilities of £73 million, the Department of Health transferred £30 million to finance initial payments. At the time of writing, however, it had not been confirmed how the balance will be met (Diversity at Work, 2006c).

In the civil service, employees of the Advisory, Conciliation and Arbitration Service (ACAS) successfully took a case based on like work.[3] It is understood that the Treasury found new money so that ACAS could comply with the tribunal's decision (conversation with author). It is also finding new money to meet the equal value claims successfully brought against the prison service, resulting in the employer having to pay out some £50 million (Diversity at Work, 2006a). Other equal pay claims in the civil service, however, have been unsuccessful so far, though litigation continues.

At this juncture, therefore, there are equal pay liabilities in the public sector generally and in local authorities in particular. Indeed, local authorities are in a Catch-22 situation. As noted above, they have no additional funding to implement the SSA, but the longer they delay implementation, the more equal pay cases are likely to be successfully brought against them, yet they will not receive additional funding to meet any liabilities they incur.

## Organisational restructuring

The second barrier to progress on public service equality is organisational restructuring which takes a number of forms: devolution and delegation, the sharing of back office services and outsourcing public service work. We deal with each in turn.

The process of devolution and delegation was started before New Labour came to power. In the 1990s under the Conservatives unified bureaucracies in the public sector were broken up into semi-autonomous units, for example, executive agencies in the civil service, so-called trusts in the NHS and the separation of the polytechnics/new universities from local authorities. New Labour, however, has not reversed this process.

So why is this policy of devolution and delegation a potential barrier to progress on equality? This is because the centre is disempowered and can no longer drive equality policies forward. It can set a framework and targets; it can disseminate good practice and sponsor networks, but it cannot control. For instance in the NHS, hospital trusts are encouraged by the centre to adopt the Positively Diverse Programme, but are not compelled to do so (NHS Executive, 2000b). In local government too, authorities have the flexibility to make as much (or as little) progress in respect of the equality standard as they think fit and considerable flexibility in the job evaluation scheme they adopt to implement the 1997 Single Status pay agreement.

In higher education too there is flexibility. For instance, guidance agreed by management and the academic unions has been issued to help HEIs to reduce their use of fixed term and casual staff (who are more likely to be women than men), but the extent to which HEIs have chosen to implement it has varied (Egan, 2003). Indeed, looking at all the sub-sectors of the public sector, research indicates that the decentralisation of employment relations has progressed furthest in education (Kirkpatrick and Hoque, 2005).

This process of delegation and devolution, far from being halted by New Labour, is being extended under its 'modernisation' arrangements. New Labour argues that to achieve customer-focused, innovative and efficient public services there needs to be:

> ...devolution and delegation to the front line, giving local leaders responsibility and accountability for delivery and the opportunity to design and develop services around the needs of local people (Office of Public Services Reform, 2002: 10).

To put this policy of devolution and delegation into practice, the government is implementing what it calls 'earned autonomy' (Office of Public Services Reform, 2002: 17), i.e. allowing certain freedoms from government control to financially viable bodies, for instance by giving managers the 'flexibility to change local terms and conditions so that they are best able to customise services' (Office of Public Services Reform, 2002: 19). To this end, the government has created foundation hospitals in the NHS and proposes to establish trust schools under the Education Bill going through Parliament at the time of writing.

Within public sector organisations too there has been restructuring with devolution to the line and, although the extent of this varies from organisation to organisation, case study research suggests that this may be detrimental to equality. For instance research by McDougall (1998: 79) indicates that devolvement of responsibility to line managers can represent 'the ultimate opt-out from gender equality'. Similarly research by Cunningham *et al.* (2004) into ill and disabled workers (and whose case studies included two local authorities) found that line managers frequently felt isolated with little or no organisational support and ill-equipped to deal with disability issues. Yet sometimes line managers failed to attend training courses and HR managers said they received little feedback from line managers. Similarly, Harris *et al.* (2002), who examined the British Library, a local authority and a probation service, found that line managers and HR specialists revealed common concerns about the effectiveness of delegation *inter alia* in relation to diversity.

Another feature of public sector restructuring is a contradictory trend to the decentralisation trend noted above: centralisation through the sharing of corporate services amongst government departments, e.g. human resources, finance, customer service centres and information technology provision (Cabinet Office, 2005b). Such a move to greater centralisation, accompanied by the procurement of such shared services from the private sector, will lead to more procurement from large organisations because of their larger capacities, and thus be at the expense of procurement from small-and medium-sized enterprises, where ethnic minority businesses are disproportionately represented (Godwin, 2004).

Public sector procurement is also at the heart of the third trend in organisational restructuring which impedes progress on equality. This is the trend to the provision of public sector services by the private sector, through for instance outsourcing and public-private partnerships. While it was previously noted that the government has sought to build equality considerations into the public sector procurement process, there are potentially adverse consequences for public sector staff who are moved to the private sector. This is because, as noted above, the private sector compares unfavourably with the public sector on numerous equality measures, so such staff are highly likely to be moving to a less equality friendly organisation. This is borne out by research on new organisational forms, including Post Office franchising, a Private Finance Initiative in the NHS and outsourcing in a central government department and a local authority. Looking at the impact of these organisational changes, the authors maintain that they 'may threaten the gains women have made in the public sector and challenge its "good employer" status in relation to equal opportunities' (Hebson and Grugulis, 2005: 234). Although these comments are made in respect of gender, arguably they also apply to other equality strands.

## The culture of uniformed public services

A further barrier to progress on equality is the culture of those in the uniformed public services: firefighters, police officers, prison officers and armed forces personnel. There is danger in these uniformed occupations and an emphasis on reliance on others, whose help may be literally a matter of life or death. Moreover, personnel often live together closely: in barracks, in police or prison housing, or sleep together in fire stations. There is an assumption that homogeneity is a necessary prerequisite to such collegiality and this leads on to an occupational norm of a white, heterosexual male, providing a hostile environment for those perceived as different: ethnic minorities, gays and women (Office for Public Management, 1996). This assumption is bolstered by the argument that women do not possess the physical ability and strength to perform certain operational duties and to accept them on a team increases potential dangers.

Indeed, in respect of the armed forces, it was only in 1994 that the Sex Discrimination Act was amended to cover service women (but to permit discrimination to ensure 'combat effectiveness') and it was not until 2000 that the ban on lesbians and gays in the armed forces was lifted.

Today, women represent less than 10 per cent of the total strength of the Armed Forces (Ministry of Defence, 2006) and an independent survey based on 9,384 responses, found that sexual harassment was rife: it had been experienced by 99 per cent of servicewomen and ranged from unwelcome comments to sexual assaults (Maley, 2006).

As to the police, recent Home Office commissioned research (Foster *et al.*, 2005) found that explicit racist language was uncommon and that managers would discipline officers using such language. The study, however, doubted whether this was indicative of a cultural change in the police service. It pointed to its own interviews, the BBC television undercover filming in 2003, which exposed racism among recruits to the police, and the report of the Morris Inquiry in 2004 on employment matters in the Metropolitan Police Service, which found disproportionality in the way black and minority ethnic (BME) officers were treated in respect of the management of their conduct (Morris Inquiry, 2004).

The Home Office Study also found that sexist and homophobic language was widespread and women, lesbian, gay and BME officers felt 'excluded, isolated and uncomfortable' and expected to experience discrimination in postings, promotion opportunities and every day interactions (Foster *et al*, 2005: 41).

At the same time, the CRE carried out a formal investigation into the recruitment, training and management of police officers and into how police forces were meeting their employment monitoring duties under the

Race Relations (Amendment) Act 2000. In short the CRE found a lack of comprehensive ethnic monitoring in accordance with the employment monitoring duty; inconsistent induction and support mechanisms for trainers of recruits; patchy delivery of equality training to serving officers; and a widespread perception that BME officers were disproportionately subjected to the disciplinary procedure compared to their white colleagues (Commission for Racial Equality, 2005b).

Racism and sexism can also be found in other uniformed public services. A formal investigation by the CRE into race equality in prisons found that racial abuse, harassment and racist graffiti were persistent features of prison life for many staff; entrenched staff cultures led to the ignoring of race equality procedures; BME staff who made formal complaints about discrimination and harassment were subsequently victimised; prison governors failed to carry out ethnic monitoring; and senior managers failed to act on Employment Tribunal findings even when a commitment to action had been made (Commission for Racial Equality, 2003b).

As to the fire service, one recent study concluded that 'the sad fact is that the culture of the service has not moved with the times' and, in doing so, noted that, in 2002, less than 2 per cent of firefighters were women and less than 2 per cent were non-white (Independent Review, 2002).

## Conclusions

This chapter has shown that the government is integrating equality into its modernisation agenda, thus giving equality a high priority. Interestingly its rationale for doing so is mainly based on efficiency and effectiveness arguments and, although the government may talk about social inclusion, social justice arguments are used to bolster the business case, not to provide the primary rationale.

As Dickens (1994, 2006) has pointed out, the business case argument is partial and contingent and can point away from equality as well as towards it (for example, there could be a business case for contracting out, even though the social justice case might point to direct recruitment from non-traditional sources). Thus the government's assumption that arguments for equality based on the business case and the social justice case are complementary is questionable and even disingenuous.

Whatever New Labour's rationale, however, it would be churlish to underrate progressive developments. These include the focus on equality in many parts of the public services and measures already taken, or in train, to foster diversity. Chief among these are the new public sector legal duties and the embedding of equality into the procurement process. In short, by and large, rhetoric is being transposed into reality.

There are certain legal flaws, for instance the weak enforcement provisions in respect of the public duties. There also are significant barriers to equality, particularly the engrained culture of uniformed public service personnel and the government's unwillingness to meet the costs incurred by failures over many years to provide equal pay for men and women doing work of equal value in the public services.

There are also contradictions between the government's activities aimed at making progress on equality and its organisational changes aimed at promoting measures that it believes (however justifiably) will lead to public organisations being more responsive to users – i.e. delegation, the sharing of corporate services and outsourcing. That being said, whereas the government's modernisation programmes have had negative effects on employment in some areas such as privatisation (as other chapters in this book demonstrate), they have had positive effects on the furtherance of equality and diversity in the public sector.

Last but not least, there have been positive effects on the equality practices of organisations in the private sector too, because the public sector has set an example. In particular, while overall the public sector compares favourably with the private sector on a variety of equality measures, many private sector organisations are being obliged to improve their equality practices as a condition of obtaining contracts for the provision of goods and services to the public sector. To sum up, although much remains to be done, by and large significant progress on equality has been achieved in the public services under New Labour.

## Notes

1. Co-financed by the South East England Development Agency and the European Social Fund.
2. The ODPM was replaced by the Department for Communities and Local Government (DCLG) on 5 May 2006.
3. Crossley v ACAS (ET/1304744/98).

# 7
# Pay and Rewards in Public Services: Fairness and Equity

*David Marsden*

One of the most notable changes in public sector rewards over the past two decades has been the erosion of the long-established salary systems which paid for grade, with seniority increments for pay progression within grades. Although such increments may not have been intended to be automatic, as the Megaw Report (1982) observed, such increments were almost never withheld for poor performance. By 2005, annual increments within grades had been replaced by those based on some measure of performance for very large numbers of public employees in central and much of local government, in government agencies, in education, and in some cases also in healthcare. Although there is an ongoing debate about levels of rewards in public sector compared with private sector employment, especially at the highest and least skilled ends, this chapter will focus exclusively on systems of rewards, and in particular on performance pay and performance management as these lie behind the sea change in public sector reward systems.

This chapter argues that we need to probe beneath the surface of these new performance-based reward systems. Although political ideology may have played its part in the initial mobilisation for change, the process of sustained continuous improvements in design and operation has continued long beyond that. It has also extended internationally. In the earliest presentations, the reasons for performance pay were framed in terms of incentives and motivation which were said to be lacking in public employment. The first study of the Inland Revenue (IR) scheme in 1991 was supported by the then Inland Revenue Staffs Federation on the expectation that it would demonstrate that performance pay was not motivating staff.[1] By the turn of the millennium, it was clear that motivation was only part of the story, and that more fundamental changes were at work within the wider context of improving the performance of whole organisations. Goal setting and appraisal for employees was but the grass-roots level of attempts to give sharper focus and better democratic accountability to civil service agencies and other public service organisations. This chapter argues that a better understanding of the reform of public service pay systems is gained if we follow the thread of renegotiation of performance instead of that of motivation. Procedural justice is an important support for effective renegotiation of performance goals and standards, but the associated procedures will work better if their design fits with management's underlying agenda of change. The chapter draws heavily on a series of studies of UK public service performance management carried out at the Centre for Economic Performance (CEP) over the past 15 years.

## Developments in Britain in international context

A recent study by the Organisation for Economic Cooperation and Development (OECD, 2005) confirms that the British experience in reform of public service pay systems is far from unique, although Britain may be among a relatively small group of pioneer countries in terms of the longevity of performance management, and the systematic way in which it has been pursued. The OECD study, which was based on reporting by senior public service managers from most OECD member countries, revealed a great deal of experimentation in the search for alternatives to long-established practices of pay advancing with seniority until grade maxima are reached. Individual performance pay was one of the more common systems adopted, but there were also experiments with collective rewards, and with performance appraisal without a link with pay. The one common feature across all countries was that the fraction of pay linked to performance was relatively small, especially for those outside senior management.

Apart from that, the study revealed a great variety in the objectives pursued, the design, and the governance of performance management systems. In addition to 'performance', other objectives included recruitment and retention, encouraging staff to take more responsibility for their work, and to engage more in organisational change. Equity was also sometimes a reason. One should not forget some of the perceived inequities of the established systems as employees saw the same rewards being given despite widely recognised variations in the effectiveness and contributions of different employees, together with the perceived failure of management to do anything to rectify the situation. The study revealed considerable variations in the design of performance pay policies. They were highly centralised in some of the 'Anglo-Saxon' countries, and highly decentralised in some of the Scandinavian countries. They also tended to be more decentralised for employees than for senior managers. Finally, it revealed considerable variation in the means of governance of these systems. In some cases, they were imposed, and operated, 'top down', whereas in others they were introduced and managed either jointly or by collective agreement with trade unions.

Underlining the need to see the reform of pay systems in a wider context, the OECD study highlighted a broad correlation between the linking of pay and performance appraisal with the degree of delegation in human resource management systems (OECD, 2005: 36). This was based on the findings of the OECD survey of strategic human resource management practices in OECD public services. At one extreme, there were the countries with low delegation and little link between appraisal and pay, including Japan, Greece, and Luxembourg, and at the other, several Scandinavian countries, Australia, New Zealand and the UK. The US, Canada, France and Italy were located near the middle, and close to the regression line.

For these reasons alone, it would a mistake to try to force one's interpretation of the British experience through the lens of 'Thatcherism', 'marketisation', or any of the ideological labels that have been used in recent years. Important as these may have seemed in individual cases, the range of political hues displayed by governments in these countries is such that one has to look deeper for the causes of dissatisfaction with established public service incentive systems, and to try to understand some of the underlying processes which these reforms seek to address.

## British public service compared with private sector practices

A rough idea of the extent of use of 'merit pay', that is pay 'related to a subjective assessment of individual performance by a supervisor or manager', can be gained from Workplace Employers Relations Survey (WERS) 2004. This shows that, in Britain, merit pay is well-established in both sectors, albeit for a large minority of employees. The figures relate to the percentages of establishments using merit pay rather than of employees covered by such schemes. In 2004, roughly 10 per cent of public sector workplaces, representing roughly 21 per cent of public sector employees, used merit pay. This compares with 16 per cent of private establishments, representing 26 per cent of private employees.[2] Performance appraisals, which are commonly used as a basis for merit pay, are now widely used in both sectors, with 65 per cent of private, and 69 per cent of public sector employees in establishments where appraisal covered all non-managerial employees.

## The experience with performance-related pay (PRP) in British public services

The government's Makinson Report, published in 2000, reviewed the experience of performance pay in the civil service network agencies.[4] Drawing on its own enquiries and on a number of academic studies conducted over the previous decade, including those of the CEP, it concluded that the existing forms of performance pay and performance management had failed to motivate many staff. Makinson noted that there was a 'stark contrast between approval of the principle and disenchantment with the practice of performance pay' (Makinson, 2000: 3). Later on the same report

**Table 7. 1   Establishments reporting use of 'merit pay' for some employees[3]**
(% of establishments in sector declaring use of merit pay)

| | Private<br>% merit pay | Public<br>% merit pay | Private<br>% merit pay | Public<br>% merit pay | Private<br>N (all estabs) | Public<br>N (all estabs) |
|---|---|---|---|---|---|---|
| Weights | Establishment | Establishment | Employment | Employment | Establishment | Establishment |
| Manufacturing | 13 | – | 27 | – | 210 | – |
| Electricity, gas and water | – | – | – | – | – | – |
| Construction | 11 | – | 18 | – | 92 | – |
| Wholesale and retail | 13 | – | 22 | – | 461 | – |
| Hotels and restaurants | 17 | – | 20 | – | 161 | – |
| Transport and communication | 9 | 29 | 25 | 21 | 70 | 50 |
| Financial services | 29 | – | 43 | – | 95 | – |
| Other business services | 19 | 0 | 33 | 0 | 274 | 17 |
| Public administration | – | 6 | – | 28 | – | 97 |
| Education | 1 | 10 | 8 | 19 | 15 | 179 |
| Health | 11 | 11 | 9 | 22 | 105 | 156 |
| Other community services | 31 | 3 | 20 | 12 | 72 | 70 |
| Total | 16 | 10 | 26 | 21 | 1557 | 589 |

also stressed weaknesses in performance management at the organisational level which would weaken its effectiveness for individual employees.

Among the weaknesses in the existing schemes were that many employees found their operation divisive. It caused jealousies among staff, and it seemed to undermine their relationships with management. Although only a few thought it had actually reduced their willingness to cooperate with management, many thought that line managers gave better appraisals to their blue-eyed staff, and that senior management manipulated appraisal scores in order to save money (Marsden and French, 1998). As a result, many employees felt that even if they did perform well, they would not be rewarded. If we follow either expectancy or agency theory, then the prediction would be that employees would become demotivated and cut back their performance.

Nevertheless, a substantial minority of line managers, who carried out appraisals of their staff, also reported that they believed that performance management had led their staff to increase the quantity of work they did. Less of them reported an increase in work quality. This, taken with other archival evidence on performance, suggests that despite apparent demotivation, overall productivity did not decline, and may have increased (Marsden, 2004). This creates something of a puzzle, which will be addressed in the next two sections.

## Procedural justice and performance management

'Procedural justice' refers to the fairness of the procedures for allocating rewards, and is often contrasted with 'distributive justice' which relates to the fairness of the allocated rewards themselves (see, for example, Cropanzano and Greenberg, 1997). Although there is some variation in the interpretation of the concept, one might say that the procedures are operated justly when employees have a fair chance that good performance will be rewarded. Several writers have argued that in the face of perceived injustice, employees will withdraw goodwill, and that when they believe that procedures are fairly applied, they will tolerate temporary departures from distributive justice in rewards (for example Folger and Cropanzano, 1998). The processes associated with performance appraisal, and the design and allocation of associated rewards all fall under the umbrella of procedural justice, and, it is argued, employees are likely to withdraw performance if they feel that management violate procedural justice norms when operating their reward systems.

In concrete terms, employees are likely to feel that procedural justice has been violated if they believe that the odds of rewards following good performance are stacked against them. Thus if they believe that:

(a) managers lack the necessary knowledge to set meaningful goals and appraise performance reliably;

(b)  managers are not acting in good faith;

(c)  performance criteria violate what they consider to be relevant in the light of their own professional knowledge and experience;

(d)  management's concept of motivation is inappropriate to what employees believe is valuable in their work and what motivates them, then they are likely to feel that their scheme is unfair. Looked at in this way, procedural justice is not just a matter of having the right procedures, but rather of having procedures that are sufficiently well-informed to lead to decisions that are considered fair.

From quite early on, the civil service agencies had adopted 'best practice' procedures as described by leading practitioner organisations such as Advisory Conciliation and Arbitration Service (ACAS) and the Chartered Institute of Personnel and Development (CIPD) (ACAS, 1990, Armstrong and Murlis, 1994). Nevertheless, the evidence of 'disenchantment' considered by Makinson embraced all four types of factor, although the mix varied between sectors and occupational groups.[5] Analysis of CEP survey data from the civil service departments, and the two trust hospitals, reveals that the quality of the appraisal process and of goal setting as judged by their recipients, had a positive and strongly significant effect on the perceived incentive of their respective performance pay schemes. They also had a comparable negative effect on perceived divisiveness (Marsden, 2004: Table 2). The same analysis showed that perceived divisiveness was stronger in the government departments than in the hospitals. An important potential cause of this is that although the procedures were the right ones for appraisal-related pay, in fact, the underlying process that was driving performance management was of a different nature, which is explored in the next section.

## Performance management and renegotiation of the employment relationship

One contributory factor to the perceived lack of procedural justice is that in fact one can detect two different agendas that were merged together implicitly in performance management: a static and a dynamic one. The static one is the traditional process of evaluating past performance, attributing rewards according to mostly subjective management judgements of employee performance, the sense WERS used to define 'merit pay' in Table 7.1 above. The dynamic one really concerns what one might describe as a renegotiation of performance standards, which can take place within performance management. It involves the setting of performance goals, followed by appraisal according to how well they have been achieved. What I should like to argue is that the tension between these two processes accounts for a large part of the perceived departures from procedural justice in the civil service agencies and in the National Health Service (NHS) hospital trusts examined by Marsden and French (1998). This explains the apparent loss of motivation, but also the sustained levels of productivity. In these cases, management were in fact using appraisal to communicate new performance standards, but mostly were not engaging their staff in the process by which these were defined. I should also like to suggest that in practice the more successful blending of these components in many schools has contributed to a better experience with performance management for teachers since 2000 than for civil servants in the preceding years.

If one looks back to the first performance pay schemes introduced into the public services in the late 1980s, such as that of the Inland Revenue (IR) in 1987, they belong to a 'static' agenda. In the words of the trade unions, they had been 'bolted onto' the long-standing civil service performance appraisal systems. These graded performance according to a long list of criteria that were applied across a very wide range of different jobs and departments, and awarded 'box markings' according to how well employees were deemed to have performed. In the IR, there were 13 such criteria covering such aspects of performance as intensity and quality of work, willingness to take initiative, cooperativeness, attentiveness to colleagues and so on. These were criteria of performance that could apply to any job, but at the same time, because of their generality, for most jobs, only a small number were relevant, and they took little account of variations in job demands, and the scope that individual employees had to vary their performance. In a sense, the thinking behind them is well-captured in the expression used in the US civil service that public servants should be 'neutral competents'. The direction of their work was to be established by the government of the day, and they were to supply competent work behaviour according to their skills and job grades. They could do this with greater or lesser degrees of effort, care and initiative: hence the logic of the appraisal criteria.

What was lacking from the appraisal system was a set of priorities. The criteria contributing to the box markings bore no particular weightings, and if the managers doing appraisals applied weightings in practice, there was no framework to guide them. As a result, appraisal did not seek to establish any specific link between individual and organisational performance beyond the general common sense idea that good individual performance is good for the organisation. Looking again at the IR experience, in the late 1980s, when its first scheme was introduced, the organisational performance indicators published in the IR's annual report and accounts were very crude. Beyond the overall financial indicators, those relating to internal efficiency were mostly based on administrative records, and related to such items as the percentage of workload completed by certain deadlines. By the late 1990s, the published indicators were considerably more sophisticated, with some based on probability sampling, and providing information on quality of performance, such as the percentage of work that was right first time, and the promptness of response to enquiries from tax payers. In its annual reports through the decade, the IR explained how it was developing new measures, and published them initially on an experimental basis. The significant point is that the IR was building a set of organisational performance indicators that related to the key inputs of any labour intensive agency, namely the time and quality of work of its employees. These provided the beginnings of a framework which would enable line managers conducting appraisal to set individual performance priorities with clearer reference to those of the organisation as a whole. If managers know that there is a higher percentage of mistakes in work from their office compared with that of others, then they know that they should give this priority when appraising their staff. The criteria of the old system were too general to assist them in this.

Without some measures to link individual and organisational performance, it is very difficult to judge whether increased employee effort has contributed to organisational performance. This works in two ways. It is hard to justify to employees why they should direct their effort to improving on the general criteria established in the appraisal system. It is also hard for managers to assess whether improvements in line with these criteria warrant additional rewards. Very often, in such circumstances, line managers come under great pressure from their immediate work colleagues to be lenient and to give people good appraisals because otherwise it is going to make work relationships difficult in the future. If top management try to combat this by insisting on forced distributions of appraisal scores, such as given percentages of employees must fall within each of the performance grades, then the scheme just appears arbitrary. On the other hand, if individual employee targets are integrated with office or department targets, and managers are then assessed on the latter, then they are under pressure to allocate good ratings and rewards to those individuals or groups who contribute most effectively to those higher level targets. This provides line managers with a clearer rationale to explain work goals to their staff, and it provides an incentive for the managers to seek to integrate staff targets with those of their office or department.

Once performance management integrates the processes of goal setting and appraisal, it introduces an element of negotiation. The key to understanding this lies in the information asymmetry between managers who have knowledge of the overall running of their departments, and their staff who have greater knowledge of the detailed nature and constraints of their work. Such information is essential to the establishment of realistic and meaningful work goals, and staff can share or withhold such information from their managers. There are different ways in which such negotiation can be approached, and there is evidence of all three in the CEP surveys of public employees. It could be a simple 'top down' imposition of work goals without discussion, and there is evidence that many public employees have experienced it in this way. In addition, many employees thought that those who achieved or exceeded their work objectives had done so because they were cleverer at negotiating easier targets than their colleagues.[6] Such tendencies would be exacerbated if line managers have few resources at their disposal to support their staff. Thus it can be zero-sum negotiation over the effort to be supplied over the coming period. There is also scope for a third approach, in which there is negotiation, but it is directed more towards problem-solving: how can individual employees alter their performance so that it contributes to improved organisational performance. This is what Walton and McKersie (1965) describe as 'integrative' negotiation, in which the two parties seek to resolve an issue in such a way that both end up better off as a result. Such negotiation contains an important technical element, assessing what options are feasible and what resources both parties can contribute, but it also takes account of their different interests.

There are limits to the effectiveness of the top-down approach in which goals are 'cascaded down' from above, and they are more serious the greater management's dependence upon employee job knowledge. If the goals are unrealistic, there is little chance that employees will achieve them, and once they see that, they are likely to become cynical about the process. This would explain some of the negative attitudes toward performance management – that it is unfair in its operation. For example, the CEP study found that perceived divisiveness of PRP schemes increased when line managers judged that their staff had no scope in their jobs to raise their performance (Marsden, 2004: Table 2). Such cynicism can have more damaging consequences, as was illustrated at the then Employment Service shortly after the survey by Marsden and French, when the *Guardian* newspaper reported in a series of articles the widespread falsification of performance target data on job placements by employees and their managers.[7] Employees and their managers feared that they would be penalised if they failed to hit their targets, and so felt under pressure to overstate the number of job placements achieved.

Treating goal setting as a zero-sum exercise encounters similar problems to those of top-down goals, and for the same reasons. The information asymmetry creates scope for employees to withhold information about their true potential for performance in their jobs. As mentioned earlier, many civil servants thought that those who achieved or exceeded their targets did so because they had negotiated soft targets. In large organisations, management has one important resource in such negotiation, notably, the ability to establish benchmarks between different departments within the organisation. The more such departments are comparable, the more such information sets parameters on how far job information can be manipulated. There is reason to believe that such negotiation played an important part in the IR's success in maintaining and even raising productivity levels during the 1990s while at the same time its performance management scheme appeared to leave employees 'disenchanted'. Many employees felt that the combined process of goal setting and performance appraisal had caused managers to set clearer targets, and where this was so, they achieved better performance evaluations. Indeed, performance benchmarking not only equipped managers to deal more effectively with misleading claims about the effort required for certain jobs, but it also set limits on management leniency. If line managers were too generous in the way they set targets and awarded good performance ratings, they stood to fall short on their own targets. One can interpret that agency's experience as a process of renegotiating the 'effort bargain' with its employees during that period (Marsden, 2004). Performance management and performance pay did not make employees feel more strongly motivated, but the clearer definitions of work goals set within this process had contributed to improved organisational performance.

Within large civil service agencies, linking individual and organisational performance will always be difficult. One of the Makinson Report's main recommendations was that in the future performance management should seek to relate individual employees' performance to group targets set at a lower level than the whole organisation, which would be more meaningful for them. It also sought to break away from the idea of fixed budgetary constraints so that if areas of organisational performance improved, more recognition could be given to employees. One of the causes of employee cynicism with regard to management's operation of performance pay stemmed from the belief that fixed budgets would not leave sufficient scope to reward improved performance. There was no equivalent of the recognition of good performance that leads, in the private sector, to increased output or sales.

The experience of performance management in state primary and secondary schools in England and Wales from 2000 provides an interesting extension to the story. Initially, classroom and head teachers were more sceptical about the suitability of performance management to their work than was the case in the civil service. Yet after three years of operation, it was clear that the initial opposition was fading, and that many heads and classroom teachers were becoming aware of certain merits in their scheme (Marsden and Belfield, 2007). Based on a representative panel survey of schools and their teachers in England and Wales, started by CEP in 2000, just before the scheme was introduced, and repeated after completion of its first and third cycles, the authors found that, in many schools, the scheme had helped managers to agree clearer goals with classroom teachers, and to integrate them better with school goals, and where this was so, pupil attainments had improved by more than the average. Probing what lay behind this, the authors argued that, in such schools, performance management had operated as a form of integrative negotiation between individual teachers and their line managers. This was justified by showing evidence from the survey responses of both classroom and head teachers that the performance management process had contained each of the four elements in integrative negotiation identified by Walton and McKersie (1965). These included identifying the source of a problem; reviewing alternative solutions; selecting the best in the light of technical issues and the preferences and objectives of both parties; their 'utility functions' in the words of Walton and McKersie; and agreeing to and implementing a solution. Arguably, this process was more successful in schools than in the civil service because of their smaller scale, and the greater control over resources held by head teachers. This meant that heads and line managers could approach the problem-solving aspects of the negotiation with the knowledge that they could provide resources to help teachers achieve the goals that were deemed important for the school. In preparation for the new scheme's introduction, the Education Department published a set of good practice cases based on existing practice in some schools. These sought to illustrate how statistical information on pupil performance across the school could be used to identify problems. For example, the boys in a given year might be underperforming compared with girls at a particular subject, and classroom teachers and their line managers could then devise a suitable teaching strategy to engage the boys more in the course material (DfEE, 1999). More generally, the school could provide additional training, or some rearrangement of work load and work times in such cases, for example, in exchange for agreement to redefine or reshape certain classroom objectives, as was evident in some schools in the CEP survey. Such actions would also help the school to reach its overall targets for pupil performance. Thus, the favourable outcome did not just depend upon the classroom teachers providing more effort, and the element of give and take, and the jointly recognised problem, enabled both parties to approach the negotiation in an integrative rather than a distributive spirit. In terms of procedural justice, the process of information sharing to find a solution and the element of give and take in such negotiation can do much to reinforce employees' perceptions of management's good faith, and their belief that their knowledge and values have been taken into account.

Nevertheless, it would be wrong to suggest that this was the experience of all schools. Many teachers wrote in replies which revealed the operation of a harder and more top-down approach to goal setting in their schools. Nevertheless, on the evidence of the panel, the number of 'reformer' schools appeared to have grown from about 10–15 per cent after the first year to about 20–25 per cent by the end of the third.

Although the school teachers' performance management system emphasises individual rewards for individual performance, and so might be thought at first sight to be a vindication of the individualistic approach that has prevailed in most British public service schemes, there are some important group elements. First, the scheme has operated with absolute rather than relative standards, despite government pressures, in the spirit that those teachers who reach the appropriate standard should progress through the system. Second, schools now operate in a quasi-market in which their reputation for good exam pass rates can influence parental choice (Glennerster, 2002). As a result, schools which fail to attract sufficient pupils can see their rolls and their income falling. School development plans are complex documents which set out each school's targets and its implementation strategies. The goal setting and appraisal elements of performance management provide a forum within which school management can have an annual dialogue with individual teachers as to how their own contribution fits into the needs of the school as a whole. Because the school's targets can be fairly specific, for example, to improve the performance of target groups of pupils who may be falling behind, these can be translated into specific objectives agreed between teachers and their line managers.

## Conclusion

Looking back at the interviews with senior managers at the IR in 1991 carried out by Marsden and Richardson on the goals of the department's first performance pay scheme instituted in 1987, it is clear that we are dealing with an emergent strategy in Mintzberg's sense (Mintzberg *et al.*, 1998). The discussion then was about providing a modest additional incentive to encourage more positive motivation among IR staff, but without making excessive claims about the likely consequences. Given the general design of the civil service appraisal scheme onto which performance pay was bolted, such modest aspirations were quite fitting. The instruments then in place could not have been used to bring about any major changes in goal setting. The new system brought into operation in 1993 represented a major step forward in this respect by introducing individual performance agreements against which staff would subsequently be appraised. At the same time, the IR was implementing radical changes in the way it measured its organisational performance, breaking away from traditional administrative measures, and adopting more focused ones based on sampling. This created the backbone for a system that would enable line managers to give greater clarity and specificity to the goals they set in appraisal, and on the basis of which they awarded performance pay. It also gave top management the means to monitor better the effectiveness with which line managers ran performance management; for example, to detect whether appraisal ratings bore any correspondence to office performance when comparisons were made across different offices. In a large department such as the IR, it is always going to be difficult to provide targets that are meaningful to individual employees in a way that will motivate them, hence

Makinson's favoured strategy of group performance incentives. On the other hand, schools are much smaller units, and have provided another framework within which to observe the operation of performance management and performance pay. It was argued that the school teachers' scheme provides a mix of individual incentives with organisational goals that are sufficiently close to the contributions of individual teachers for performance management to involve a significant degree of integrative negotiation at the individual level.

Procedural justice is an important factor in the engagement of employees in performance management. Although the focus of performance management has been at the individual level, Marsden and Belfield (2007) have argued that organised employee voice, through their unions and professional associations, can provide substantial support. This comes through their ability to articulate employee views about the importance of information asymmetries in goal setting, and about employees' values that underpin both their motivation and what they feel important about their work. Such organisations can also assist by monitoring the good faith with which management operates its pay systems in a way that individual employees cannot.

If the integrative negotiation component of performance management is to develop, it needs to be more fully recognised. The emphasis needs to be shifted away from 'cascading' goals from the top-down and then seeking to motivate people afterwards, towards more flexible and interactive methods for agreeing work objectives. If organisations are to pursue integrative negotiation within performance management, then they will need to build sufficient flexibility into the definition of organisational goals so that there is enough breathing space at grass-roots level for integrative negotiation between line managers and their staff. This need not be a recipe for blurring the clarity of organisational goals because integrative negotiation also improves the information base on which goals are set, often making them more realistic. Finally, these observations extend beyond the highly qualified who currently have more scope to determine their objectives than the less qualified. One should not neglect the scope for this among less qualified employees. At present, the way their work roles are constructed often limits their scope for active involvement in selecting work goals, and lack of scope to change their performance can make performance pay seem unfair to them. However, work organisation need not be so restrictive, and one of the lessons of research on Japanese patterns of work organisation is that even relatively unqualified employees can contribute to problem-solving activities and this can in fact enhance what Koike (1997) has described as 'intellectual skills' among workers in such jobs. This requires a degree of flexibility by top management in the definition of organisational goals so that enough breathing space is left at grass-roots level for integrative negotiation between line managers and their staff.

## Notes

1. The study is described in Marsden and Richardson 1994.
2. It is possible that the definition used by WERS understates the true extent of performance pay in the public sector as the system of performance management in primary and secondary schools, for example, restricts the degree to which managers' subjective assessment can influence both threshold assessment and subsequent progression along the performance-related upper pay scale under the system of performance management introduced in 2000.
3. Notes: '–' denotes less than ten establishments in the weighted sample. Establishment weights correct for the sampling fractions used in the survey. Employment weights take account also of the number of employees in an establishment. percentage relate to establishments paying merit pay as a percentage of all establishments in the sector. Private sector includes public and private limited companies, companies limited by guarantee and partnerships and self-proprietorships, and the public sector includes government-owned companies, public service agencies, public corporations, QUANGOs and local and central government, including the NHS, Local Education Authorities (LEAs), and schools. These are based on *astatus*1 = 1–4, and public sector *astatus*1 = 8–12.
   *Source*: WERS 2004
4. These were the Inland Revenue, the Benefits Agency, the Employment Service and HM Customs and Excise.
5. The survey evidence on employee attitudes and experiences of their performance pay schemes available to the Makinson team included that of Thompson (1993), Kessler and Purcell (1993), Marsden and Richardson (1994), Marsden and French (1998) and Heery (1998). These surveys covered a wide range of public employees from across the public services, and contained many similar findings, most notably, that performance pay had not proved an effective motivator for the majority of employees, and that its operation had often proved divisive despite quite widespread support for the principle of linking pay to performance.
6. Marsden and French (1998) found that two-fifths of their Inland Revenue respondents were of this view.
7. *Guardian* (29.3.97), 'Jobcentres fiddled figures to boost employment statistics'; *Guardian* (1.4.07) 'McDonalds' job data abused'; *Guardian* (16.4.97) 'Fake job figures scandal exposed'.

# 8
# 'Employment Security' and 'Job Insecurity' in Public Services: Two Sides of the Same Coin?

*Pauline Dibben*

Employment security is a key issue for public service workers in Britain. A traditional caricature of the public servant has been of someone who seeks to serve the public good, and deserves a 'job for life'. But these perceptions have been gradually eroded over time, not least as a result of 'public choice' arguments that have characterised public sector workers as self-interested and bureau-shaping bureaucrats. The professional autonomy of the public servant has been undermined, and in the 2005 general election, all three of the main political parties attempted to win votes through pledging public sector job cuts. At the same time, those who provide cleaning services, or assistance in classrooms, hospitals and nursing homes have apparently been regarded as external to the smooth running of public services. Against this background, this chapter aims to explore the different dimensions of employment and job security, recognising that insecurity has affected different groups of workers in different ways.

## 'Employment' or 'job' insecurity?

'Employment security' and 'job security' are often used interchangeably, which can lead to a loss of conceptual clarity in relation to causality and effect.[1] For the purposes of this chapter however, 'employment security' will be used as a macro-level concept, taking into account relevant labour market trends, the responsibility of the State, and national-level engagement by the trade union body. In contrast, 'job security' will be used as a micro-level concept, focusing on individual perceptions, the employment relationship between public service workers and their employer, and the role of trade unions in providing workplace and individual support. Table 8.1 on page 122, outlines this range of factors and influences.

Although providing the basis for investigating insecure work in Britain's public services, this framework does not attempt to capture all related

**Table 8.1   Conceptualising insecure work in Britain's public services**

|  | Macro-level 'employment security' | Micro-level 'job insecurity' |
|---|---|---|
| **Trends** | Labour market trends<br>– Job tenure and job loss<br>– Defining and evaluating levels of insecure work | Individual perceptions<br>– Quantifying job insecurity<br>– Determining levels of perceived job insecurity |
| **Role of Government** | As State<br>– Employment benefits<br>– Legislation | As employer<br>– Downsizing, delayering and redundancy<br>– Outsourcing |
| **Role of Trade Union** | National level<br>– Influencing legislation and policy<br>– Sectoral collective agreements | Individual /workplace level<br>– Direct intervention<br>– Cooperation with employer |

aspects. Such a task would be immense, and include, for example, reference to low income (see for example Gregg *et al.*, 2000), stress (c.f. Nolan *et al.*, 2000; Burchell *et al.*, 2002) and training (c.f. Heery and Salmon, 2000; Guest, 2000). In addition, it does not include government supply side initiatives related to job creation, or public expenditure decisions, through which it could influence levels of insecurity.

The chapter examines, in turn, the macro- and then micro-level aspects of: trends in insecure work, the role of government, and the response of trade unions. Although the focus here is on public services, the uneven quantity of published material means that it is difficult to draw exclusively on such material (Morgan *et al.*, 2000). Nevertheless, where such evidence is available it is used to offer insights into the above dimensions.

## Trends in insecure work and job insecurity

Measuring job security is complicated and critics of the 'insecurity thesis' advanced by Heery and Salmon (2000) question whether work in Britain is more insecure in current times than it has ever been in the past (Green *et al.*, 2000). One means of measurement is the level of employment. Public sector employment has fallen over recent years, from 7.5 million in 1979 to 5.1 million in 1996 (Morgan *et al.*, 2000), but in the first quarter of 2006, public sector employment was nearly 6 million, and private sector employment was 23 million (ONS, August 2006b). Case study and survey evidence in the NHS, Education and local government suggest that there has been an increase in the use of redundancy as a result of restructuring, and that job losses have resulted from contracting out, although the rates still compare favourably with the private sector (Morgan *et al.*, 2000). Cuts in public sector jobs have, however, been very much on the agenda in recent years. The Gershon Report (2004: 3–6) explained how efficiency gains of over £20 billion in 2007–8 had been agreed, resulting in the loss of 84,000 posts across the civil service and military personnel, with 'efficiency review workstreams' for central government and 'all devolved services', a review of policy, funding and regulation to include local authorities and primary care trusts, and 'productive time' applied similarly to teachers, doctors, nurses and police as well as central government staff (Gershon, 2004: 11).[2]

Another means of measurement is the mean length of time of jobs. In this respect, there was little overall change in mean job tenure between the 1970s and 1990s, although there is evidence to suggest that tenure has been shorter for manual and public service workers, part-timers and ethnic minorities (Herzog, 1997; Burgess and Rees, 1998; Gregg *et al.*, 2000). It could be argued that job tenure is not necessarily a good measure of perceived security since people who stay in their current jobs may fear being able to find an alternative job, especially during a recession (Robinson, 2000; Edwards, 2001). Also, average tenure may have changed due to either permanent dismissals or voluntary quits (Turnbull and Wass, 2000). An alternative and arguably better way of measuring levels of job insecurity over time is through examining the proportion of employees on non-permanent contracts.[3]

## Defining and determining levels of 'insecure' work

There are many ways of defining atypical and/or insecure work. These include: non-standard, contingent and flexible employment, marginal labour and the peripheral workforce, and include part-time, temporary and self-employed workers, sub-contracting employees and self-employed consultants, directly employed and agency workers (Purcell *et al.*, 1999). The term thus includes a wide variety of workers, including low-paid home workers and independent professionals (Edwards, 2001: 3) and not all forms of atypical work are contrary to the best interests of workers. For example, Druker and Stanworth's (2004) study of temporary agency work suggests that some temps appreciate the flexibility to try different things, or choose this form of work because they do not want to accept the work discipline of permanent work or want to get a foot in the door of a new workplace. Other forms of work include 'interim management', where managers are used in project work where there are no in-house experts, to replace someone for a few months, or as 'company doctor' to turn round an ailing business over a limited period of time (Stredwick and Ellis, 2005).

Part-time work is another type of work that is generally referred to as 'atypical work,' but may or may not be included within the concept of 'insecure work'. Part-time work can lack training, be gendered, and is often temporary (Purcell, 2000). However, in some European countries full-time and part-time hours have converged as a result of an increase in part-time and reduction in full-time hours of work, or it receives equal provision under the law. Also, where statutory regulation is low, and full-time jobs are not covered by collective agreements, full-time jobs may not offer more protection than part-time ones (Bosch, 2004). In Britain, amendments in 2002 to the Part-Time Workers Regulations 2000 means that it is unlawful for employers to give part-time workers less favourable terms and conditions of employment than full-timers, irrespective of contract, unless different treatment can be objectively justified, and full-time employees now have the right to request part-time work to suit their work-life balance, especially after maternity leave. While it is accepted that part-time work can sometimes imply lower terms and conditions than full-time work, for the purposes of this chapter, the term 'insecure work' generally implies that it is also temporary in nature, or that a perceived threat of job loss exists.

In contrast, annualised hours is a form of work that can be both unpredictable and insecure. It is commonly associated with the manufacturing sector, but has more recently been extended to public services and involves the replacement of a weekly hours' contract by one covering the whole year, with both planned and reserve hours varying greatly throughout the year (Stredwick and Ellis, 2005). Nevertheless, there is usually a ceiling set on the number of hours worked in a year, and although weekly hours vary, they are tied to a set salary level.

Another method which is more commonly used now than was previously the case is temporary agency work. Contracts for temporary agency workers in Britain have often been renewed on a week-by-week basis, an arrangement that is legally prohibited in some other countries, and although in 2002 the amended regulations for part-time fixed-term workers were applied to both employees and non-employee workers, employers can still justify different treatment on 'objective' grounds. While temporary jobs in the UK stabilised at the end of the 1990s, and between 1997 and 2002 actually fell (TUC, 2004), placements through temporary work agencies continued to grow, and in some cases, workers recruited through temporary work agencies have in effect become the 'core', in that there are larger numbers of temporary than permanent workers and since their use changes a workplace's culture and dynamics (Ward *et al.*, 2001). Moreover, there has been a growth in different forms of work such as zero-hour contracts, where there are no minimum hours, and workers are not paid to be 'on call' but only for the hours worked (Purcell *et al.*, 1999). These employees have often been paid below the National Insurance threshold, making them ineligible for maternity pay, sick pay and a state pension, and they have also been excluded from time off for national holidays or for meal breaks (Purcell, 2000).[4] Although the Employment Relations Act 1999 did make many of these abuses of employee rights illegal, differences in treatment still remain.

In terms of the numbers of those in temporary employment, during the 1990s, this form of work increased in most developed countries, except Italy and Denmark (Grunberg, 1999). However, in 2003 only about 6.5 per cent of UK workers were on temporary contracts, compared to 32 per cent in Spain and over 10 per cent in France, Germany and Japan (Stredwick and Ellis, 2005). More recent figures from the Workplace Employee Relations Survey (WERS) (2004) show that 30 per cent of workplaces in Britain had employees on temporary or fixed-term contracts, and 17 per cent had employees who were temporary agency staff. Meanwhile, 5 per cent of workplaces offered zero-hour contracts to employees (Kersley *et al.*, 2006). More specifically, in public services there has been cost-cutting and a reduction in the terms and job security of workers, particularly for those who work part-time, as well as female and ethnic minority workers (Escott and Whitfield, 1995; Conley, 2002; Sachdev, 2001; Bach, 2002). Such workers have often been placed on temporary or casual contracts, and within local government this has been, at least in some cases, a political manoeuvre, aimed at reducing the figures for compulsory redundancy, recruitment and redeployment (Conley, 2002, 2006).[5]

## Measuring individual perceptions of job insecurity

Feelings of insecurity are difficult to quantify, since they tend to be related to the usual factors associated with segmented labour markets, and with individual risk assessment (Gallie *et al.*, 1998; Guest, 2000; Doogan, 2001; Burchell, 2002). Thus, for example, employees who have marketable skills are less likely to feel insecure (Charles and James, 2003), while those who have previous experience of unemployment are more likely to fear job loss – a situation that is more often the case for those in manual occupations.

There have been many debates as to how job security should be measured. One approach is to question people about their perceptions/and or satisfaction with their 'job security' or how they perceive the risk of job loss and unemployment in a specified future period. These have been otherwise termed as affective and cognitive dimensions (Green *et al.*, 2000). Another approach is to take into account both quantitative job insecurity (the likelihood of job loss) and the wider definition of qualitative job insecurity (the loss of job aspects or features such as salary development, employment conditions and career opportunities) (Ashford *et al.*, 1989; Sverke and Hellgren, 2002).

Irrespective of the way in which perceptions of job insecurity are measured and defined, there is a large body of evidence to suggest that it has a significant impact on workers. One area of impact can be grouped under the term 'work effort' (Brockner *et al.*, 1992). In British public services, local authority workers contracted out under Private Finance Initiative (PFI) experienced a decline in job security following a series of redundancies, and this limited their willingness to put in extra effort (Hebson *et al.*, 2003). Again, a survey of contingent workers in local government (Coyle-Shapiro and Kessler, 2002) showed that they were less likely to have positive attitudes and behaviours than permanent staff. Meanwhile, although a study by Gould-Williams (2004) found that job security did not have a statistically significant effect on the attitudes of workers in local government, it was later found that this was because workers did not believe that it was possible to further reduce the numbers of staff responsible for providing the service without removing the service completely. Other effects of job insecurity relate to health or to health and safety: job insecurity can be associated with mental health problems, stress and declining physical health (Sverke and Hellgren, 2002; Wichart, 2002) while those on temporary contracts can be more prepared to accept riskier working conditions, for fear of losing their jobs (Johnstone and Quinlan, 2006; Mayhew and Quinlan, 2006). At the same time, illness can also be a causal factor of job insecurity (see, for example, Dibben *et al.*, 2001; Cunningham *et al.*, 2004).

The impact of job insecurity is difficult to assess, both due to the differential impact on groups of workers, and also since factors such as the different personalities of workers, the relationship between different dimensions and outcomes of job insecurity, and mediators such as perceptions of fair treatment and the support given by managers and unions are also relevant (Sverke and Hellgren, 2002). Furthermore, the management of uncertainties by employers also affects employee response (Hallier, 2000) as do employees' own coping strategies. For example, in Armstrong-Stassen's (1994) study some workers were more likely to engage in control-oriented (proactive) coping rather than escape-oriented (avoidance/denial) coping.

In general terms, most workers in Britain seem to feel that their jobs are secure. For example, the Working in Britain Survey (Taylor, 2002) based on in-depth interviews with up to 2,466 employees found that only 1.5 per cent expected to lose their jobs in the next 12 months due to closure of their workplace, and 2.2 per cent due to redundancy. Again, Clark's (2005) analysis of data from the International Social Survey Programme (1989; 1997) and the British Household Panel Survey (BHPS) (1992–9), although indicating a lower percentage, similarly showed that high numbers reported that their job was secure (around 70 per cent). Meanwhile, in 2004, 63 per cent of employees participating in the British WERS survey were either very satisfied or satisfied with their level of job security (Kersley *et al.*, 2006). However, it seems that there is some variation between types of workers. Burchell's (2002) analysis of various surveys undertaken in the 1980s and 1990s suggests that those in higher-paid occupations, the construction and financial services, those who had been in their jobs for over ten years, and the self-employed had become more insecure. Other surveys have indicated the increased job insecurity of temporary workers and those with very long and short job tenure, the former presumably because their skills might be obsolescent (Green *et al.*, 2000).

Much survey data does not carefully distinguish between public and private sector workers, but in the 1990s, it does appear that although the percentage of public service workers who felt insecure rose, they were still more likely to be satisfied with their level of security than private sector workers (Morgan *et al.*, 2000). The modernisation of public services has, however, been influential in increasing perceptions of job insecurity, as shown in public transit systems in the United States (Ugboro and Obeng, 2001) and in local authorities in Scotland and Wales (Webb, 2001). Similarly, increased insecurity has resulted from Best Value reviews. Richardson *et al.* (2005) carried out a study of workers within a local authority, comparing the perceptions of job security of those that had undergone Best Value reviews with those who had not. The Best Value reviews had led to cuts in the number of core staff, and the subsequent restructuring and reorganisation of work had led to feelings of insecurity. These feelings were reportedly played upon by managers who gave regular announcements about the threat of outsourcing. In those departments that had not undergone review, more workers felt secure, but also feared the prospect of future reviews.

## The role of government in determining employment and job insecurity

The role of government will vary according to a range of factors including: the macro- and micro-economic environment, political conditions and the positions adopted by parties, and the institutional context (Flynn, 2002). However, it can have an important role in determining the insecurity of work at both the macro level as legislative state and at the more micro level as employer.

### Government as State: employment benefits and legislation

Unemployment benefits and sickness benefits, as well as the means by which they can be claimed, can increase/reduce the fear of job loss, and reductions in benefits can contribute toward heightened perceptions of job insecurity. The post-war system was based on the contributory principle laid down in the Beveridge Report 1942, and provided low, flat-rate benefits paid through flat-rate contributions. This was made more generous in the 1960s and 1970s by introducing earnings-related supplements to unemployment and sickness benefits. After the problems faced in the UK economy during the 1960s, the link between earnings and benefits was cut, linking them instead to prices, while the earnings-related top-up and supplementary allowances for dependent children were abolished in the early 1980s, with an increase in means-tested benefits, as well as more stringent contribution requirements and longer periods of disqualification for rule infringements. For example, the time for disqualification from benefits if an employee left a job without good cause was extended from 6 weeks to 13 weeks and then 26 weeks. Claimants were increasingly required to be 'actively seeking work', and in 1996 unemployment benefit was defined as 'jobseekers allowance' and made available for six months, after which time it was means-tested. With the new 'Welfare to Work' system, failure to comply with job search included the threat of benefit reduction or withdrawal. Thus, changes in the level and conditionality of benefits have acted to increase the potential costs of job loss (Ladipo and Wilkinson, 2002). The UK is an extreme case in this regard, and together with Ireland it provides a lower level of protection for both permanent and temporary workers than most other European countries (Maurin and Postel-Vinay, 2005).

Legislation relevant to employment security includes that relating to redundancy, fixed-term contracts, public sector outsourcing, health and safety and dismissal. In Britain, in order to 'downsize' through redundancy, the only statutory requirement is that the employer must experience a 'reduction of cessation of work of a particular kind', and in the employer's opinion, less workers are needed to perform the work in question. Employees must give prior notice, but this involves consultation rather than negotiation, and apart from regulations prohibiting discrimination on the basis of race, gender and trade union activities, employers can develop their own criteria. In addition, although employers are required to give at least 30 days' notice for 20–99 redundancies and at least 90 days for 100 or more, employers 'buy out' statutory notice periods, which leads to less time for retraining (Turnbull and Wass, 2000). In 2005, the government did, however, honour its Warwick Agreement pledges to extend the period of protection from dismissal for striking employees and also increased redundancy pay (Bewley, 2006).

In addition to legislation on downsizing and redundancy, other relevant legislation for employment security relates to temporary work. The Employment Rights Act 1996 introduced the concept of 'worker' as opposed to 'employee', extending some employment rights to temporary workers (Biggs *et al.*, 2006). Then in 1999 the Employment Relations Act prohibited the use of waiver clauses relating to unfair dismissal (Stredwick and Ellis, 2005). Meanwhile, in relation to fixed-term contracts, the Fixed-Term Employees (Prevention of Less Favourable Treatment) Regulations 2002 stated that employees on fixed-term contracts must not be treated less favourably than comparable permanent employees, including pay and benefits such as occupational pension schemes and training, unless this is objectively justified. It also made it unlawful for workers to waive their right to a redundancy payment, with a maximum period of four years for a succession of fixed-term contracts (TUC, 2005).

However, agency workers are not included in this legislation but are covered under the Employment Agencies Act 1973 and the Conduct of Employment Agencies and Employment Business Regulations 2003. A proposed Temporary Agency Workers Directive offered temporary workers the same employment conditions as fixed-term workers from day one of employment, but was blocked by a minority of States in April 2005 (Stredwick and Ellis, 2005; Bewley, 2006). Furthermore, although in most EU Member States the agency worker is, by law, an employee of the temporary work agency and enjoys the same or similar protections and rights as other employees, there is no requirement under UK law for agency workers to be employed either by the agency or by the client company, and most are not employed by either (TUC, 2005).

In public services, the outsourcing of work has arguably led to more insecure work. Until the 1980s most services were provided directly, but by 1983 the NHS was using competitive tendering for catering, laundry and domestic work, followed by local government in 1988 (although Direct Service Organisations were first affected in 1980) and from 1993 the whole civil service (Ladipo and Wilkinson, 2002). In 1981, Transfer of Undertakings (Protection of Employment) Regulations (TUPE) were enforced for private sector work, then amended in 2003 so that new employees taken on after an outsourcing transfer of employees from the public sector must have no less favourable terms than those of TUPE-protected staff (Stredwick and Ellis, 2005). Nevertheless, those outsourced under TUPE often experience job insecurity and concerns about the future of their work, as demonstrated in research by Cooke *et al.* (2004) which investigated the impact of outsourcing on a council housing benefit service in local government, and also on estate maintenance and hotel services under an NHS hospital Private Finance Initiative, and found insecurity among each group of workers.

A further area is health and safety legislation. There were concerns within the labour movement in 2005 about the impact of the draft EU Service Directive on health and safety since it was feared that the country of origin principle – which allowed firms providing services on a temporary basis to operate according to the laws of their home country – would undercut labour standards (Bewley, 2006: 364). Such legislative changes, in common with those relating to collective rights such as those provided under the Employment Relations Act and subsequent amendments, also impact upon the rights of insecure workers. However it is beyond the scope of this chapter to discuss them at length here. More detail is provided, where relevant, within other chapters of this volume.

Finally, legislation relating to dismissal has been changed over recent years. The minimum qualifying period for unfair dismissal has been changed from two years to one year, but this is still higher than the six months in place before 1980. Meanwhile, rights to representation in grievance cases were improved under the Employment Relations Act 1999, but the new rules on tribunal applications, dismissal and disciplinary procedures under the Employment Tribunals Regulations 2001 and the provisions of the Employment Act 2002 have effectively reduced applications to Employment Tribunals. This is at least partly due to the potential costs to applicants (Pollert, 2005).

## Government as employer: downsizing, delayering and outsourcing

Governments can impose minimum standards across the labour market through the direct regulation of employment, but can also exercise influence over employment practices in their role as employer (Bewley, 2006: 351). The government has traditionally been seen as a 'model employer', encouraging a high degree of job security, and in doing so setting an example for the private sector. There has been higher support of lifetime employment and a reduced tendency to use a non-permanent workforce to cut expenditure (Boyne *et al.*, 1999). However, from the 1980s this was arguably reversed: public sector employers were encouraged to copy private sector practices, with a massive reduction in public sector jobs (except in areas such as Higher Education and the emergency services) and a movement toward flexible working and casualisation, particularly in higher education, nursing and local government (Morgan and Allington, 2002). Although the concept of flexibility has been previously applied to non-core workers (see for example Atkinson, 1984) in the 1980s and 1990s it tended to be the core labour market that was exposed to numerical flexibility with continued divisions, inequalities and exploitation (Pollert, 1991). At the same time, downsizing and delayering – reducing the number of vertical hierarchies – were encouraged.

Moreover, there has been increased pressure by governments to use suppliers rather than provide services in-house, referred to variously as: outsourcing, sub-contracting, market testing, contracting out, and externalisation (Sachdev, 2001). There have been high profile failures in a number of cases of public sector outsourcing, while winning contracts has often been secured by cutting jobs (Hebson *et al.*, 2003; Stredwick and Ellis, 2005). In the 1980s, those most affected appear to have been manual workers including contract workers in cleaning, catering and security services, where employment was only guaranteed for the duration of a particular contract. When contracts were lost, employees could transfer to a new employer, but often with different and inferior terms and conditions. Over the course of a decade from the mid-1980s, various estimates of job loss have been provided, with some as high as 40 per cent, while similar increases have been reported for the numbers of those on temporary contracts, a large proportion being women (Sachdev, 2001; see also Toynbee, 2002).

## Trade unions: prioritising employment and job security

Union membership is widespread in the public sector, so that while only 22 per cent of employees in private sector workplaces are union members, the figure rises to 64 per cent for the public sector. Similarly, while there is union density of 50 per cent or more in only 8 per cent of private sector workplaces, in public sector workplaces, the equivalent figure is 62 per cent (Kersley *et al.*, 2006). This is irrespective of the strain placed on trade unions during the 1980s and 1990s due to structural reform, privatisation, marketisation, and organisational devolution (Duncan, 2001).

Job (in)security has arguably been central in shaping industrial relations (Hyman, 1997). Thus, unions have been described as,

> ...the flag-bearers in the promotion of justice in the workplace and in the promotion and protection of jobs (Guest, 1997: 349).

This statement is backed up by evidence from WERS 4 data, where security of employment for trade union members was second in the list of priorities of union representatives, and 40 per cent of union respondents had spent time on this issue in the previous year (Cully *et al.*, 1999). Again, among union members, various studies have identified a strong demand for job security to be a priority for the labour movement, while job insecurity stimulates demand for trade union representation (Heery and Abbot, 2000).

In practice, however, it has been argued that unions tend to neglect job security. Some have argued that they have attempted to raise the price and govern the supply of labour, leading to a cut in output and employment, and therefore increasing job insecurity. Others have argued that the focus on pay has been due to its centrality to members' concerns, and is an area where it is possible to develop clear and well-defined bargaining strategies. At best, it can be argued that their role is 'theoretically ambivalent' (Green *et al.*, 2000: 871). In public services, amidst Compulsory Competitive Tendering (CCT) and then Best Value, unions have similarly faced a dilemma: whether and to what extent they should attempt to protect employees' existing terms and conditions when this might lead to a rise in the cost of in-house jobs and therefore a greater likelihood of contracting out (Sachdev, 2001). Meanwhile, a newer issue has been raised in relation to equal pay, and the challenges faced, for example, by the public sector union Unison, having negotiated compromise deals with employers to prevent redundancies.

### The role of trade unions: national level

In dealing with temporary workers and the casualisation of work, unions generally have three lines of attack on regulatory initiatives: restrictions on temporary employment, the level of rights and benefits compared to permanent workers, and the level of compensation for perceived disadvantages. Research carried out in Australia, where casualisation is a topic of some debate, shows that unions have tended to focus on the first of these, and the third has tended to be viewed with suspicion as it involves trading in rights and benefits for money. The second is also important, however, as employers may choose temporary workers for cost-cutting reasons (Campbell, 2005). Meanwhile, in Europe there has been a shift from focusing on the imposing of restrictions to tackling the differences in protection. While no European country has a complete prohibition on fixed-term employment, it is generally subject to special rules and regulations which relate to reason, duration, renewal, conversion to a permanent contract, and compensation at the end of the fixed term (Campbell, 2005). In many European countries, there are also legally codified systems of co-determination and long-standing traditions of partnership (Bach, 2002).

In Britain, it seems that relatively little national-level action has been taken with regard to casualised workers, although a motion 'against casualised employment practices' was carried at the Trade Union Congress (TUC) conference in 2001 (Heery *et al.*, 2002). Senior policy officers from 56 unions, when questioned about their activities, admitted that legal and political action was undertaken by only a minority of unions, and was mostly directed toward part-timers. A breakdown of activities is shown in the following table:

**Table 8.2  Legal and political action on behalf of part-time and temporary workers (percentages)**

| Category | Sponsorship of test case | Special legal advice | Response to Government consultation | Lobbying UK Government | Lobbying European commission |
|---|---|---|---|---|---|
| Part-time | 25 | 23 | 21 | 25 | 11 |
| Fixed-term | 11 | 16 | 16 | 21 | 9 |
| Agency | 4 | 14 | 14 | 16 | 4 |
| Freelance | 4 | 11 | 7 | 9 | 5 |

N=56
*Source*: Heery *et al.*, 2002: 11.

In seeking to analyse the success of trade unions in defending the rights of contingent workers, Heery and Abbot (2000) explain how at the national level they have employed a 'dialogue' strategy, which includes lobbying on the issue of job security, and seeking to change regulations on the conditions of temporary and agency staff to prevent undercutting. To some extent, this seems to have been successful, so that the Employment

Relations Act 1999 reduced the qualifying period for protection from unfair dismissal, brought in changes in financial compensation for such behaviour, and introduced representation during disciplinary and grievance procedures, while the union movement has sought to secure agreements on the two-tier workforce. More recent attempts also include the TUC's push for a Trade Union Freedom Bill to deal with the massive loopholes evident after the 'Gate Gourmet' dispute.

Unions have also sought to influence policy and regulation on public sector modernisation, and since the 1990s the British government has involved trade unions in discussions about public sector modernisation under the social partnership banner. However, unions have been concerned about insufficient consultation on the actual implementation of initiatives (Bach, 2002). Furthermore, although Unison has promoted a 'Best Employment for Best Value' agenda, research sponsored by the union has been highly critical of job loss under Best Value, and in the 2000 national conference the union voted to oppose Best Value (Geddes, 2001).

## Individual-level activity

At the individual level of employment relationships, the attitudes of those in contingent or insecure work toward unions seem to vary, according to the level of union representation in the workplace (Macais, 2003) and the availability of other forms of support. However, the evidence based on the attitudes of insecure workers toward trade unions is admittedly relatively weak, so is not in any way conclusive. Again, the availability of evidence on the union representation of insecure members is also limited, although it is recognised that the organisation of contingent workers can be difficult because they can be scattered among many work sites and their employment tenures are short (Kochan *et al.*, 2004). Most unions have not tended to invest in the dedicated recruitment of part-time and temporary workers, nor have special measures to help these members participate, nor have they offered special services such as financial services, employment advice or education and training for them (Wilkinson and Lapido, 2002).

More has been written about the relationship between unions and employers and issues of job security, but attention has tended to focus on the private sector, and the problematic outcomes resulting from collaborative employment relations (Hyman, 1997: 323). Although unions can encourage employers to make agreements to avoid compulsory redundancy – offering employment security in return for flexible working practices (Guest, 1997; 2000) – some deals have had dubious results. One union agreed to a restructuring programme and more flexible working practices on the basis that the employer (a bank) would redeploy staff whose jobs were lost, but the bank reduced its recruitment of permanent staff and increased its use of temporary workers (Ward *et al.*, 2001). Again, in Bacon and Blyton's study of two steel plants (2004, 2006) job insecurity led cooperative unions into 'coerced cooperation', where managers took advantage of labour cooperation, but union militancy led to employee benefits.

In relation to public services, unions have also cooperated with management. Cooke *et al.*'s (2004: 8) study of an outsourced housing benefits service revealed that the trade union was involved to secure cooperation and to provide a 'dignified exit' for the employees. Meanwhile, in hotel services outsourced from the NHS, the union negotiated with management without consulting with staff until decisions were taken. Richardson *et al.*'s (2005) study of Best Value in local government (referred to above) provides a particularly interesting insight into the union dilemma. The unions initially supported the replacement of CCT with Best Value. However, when they realised that services might be outsourced, they became more deeply involved in Best Value steering groups, in order to influence changes to the labour process, job security and quality of working life. Keeping services in-house was regarded as the best way to defend existing jobs and pay, and they worked with senior management to develop restructuring plans to achieve service improvements so that this would happen. The outcome was that both the payroll and the local taxation departments kept the service in-house, but in the taxation department staff numbers were gradually reduced from 134 to 104.5 full-time equivalent positions, and the long-term plan was to reduce the service to 77 staff. Thus unions were successful in keeping services but not in keeping jobs. The authors' conclusion is that,

> ...partnership poses real dangers to employees and their unions should co-operation and consensus be vehicles for work intensification and job loss (Richardson *et al.*, 2005: 727).

## Conclusions

Using a conceptual framework that encapsulates both macro-and micro-level concerns for public service workers, this chapter has investigated trends in employment and job insecurity, and examined the role of both government and trade unions. The evidence base for the dynamics of the employment relationship in respect of employment and job security appears to be weak. Nevertheless, some tentative conclusions can be made. In summary, it appears that the modernisation of public services may have led to more insecure work. This is the case, irrespective of which 'side of the coin' we look at – 'employment security' and the economic political and institutional environments in which work takes place – or 'job insecurity' which presumes an individualised job and specific anxiety (c.f. Doogan, 2001: 438).

At the macro level, although there has been an overall increase in the length of tenure, and a reduction in the numbers of those undertaking temporary work, there has also been a greater tendency toward ever more insecure forms of work in public services, including, for example, temporary agency work and zero-hour contracts. There is also some evidence to suggest that casualisation – moving from more secure to less secure or temporary jobs – disproportionately affects those who are already more vulnerable: particularly in public services, it appears that employment and job insecurity are both experienced and felt particularly by women, ethnic minorities, the lower skilled and older population.

Against this background, to what extent have recent governments helped to prevent or alleviate these experiences? The requirements for receipt of employment benefits have been tightened, leading to greater fear of job loss, but at the same time, legislation has been brought in to address insecure work, albeit that this has tended to come about as a result of directives at the European level. Nevertheless, although there have been improvements in relation to redundancy, dismissal, and for those working on fixed-term contracts, the concerns of agency workers still need to be more effectively addressed. Moreover, the record of the government as 'model employer' in relation to job security is questionable, particularly in the light of more recent movements toward wider scale job reduction and contracting out, particularly for those in low-paid occupations.

In this context, to what extent and how should trade unions react? Trade unions have conflicting priorities between employment/job security and raising wages. They have traditionally campaigned on pay, with clear and well-developed strategies, and job security comes at a price. Nevertheless, trade unions arguably have a duty to protect those who are most vulnerable in the workplace. At both the national and local level, the restructuring of public services appears to have put trade unions on the defensive, while 'partnership' deals that provide cooperation with employers have often failed to protect jobs for any length of time. While 'employment security' and 'job insecurity' might indeed be two sides of the same coin, it appears that the different dimensions of both aspects therefore merit further investigation.

## Notes

1. Definitions of employment security and job insecurity have been advanced by, for example, Standing (1999), Robinson (2000), and Charles and James (2003). The 'insecurity thesis' outlined by Heery and Salmon (2000), centres around the causes, extent and effects of insecurity, but although it encapsulates both individual and broader macro-economic causes and effects it does not clearly distinguish between them. Doogan (2001: 438) perhaps comes closest to the definition advanced here, suggesting that precarious employment is considered in terms of wider social and economic security, and that job insecurity presumes an individualised job and specific anxiety. Similarly, Burchell (2002) defines job insecurity as the subjective feelings about job loss, as expressed by employees themselves.
2. In response, the 2004 pre-Budget Report (PBR) committed to a net reduction of 70,000 civil service jobs by 2007/8 (Bewley, 2006).

3. It is noted, however, that where job protection for permanent workers is weak, their jobs could also be insecure (Burchell, 2002).
4. In Australia, some temporary workers are referred to as 'casual workers' and have limited protection against unfair dismissal (Campbell, 2005), while in the United States temporary workers earn about 14 per cent less than permanent workers and are about half as likely to receive any employer-provided healthcare (Capelli, 1999: 136).
5. An exception is Teaching Assistants in local education, where attempts have been made to increase job security and tenure. But these workers still perceive themselves to be peripheral, and feel uncertain about their role and the organisation of their work (Bach *et al.*, 2006).

# Part III

# The Dynamics of Collective Employment Relations and the Performance of Services

# 9

# Sustaining New Industrial Relations in the Public Sector: The Politics of Trust and Cooperation in the Context of Organisational Dementia and Disarticulation

*Miguel Martínez Lucio and Mark Stuart*

The development of partnership in employment relations has been a central feature of New Labour's policy for the public sector. The present chapter takes note of this attempt to encourage, strategically, partnership-based approaches to employment relations change and thereby inculcate a culture of labour-management cooperation which moves away from traditional industrial relations and towards a new commercially oriented approach. It also, however, notes that within the study of the public sector, and the private sector for that matter, the evidence for change in this direction is patchy. Indeed, there are serious differences of opinion regarding the uses and realities of partnership (Beale, 2005; Gall, 2005) and, overall, the evidence has tended towards a critical position arguing that we have not witnessed major change and that in many cases partnership has been inconsistent or linked to a strategy of drawing trade unions into compromising positions.

Against this background, the present chapter tries to evaluate the challenges to partnership in local authority contexts where the regulatory framework and organisational traditions should be supportive of mutually beneficial outcomes. It does so for two reasons. First, because much of the above criticism of partnership focuses on the fact that in the United Kingdom (UK) we are developing partnership without regulatory supports akin to those of western and, in particular, northern Europe (Stuart and Martínez Lucio, 2006). Secondly, because rarely are the challenges of sustaining partnership discussed in relation to cases where there have been 'positive' agreements as far as the main participants are concerned. Notwithstanding that, it is in such contexts that one begins to see how the 'new public sector' and the more market-based approaches it encompasses make the business of good employment relations very difficult.

The chapter begins by exploring the meaning of partnership, the debates which have taken place in relation to its benefits and drawbacks, and what light the available evidence sheds on them. Details of the two case studies which form its central focus are then provided and some brief insights provided into the nature of public sector employment relations. Finally, key findings from these studies are detailed and some concluding observations made as to the potential for, and sustainability of, partnership in the context of the UK public sector.

## Partnership: caught between dire cynicism and curious optimism

Whilst the definitional status of partnership is a matter of some debate, with most commentators arguing that it is a vague, ambiguous concept, formally there has been an astonishing amount of interest in the concept (Ackers and Payne, 1998; Bacon and Storey, 2000; Guest and Peccei, 1998, 2001; Haynes and Allen, 2001; IPA, 2001; Martínez Lucio and Stuart, 2004). Much of this interest has centred on the perceived benefits, or otherwise, of labour-management cooperation around strategic matters of organisational change. For some, cooperative employment relations represent the only route to competitive success in increasingly competitive international markets (Cooke, 1990) and for trade unions to increase their 'institutional centrality' (Ackers and Payne, 1998). Others disagree given the definitional ambiguity of partnership.

More generally, the partnership debate has become clearly associated with a number of key academic interventions, in response to developments at a policy level. Kochan and Osterman's (1994) work in the USA on the 'mutual gains enterprise' has been particularly influential (but see also Cooke, 1990). Drawing from a more long-standing engagement on the potentially positive contribution of trade unions to economic competitiveness (Beer *et al.*, 1984; Katz *et al.*, 1983; Nolan, 1989; Voos, 1987), Kochan and Osterman's (1994: 46) intervention stressed a series of guiding principles of mutual gains enterprises, based on the extension of employee voice at three levels of organisational decision-making: the strategic, the functional level of human resource policy and the workplace. By respecting and guaranteeing the rights and roles of organised labour – sustainable through supportive public policy – it was argued that employers and managers have much to gain in negotiating and involving them in change. It is important, however, to recognise that the role of organised labour within such partnerships is seen as distinct from more macro-level and politically-driven understandings of labour involvement.

In the UK context, the emergence of interest in partnership was summarised in the wake of the Labour Party's electoral victory in 1997 by Ackers and Payne (1998). Given the ongoing difficulties management faced in responding to the imperatives of change, the pressures for more ethical business practice and the likely impact of a potentially more labour friendly political environment (in the UK, but also increasingly from the EU), Ackers and Payne argued that management could not proceed to progress change without bringing unions on board in terms of decision-making. At a broader level, the Trades Union Congress (TUC) and organisations such as the Involvement and Participation Association (IPA) established a series of partnership principles to guide the effective implementation and practise of partnership (Martínez Lucio and Stuart, 2002; Stuart and Martínez Lucio, 2002).

Whilst a number of initial studies questioned the potential benefits of partnership and suggested that trade unions, in particular, faced very real challenges and risks with partnership engagement (Claydon, 1998; Kelly, 1998, 2004; Taylor and Ramsay, 1998), the agenda set by Kochan and Osterman and Ackers and Payne has led to a significant and sustained empirical assessment of partnership. Further discussions on the question of the positive aspects of partnership for performance have also emerged (Guest and Peccei, 2001). Much of this assessment has focused on specific manifestations of partnership and has largely involved case study assessments of the merits of partnership-committed organisations. Three discernible lines of analysis can be delineated within this work. The first has considered the extent to which partnership 'diminishes trade union representative capacity (critics) or enhances it (advocates)' (Terry and Smith, 2003: 2). Kelly's review (2004) of leading partnership agreements in the UK, for example, found no association between the introduction of a partnership agreement and increased trade union membership, whilst Taylor and Ramsay's (1998) study of a high street supermarket chain showed how partnership-based arrangements could draw trade unions into a management strategy of enhancing surveillance and work intensification. A key concern has therefore been the extent to which trade unions become incorporated into the structure of companies. Certainly, studies by Beale (2005), Danford *et al.* (2002), Gall (2005) and others reveal how union engagement in partnership can lead to the downgrading of membership-led and resistance-based strategies and a marked disjuncture between the interests and experiences of members and the more political concerns of full-time officers with partnership. Some of these latter authors, it should be pointed out, used the public sector as an area of their research.

Noting the over-emphasis in much of the partnership literature on the role of trade unions, an increasing number of studies have meanwhile sought to examine the experiences of employees in partnership companies and the broader extent to which genuine mutual gains for all stakeholders are delivered (see Stuart and Martínez Lucio, 2005a). Assessed against the claims of advocates that partnership agreements aim to deliver job security, increased employee voice, improved quality of working life and enhanced levels of employee commitment, the evidence is, again, far from positive. For example, Richardson *et al.*'s (2005) research in aerospace and local government explicitly links the furtherance of partnership practices with increased levels of employee stress, work intensification and job insecurity.

Much of the empirical literature has, then, typically involved an assessment of the extent to which mutual gains have been generated by the introduction of a partnership agreement or approach, with the findings drawn against either a critical or a supportive view of partnership. Less concerned with measuring the impact of specific features of partnership agreements, a third body of work has further sought to locate the development of partnership within historical changes in employment relations. These have tried to tease out the motives behind trade union-management engagement with partnership and unpack the specific internal and external organisational conditions that shape differential forms of partnership (Ackers *et al.*, 2005; Deakin *et al.*, 2005; Oxenbridge and Brown, 2002, 2005). Differentiating between 'robust' and 'shallow' partnership arrangements, Oxenbridge and Brown (2005) show that 'robust' and effective labour-management cooperation is far more likely in 'nurturing' organisations, where traditional bargaining relations are well established and recognised by management and trade union membership is relatively high (see also Martínez Lucio and Stuart, 2004; Terry, 2003). For Taylor (2004) this represents something of a riposte to those critics of partnership that often situate labour-management cooperation in binaristic opposition to more militant trade unionism underpinned by collective bargaining. For him, the 'critics of the partnership model fail to recognise that the most effective examples of this approach can be found in companies with a history of powerful and successful workplace organisation' (Taylor, 2004: 12).

Partnership is therefore a contested concept. In particular, there are concerns about the effective sustainability of cooperative industrial relations and how such relations can be sustained without compromising trade unions in terms of their strategies. Yet one should be cautious of a binary approach that fails to understand how partnerships evolve and the complexities involved in their development, even in regulated contexts such as the public sector where the issue of worker voice – central to many of the critiques – should not be an issue. Thus, even in such a context with its supposedly 'positive' developments, ironies and tensions remain, as we illustrate below, an issue due to strategic and structural factors.

Methodologically, then, what is needed is the paying of closer attention to the issues McBride and Stirling (2002) raised in terms of partnership outcome, process and ideology. There has been a lot of work on the former (outcomes), some on the latter (environment) and not much at all on process. More specifically, what is required is longitudinal work about the difficulty of building and sustaining partnership as a process, which we acknowledge is difficult given its contested nature. In addition, as the early work of Cooke (1990) suggests, modes of cooperation require facilitation but this issue is relatively unexplored within the UK work on partnership. Hence, we need to look at how partnership evolves, and becomes shaped across time, and how it is the focus of attention of a variety of actors and players. In effect, we need to prize open the new public sector and its new institutional contours if we are to understand strategies of cooperation within it.

To this end, in what follows, we draw on our ongoing research into the development of labour-management partnerships and the modernisation of employment relations. This work has involved a number of empirical-based studies since 2000. Here, we draw on the findings of two of these studies. The first was a study of new consultation arrangements in the public sector, which included local authority A. The second followed a Department for Trade and Industry (DTI) Partnership Fund supported initiative at local authority B, as it evolved over a 12 months' period. In both cases, semi-structured interviews were conducted with key Human Resource (HR) managers, line managers and trade union officers. We were also able to collect relevant documentary evidence and, in the case of local authority B, attend and observe workshops and meetings of working groups. In both cases, the Advisory, Conciliation and Arbitration Service (ACAS) played a role in 'facilitating' the 'turn' to partnership and we additionally conducted interviews with the key ACAS representatives involved.

## The public sector context

The public sector when compared to the private sector remains highly regulated, unionised and subject to political contingencies (Jenkins *et al.*, 1995). For all the changes in terms of structures and cultures (see Kirkpatrick *et al.*, 2005), let alone the drive to greater Taylorisation (Kirkpatrick, 2006), it remains driven by a collective and professionals-based culture.

The development of partnership in local government consequently raises a variety of issues. Firstly, local government trade unionism is complex and varied, with a large number of trade unions operating across the different departments and services offered to the public, and national processes of regulation still play a significant role. Secondly, management cultures vary across departments due to a host of reasons. Thirdly, the political context of local government means that there are players such as Councillors who are part of decision-making processes, with the result that local political contingencies are a major factor in shaping local industrial relations issues. Fourth, local government is changing due to the pressures of commercialism and reorganisation. Moreover, the increasing use of strategies such as 'Best Value', with its emphasis on improving quality and efficiency and prompting new forms of service provision, carry a view of partnership that involves broader stakeholders and raises a question mark over how this wider conceptualisation sits with partnerships between unions and management (Roper *et al.*, 2005). A question mark of considerable import given that one of the espoused goals of the government since 1997, when the Labour Party became elected to power, has been the development of a policy of industrial relations partnership which has sought to involve trade unions in a more strategic manner in the public sector but with the aim of contributing to greater efficiencies and to a climate of cooperation where business agendas are as important as social ones (Beale, 2005; Gall, 2005). An aim which means that the 'partnership turn' has not represented a shift back to the 1970s but a restructuring of the language of involvement in terms of customer- and market-related issues (Stuart and Martínez Lucio, 2000: 310–13).

## Local authority A

### The development of partnership

In 2001, the Council in City A was facing a variety of problems. It had a poor industrial relations record and a lack of consistent and effective consultation. There were notable differences in the approaches and styles of management in different departments and in their relations with different trade unions. There had also, against this background, not been any systematic attempt to renew the processes of consultation.

The different industrial relations cultures and competing management styles operating across the Council meant that it was very difficult to develop a consensus on the question of change and modernisation. In addition, there was a broader political problem. A crisis in City A Council brought on by a high profile financial scandal further contributed to a widespread demoralisation amongst management and staff alike. In this respect, the Council faced industrial relations problems compounded by a broader political dilemma. The high profile nature of this crisis provided the Council with a very extensive set of problems in terms of motivation and the ability to face up to and respond to the pressures of change that confronted it. However, it also brought a general desire for reform amongst Councillors, key managers and senior trade unionists who felt that action was needed in order to avoid a further downward spiral.

ACAS was approached for help by the Council in 2001 due to its previous role in resolving specific industrial relations issues within the organisation. The personnel department's approach was supported by trade unionists since ACAS was seen as impartial and independent. Leading Councillors played a significant role in providing this link and in driving the process forward, as they saw the reform of industrial relations within the Council as part of a wider attempt to give it a fresh start and completely new image.

There was also a feeling from functional directors that the pace of change was such that they needed more fluid decision-making processes and consultation machinery.

A series of ACAS-facilitated workshops – attended by Councillors, management and trade union representatives – was conducted to assist participants to identify key issues concerning the employment relationship. From these workshops, a working group was established. The working group was set up to implement identified action points regarding consultation, apply for DTI partnership funds in order to support the move to a 'working together' culture (see further below), and communicate a new vision of industrial relations to the staff. ACAS supported this working group in terms of taking the action plan forward by attending a number of its meetings.

Firstly, an employee attitude survey was conducted to elicit and understand the concerns of the workforce. This was a major output from the earlier discussions and was a way of discovering the key concerns of the workforce and of sending a strong signal that their concerns were being taken seriously. Secondly, the Workshops and Joint Working Parties were complemented with the use of larger conferences that brought together Councillors and large numbers of line management and staff from a wide range of departments. These were highly publicised events meant to herald a change in the way industrial relations would be conducted. This added a novel feature to the project by ensuring a broad dissemination of ideas and proposals, and a wider dialogue and sense of ownership. The conferences were led by senior figures within the Council's political and executive quarters, and there were national political leaders invited as a means of according recognition to the Council's decision to progress and change.

The immediate outcomes of the project were positive and varied. The Joint Working Party, by bringing together management and trade unionists to discuss a range of issues, helped establish a closer relationship between unions and the personnel department. Issues regarding labour deployment, for example, were discussed in a more open manner and there was a joint recognition of the need to reconsider the way employees worked within their posts, and how they could be redeployed within the Council as a whole. There were also initiatives on employee health, and on matters related to work-life balance, with the former acting to link the project of change into a tangible experience within the workplace of individual employees. Meanwhile, department-based middle managers gained a greater understanding of the nature of worker concerns and the importance of adopting a new approach.

The most important long-term benefit was the steady erosion of the sense of despair that faced the Council and its employees. According to one trade unionist, the initiative to bring in ACAS and build a new dialogue regarding the challenges facing the Council in terms of employment issues was a major reason for this change-around: 'they were important because it meant that the changes would be discussed openly'. The commitment to change from senior Councillors and management was reflected by trade unionists, and it was communicated to the workforce through a wide range of communication events and workplace meetings in some cases. This display of common interest and concern marked an important change in the way employees were involved. Industrial relations renewal was, then, not simply a case of fine-tuning forms of consultation, but also of tying them to the concerns and needs of line managers and staff. The broader conferences were '*vital*' according to a senior personnel manager in 'including those in the field delivering the services'. This was a key issue in the case. Personnel managers and trade unionists acknowledged the importance of involving people consistently across various departments that had a variety of cultures.

## Challenges

However, there were challenges. The first was sustaining such a dialogue in a consistent and even manner. ACAS returned to the Council soon after its involvement with the aim of enhancing the gains from the developments of the previous two years. Further workshops were held to draw out some of the positive developments and experiences. The main objective was, then, on the focusing and narrowing of the structures of working together in terms of the establishment of a smaller group.

One of the difficulties of consultation in the public sector, especially in terms of health services and local government, is the sheer breadth of actors in terms of management departments and trade unions. It is not uncommon to see committees or working parties with 30 or so individuals. In the case of City A, the decision to move to a smaller group, whilst not universally well received, was considered a necessary development in order to allow for more focused discussion and tighter decision-making processes in the face of ongoing pressures for change. This, however, created difficulties amongst some of the trade unions, as they had to delegate their roles, according to one representative. It therefore raised the problem of how voice is structured and how interests are represented even in such a regulated context. The Council began to consider a broader strategy of capacity building for trade unions by developing new skills and resources to deal with the new challenges of public service delivery. The view of trade unions as assets within change is something that had become very transparent according to senior managers and clearly linked into government initiatives regarding trade union modernisation in 2004 and 2005. However, the demands of new forms of service delivery and financial pressures meant that involvement had to be reshaped, according to management, around more 'focused' and less 'participative' mechanisms. Trade unions saw this as a potential challenge to attempts to get consistent processes of consultation and a broad culture of both direct and indirect involvement. This remains the key challenge, developing participation strategies and involvement mechanisms in a more decentralised system of public service delivery.

The main challenge facing any consultative process within local government is the manner in which local government is being reorganised. With greater outsourcing and arms-length management, and the move towards cost centres, each department and section begins to develop its own idiosyncrasies and culture. Representing all staff and management within that context becomes a major challenge. Ensuring that participation is a feature of all sections and that there is a culture of inclusion in terms of decision-making and employee relations is consequently not easy. Indeed, some thought that this context would probably undermine attempts at creating a cohesive culture of consultation due to the sheer extent of change:

> ... the ALMOs are starting to come up now – Arms Length Management Organisation – within the homes and housing and it's going to be a massive transfer. So that's going to be a big issue and people are going to move from the local authority over to an Arms Length Management company. So there's a lot of consultation on that, there's the job evaluation that needs a lot of consultation there. ... The whole authority is within the green book, and its terms and conditions (Trade Union Representative).

A further problem was – in effect – the mortality and mobility of strategic individuals. The changing nature of leadership, the absence of key individuals who had been heavily relied on due to illness, and the shift in inter-trade union relations meant that sustaining relations and reciprocal arrangements proved difficult especially given the broader landscape and flexibility of joint decision-making and consultation (see Stuart and Martínez Lucio, 2005b).

## Local authority B

### The development of partnership

The Council in City B was larger. It had a tradition of good management and had been well regulated. It had established what the main actors considered to be traditional industrial relations; in collective terms there was a pattern of bargaining and consultation that was effective and rarely led to disputes. However, the individual level of industrial relations was seen to create more tensions. Individuals within management considered the Council to be undermined by high levels of grievances that took up many resources. They believed that workers at the Council were using grievances in a haphazard manner. Hence, there was much talk of a 'grievance culture'. Some individuals, though, felt that the problem was the failure of senior management to appreciate the tensions and stresses on local departments and the untrained and unsympathetic nature of line managers. In fact, one of the criticisms was that the Council had not actually studied the problem in detail and had not collated data that permitted a developed understanding of the causes, nature and focus of the grievances.

Regardless of such views, the Council decided to put in an application, ultimately successful, with the trade unions to the DTI Partnership Fund. The Labour Government had developed this Fund in the late 1990s as a way of getting employers and trade unions to improve their industrial relations and develop a more partnership-based approach. Under it projects developed between trade union representatives and management could receive financial support of up to £50,000 as part of an attempt to establish benchmarks that would act to crystallise the partnership culture and rhetoric.

The project focused on a series of workshops that would modernise and reform the grievance procedure. The timeframe was approximately 12 months. The different workshops aimed at developing an understanding of joint working and partnership while also covering such substantive issues as mediation, decision-making and the law related to grievances and discipline. Their overall aim was to help secure agreement to renewing the procedure in such a way that it would make it easier to resolve the cases. The idea was that by bringing together the main trade unions, representatives of key departments, the personnel department, and selected individuals (e.g. the Local Government Management Board and Councillors), the resulting agreements would be collectively owned and supported.

The sessions also involved interventions by ACAS (who tried to get the group to agree with what they meant by partnership through a review of established principles and approaches) and the TUC's Partnership Institute. This was an innovative process of learning and discussion. It was also one which eventually yielded an outcome where mediation was included at an earlier stage in the procedure and some of the later stages were reformed (e.g., in future Councillors were only to be involved in appeals and not final hearings).

## Challenges

Regardless of such innovative and positive outcomes, which would leave partnership exponents salivating, the reality was more complex and much of that complexity was due to the nature of change in the public sector. This complexity gave rise to a series of issues and challenges which seriously questioned the ability of such local state structures to create a space for partnership-style approaches and new forms of industrial relations. Central to these – even in such a regulated context, were issues of voice and representation.

Firstly, due to the reforms in the education department and industrial relations differences within what was becoming a stand-alone, semi-privatised management section, the education unions refused to attend the sessions. This was a major problem and located the discussion around only one part of the local Council.

Secondly, problems of consistency as to who attended, and who did not, in terms of departments and trade unions were such that there was only a small core of personnel who attended regularly; a problem compounded by the fact that Councillors, although asked to, chose not to attend. The upshot of this situation was that some key departments with major issues in terms of grievances would attend sporadically, and the lead union Unison faced difficulties in reconciling the differing viewpoints of branch and regional full-time officers. In addition, the variety of trade unions involved meant that although certain unions took a lead role, they did not have the ability to speak on behalf of the 'union constituency' as a whole. These features, in turn, meant that the recalling and remembering of decisions and the need to clarify what had been agreed and what the key principles of partnership were, all became sources of difficulty. This was particularly so given that, curiously, the role of ACAS was for the most part limited to initialising the process rather than going on, as in the previous case, to oversee developments and attend all meetings. Thus, it could not play the role of witness and recollect activities and agreements on behalf of the group. This meant that it was hard to establish the development of ideas and issues and, at times, the sessions became more 'tasters' of innovative employment practices.

This contributed to competing agendas. There was a consensus on 'soft' issues such as mediation and the need to use mediation at earlier stages of the grievance procedure. However, certain members of the personnel department had to be reminded that mediation, whilst useful, could not replace key stages of the grievance procedure. In this respect, one began to detect that within the personnel department there was a tension related to regulatory procedures, with newer personnel managers feeling that they should have greater discretion over such matters. This came to a head when the question of appeals was discussed and it took experienced trade unionists a substantial amount of time and effort to explain that there were procedures backed by ACAS that made reform or withdrawal of such stages difficult. This led to a further problem. Tensions emerged around the relations and roles of key individuals. It was never clear who was meeting with whom in informal terms and what was prepared and by whom in terms of different stages of the project. Within the new partnership, there remained an individualised and obscure trust-generating mechanism based on informal relations and discussions.

Thirdly, alongside these issues of voice and the complexities of local government was the key issue of middle management. It was felt amongst many management interviewees, let alone those from the trade union that much of the problem in terms of grievances was not just procedures and their bureaucratic nature but a failure of network managers to create effective communication systems between line managers and between middle managers; many managers were 'acting up', taking up higher positions on a temporary basis, and there were real knowledge and resource issues in relation to them. These 'networking' problems were, moreover, echoed in the partnership process itself. Different committees dealing with the question of bullying and harassment were aware of developments in terms of the grievance partnership project but there were few synergies. The same was true with regard to the parallel discussions taking place on the Council's sickness procedures. Partnership, as a result, appeared to be fragmented and 'locked' into project management silos. In this respect it was different to the more culturalist – albeit partly flawed – approach outlined in the first case. Hence, the existing management and organisational structure worked against the development of 'new ways of joint working', irrespective of the political ambivalence of some trade unionists towards partnership as a concept. The increasing divisionalisation of the Council in terms of spatial zones, and the increasing proposals to move towards a more arms-length management system only threatened to worsen further this situation.

Yet there was also a specific problem relating to the generation of trust and the creation of new forms of working. These related to memory and individuals. Throughout the partnership process, key players were opting in and out. Indeed, the main instigators of the project moved on and the personnel department changed shape and character after the commencement of the project and the arrival at some tentative agreement. This created a situation where the agreements, the events and the discussions tied to the project were in effect lost. This meant that the researchers – the authors in question – were invited back to remind the Council personnel staff of what they had achieved. The sheer logistics of using innovative decision-making procedures at the margins of established consultative mechanisms, with their capacity to record and regulate processes, then, throws light on the perils of working on the margins and in 'flexible' ways. The cult of discussing issues without recourse to one's interest – 'leaving the baggage at the door' – presents other avenues to risk other than those which already exist in relation to partnership more generally (Martínez Lucio and Stuart, 2005). It is, as a result, perhaps unsurprising that, in contrast to the two cases reported here, other organisations studied by the authors have chosen to revamp joint regulation and consultation, and enhance the skills and increase the capacity of members in such forums, rather than create new mechanisms of joint working.

## Conclusion

Partnership varies. It is mistaken to believe that a new culture of cooperation is taking root. Even when it appears to have led to changes, as in the cases above, it still varies in terms of its form, structures and outcomes. In this respect, there is still a strong voluntary element even in the regulated public sector. The weakness or ambivalence of regulation in the UK still maps itself onto the experience of the industrial relations system. In a context of ongoing decentralisation, this is increasingly the case in the public sector.

What the chapter shows is that there are strategic and structural challenges to the remoulding of trust relations in the public sector. The structural challenge is one of engaging trade unions and managers around new participative arrangements in what is an increasingly fragmented context of public sector organisations. Greater decentralisation, local management cultures, and local political factors mean that finding long-term reciprocity between management and unions – *quid pro quos* around social and economic issues – is a challenge in a context of marketisation. As regards strategic factors, these relate to the fact that such structural pressures and developments require, ironically, strong informal and personal arrangements (see Oxenbridge and Brown, 2005 for a discussion of the latter). The role of key players and the role of direct communication between them become essential to hold the fragments together in a context of two problems. The first is the capacity of management and trade unions to play a more complex game of consultation around broader agendas. The second is the pressures it places on key individuals in terms of their time, focus and health; pressures that simultaneously can prompt a reliance on external agencies and third parties such as ACAS and create difficulties in relation to their utilisation and the evaluation of their value (Stuart and Martínez Lucio, 2005a, 2006).

In the two local authorities studied here, recalling key developments and improvements in industrial relations because of ACAS intervention was not straightforward. Key interviewees within the organisation did not always keep systematic records of agreements and events and the content of activities was not easily recalled – although case A had less of a problem in this respect as it relied on ACAS more effectively. Nevertheless, in both organisations there were key players – sets of individuals – within them who created strong relations amongst themselves, both formally and informally, which allowed for a degree of reciprocity and mutual trust. However, the absence of such individuals due to transfers to another organisation, or illness, created a memory gap – an organisational dementia – that precluded institutional players from recalling developments or the precise features of joint working activities and outcomes. These developments, ironically, allowed third parties to play a prominent role in keeping records and memories of events. The ACAS advisor played a pivotal gatekeeper role about previous developments and events due to this ever-changing roll call of personnel and personalities. Even with a rigid structure for voice mechanisms in the area of local government, there was a need to involve a broader set of players in order to generate consent and reinvigorate organisational memory. For some this raises issues related to knowledge management and the need to preserve strategic memory (Jennex *et al.*, 2003); however, it also means that internal labour market and employment stabilisation strategies may assist in longer-term planning (Guest, 2000) due to the implications on knowledge. However, public sector change appears to mitigate against these two factors.

In their work on partnership in the public sector Danford *et al.* (2002) argue that partnership has led to outcomes related to greater work intensification. We agree, but point to the irony that the very establishment of partnership was institutionally challenging – even in apparently supportive environments – and this was partly related to the way the climate of organisational change and work intensification (whether brought on by partnership or not) undermines the capacity for support in terms of key participants. It undermines the process let alone the outcomes.

Mortality and the sphere of the personal is an issue in industrial relations. It links to the interest in the 'informal' in industrial relations. However, making partnerships without secure structures – or relying on focused and more limited and even concealed structures – raises issues of vulnerability and sustainability in the face of our physicality. It calls forth the need for guarantees and guarantors. A new form of state is required that goes beyond process and systems of representations, towards a more complex internal arrangement of actors and players. The changing state requires changing internal relationships and more than just a guarantee of voice mechanisms. The importance of informal links, networks and dialogues is central. The public sector has therefore become an object of intervention in its own right as it moves towards a new, marketised system of regulation (Stuart and Martínez Lucio, 2006). That is to say that as the public sector changes and becomes similar to aspects of the private sector, state agencies such as ACAS find that they intervene increasingly in the realm of the public sector. Much of this has to do with forcing the public sector to recall its legacies and practices as a 'good employer'. This is itself an irony worth noting given the role the public sector was meant to play, and it raises further issues regarding memory.

# 10
# Trade Unions and the Public Sector: A Story of 'Internal' Institutional Stability and Declining 'Regulatory Reach'

*Ian Cunningham and Phil James*

Trade union membership, recognition and organisation are widespread within the British public sector, with the result that unions play a central role in determining the terms and conditions of those employed in the sector as well as, more generally, shaping the nature of employment relationships within it. At the same time, the environment within which unions have operated in recent decades has undergone a profound process of change. Employers have sought to reform their human resource strategies and policies, including *via* the introduction of more extensive systems of performance-related pay, and governments have imposed a seemingly never-ending stream of performance management arrangements encompassing the laying down of performance targets and the use of systems of audit to monitor compliance with them. Meanwhile, a range of governmental initiatives have been introduced aimed at exposing public service provision to market-based forms of competition that have resulted in a substantial growth in the sub-contracting of services to private and not-for-profit organisations.

Against this background, the objectives of the present chapter are to consider how far this picture of change has been accompanied by changes to the institutional position and role of unions in relation to those directly employed in the public sector, and to examine how the ongoing drive by government to encourage the outsourcing of public sector work has challenged the capacity of unions to regulate the employment relationships of those engaged in externalised activities and hence detrimentally affected their 'regulatory reach'. The analysis provided falls into three main parts. In the first, attention is paid to how union membership, organisation and activity within the sector have changed since the early 1980s. This is undertaken through an analysis of changes to workforce unionisation, union recognition, the coverage of collective bargaining activities and structures, and the spread and strength of workplace organisation and activism. In the second, the potentially adverse implications that externalisation has for the role that unions play in regulating the terms and conditions, and more general employment situation, of those engaged in outsourced work are explored. Finally, the extent to which these implications are being realised in practice is examined by reference to research evidence drawn from the social care sector, this sector being chosen because, as will be seen, it is one of those where outsourcing has been most widespread.

## Trade unions and public sector employment

### Public sector unions and their membership

The public sector is marked by a multiplicity of unions that differ widely in terms of their size, functions/nature and the types of workers they seek to recruit. For example, unions involved in it include large general ones, the Transport and General Workers' Union, Amicus, and the GMB, which have traditionally recruited in both the public and private sectors. They also include others that have historically operated only in the former – the largest of these being Unison, the National Union of Teachers and the Royal College of Nursing (RCN)[1]. Those falling in the second of these categories also exhibit significant differences with regard to the parts of the public sector that they focus on, the categories of workers they seek to recruit and the extent to which they, like the RCN and smaller organisations such as the Chartered Society of Physiotherapists and the Royal College of Midwives, combine the roles of a trade union and a professional association.[2]

This complex pattern of union representation exists alongside levels of membership which are relatively high, and much higher than those found in the private parts of the economy. Indeed, as membership in the latter has fallen dramatically over the last 20 or so years (see Millward *et al.*, 2000 and Kersely, *et al.*, 2006 for summaries), the disparity between the two sectors in this regard has grown. This is not, however, to say that the public sector itself has been immune to membership decline.

Labour Force Survey data covering the years 1989–96, for example, shows that the density of union membership fell across the public services during this period from 80 per cent to around 55 per cent, with this overall decline subsuming notable falls in central government and the health services, but relative stability among some groups of staff such as teachers, fire fighters and nurses (Bird and Corcoran, 1994; Cully and Woodland, 1996). More recent data covering the period to 2005, however, indicates that this process of union density decline has largely come to a halt, with membership levels having declined by only a few percentage points during the years from 1996 (Grainger, 2006).

There has, then, been a clear rise in the proportion of staff that have either never joined a union or chosen to relinquish their membership over the last 15 or so years. The reasons for this growth in non-membership in the context of virtually universal union recognition would seem to be potentially the product of four rather different dynamics (Charlwood, 2003; Bryson and Gomez, 2005; Prowse and Prowse, 2006). First, a reduction in the degree to which union membership constitutes a 'social custom' in the workplaces where they work. Secondly, an 'instrumental' calculation that the benefits of such membership are less than its costs, where these costs include the cost of subscriptions and the perceived negative impact of membership on career progression and more general relations with the employer. Thirdly, the adoption by workers of attitudes and values which are ideologically less supportive of the role of unions than those previously held. Fourthly, the compounding of these three contributing factors by another wider one: a decline, at least at the aggregate level, in the degree of workplace union activism and the related availability of representatives to encourage membership (Waddington and Kerr, 1999; Millward *et al.*, 2000; Terry, 2003).

The precise role played by these factors remains difficult to specify with any precision. It would, though, seem that an increase in 'anti-union' attitudes has played a relatively small role (Charlwood, 2003; Bryson and Gomez, 2005). Consequently, a decline in the social custom and perceived utility of union membership would appear to have been most influential, with both of these, in turn, being linked to some extent to a relative decline of union activism. It is, inevitably, unclear how far this downward trend in union membership will continue. In the light of the above observations, however, there would seem grounds for believing that future trends will be influenced strongly by the degree to which unions are able to mobilise, maintain and extend effective workplace organisation, and hence influence perceptions regarding the value and 'appropriateness' of union membership (Kelly, 1998).

### Trade union recognition, employment regulation and workplace organisation

As has been the case throughout the post-war period, trade union recognition for the purposes of negotiating pay and conditions remains close to universal across all parts of the public sector. The findings from the latest Workplace Employment Relations Survey (WERS), for example, reveal that in 2004 such recognition existed in 90 per cent of public sector workplaces, compared with 16 per cent of private sector ones (Kersely *et al.*, 2005). As a result, the majority of public sector staff has their terms and conditions set *via* collective agreements.

The role of collective bargaining in determining the pay of staff has, however, declined and expanded during the course of the last quarter of a century, primarily as a result of the expansion and contraction of the remit of independent national pay review bodies (Millward *et al.*, 2000; Bach and Winchester, 2003.[3] Currently, according to the latest WERS findings, the proportion of staff covered by collectively determined pay stands at 82 per cent, while collective bargaining takes place in more than three-quarter of workplaces in the sector (Kersely *et al.*, 2005).

The structure through which collective bargaining over pay (as well as other terms and conditions) takes place now sometimes differs from the centralised national, 'Whitley', style arrangements that predominated from the end of the Second World War up until the end of the 1970s (Beaumont, 1992). For example, in the civil service negotiations take place at the level of individual agencies and departments (Corby, 1998) and in further education in England and Wales many colleges have chosen to either negotiate local agreements or unilaterally impose pay settlements, notwithstanding the existence of a national negotiating framework (Williams, 2004). Meanwhile, in local government a small number of authorities have similarly elected to break away from national negotiating arrangements, and the pay of the new grades of 'health care assistant' and teaching assistant' in the health and school sectors are determined locally (Bach and Winchester, 2003; Upchurch, 2003).[4]

Insofar as pay bargaining has been decentralised, it has served to increase the workload of full-time union officials while also acting to expand the negotiating role of local workplace union organisations. Even where bargaining has remained centralised, however, similar trends can be discerned. In part, as a result of the growing use of external contractors and the implications this has for the job security and transfer of staff. It is also, in part, due to the establishment of new harmonised, national job evaluation-based grading structures in the National Health Service, local government and higher education that need to be jointly implemented at the local level.[5]

One important consequence of these developments has therefore been that workplace union organisations have been acquiring a more important role in public sector industrial relations. Another, which links back to the earlier discussion of what the future holds for union membership in the sector, is that perceptions of the attractiveness and relevance of union membership are likely to be shaped much more now by the activities and effectiveness of these organisations.

Existing case study evidence, however, provides a mixed picture regarding the vitality and strength of union organisation at the workplace level, with examples of both strengthening and weakening being noted (Fairbrother, 2000). Meanwhile, surveys suggest that while such organisation is relatively widespread, both its coverage and strength has been tending, at the aggregate level, to be declining. For example, findings from the 2004 WERS indicate that the period from 1998 saw a decline, from 55 per cent to 45 per cent, in the proportion of members of recognised unions that had access to a lay representative at their own workplace and that this decline was greatest among small workplaces and in the public sector (Kersely *et al.*, 2006).

At the same time, these figures have to be tempered with findings from the same study relating to what union representatives in the public sector do. Thus, these indicate a continued high profile for those representatives that remain. Indeed, they point to the fact that public sector representatives spend longer hours on their duties than those in the private sector, especially those in public administration (Kersely *et al.*, 2006).

The above summary, then, highlights a continuing relative resilience of union organisation among directly employed public sector workers. Attention now turns to a consideration of how far unions have managed to extend their organisation, and hence regulatory reach, to externalised workers undertaking public sector work in the sub-sector of social care within voluntary sector organisations. This is, with the purpose of shedding light on whether the externalisation of such work is acting to undermine their capacity to regulate the employment conditions of those undertaking tasks that would previously have been covered by in-house regulatory arrangements.

## Outsourcing and public sector unionism

The advent of a Conservative Government in 1979 saw the beginnings of a long-standing move on the part of successive Conservative and Labour administrations to open up public services to external competition and thereby encourage the transfer of work to private sector and not-for-profit organisations. These two related objectives, which have been pursued in different ways, both across different parts of the public sector and over time, have met with much union opposition. This has partly stemmed from the implications that externalisation can have for the quality of transferred work. But also because of its potential impact on union membership, and the role of unions in regulating the terms and conditions of staff working for outside contractors, as well as the possible way in which any reductions in them might subsequently impact on those of 'in-house' personnel.

From a legal point of view, the Transfer of Undertakings (Protection of Employment) Regulations (TUPE) provide unions with some protection in relation to these last areas of concern. Thus, by virtue of their provisions, where staff are transferred away from the public sector, union recognition is also transferred, along with their existing terms and conditions of employment. However, this protection is limited since there are no requirements under the regulations for the new employer to extend this recognition to other staff used to undertake the required work or to provide them with the same terms and conditions. Nor is there anything to stop them from subsequently deciding to derecognise the union. On top of this, unions recognised for transferred staff can potentially find themselves operating in a much more challenging environment in which their role is less accepted and there is a lack of access to the strength and expertise of a wider workplace union organisation. A potential that is highlighted by case study findings which suggest that, in situations of sub-contracting, union's 'voice is particularly susceptible to fracture and fragmentation' (Grimshaw *et al.*, 2006).

National level union action has gone some way to alleviate the above weaknesses in the TUPE regulatory regime. In 2003, the Labour Government, in the face of union pressure, published a Code of Practice on Workforce Matters in Local Authority Service Contracts which provided for external contractors to employ new recruits on terms and conditions that broadly matched those of transferred staff. Subsequently, in 2005, the provisions of this code were, then, extended to cover other parts of the public sector. Meanwhile, also in 2003, regulations were introduced under which certain categories of National Health Service (NHS) staff transferred to new hospitals built through the Private Finance Initiative (PFI), and hence operated by outside private sector companies, would work on a secondment basis and hence remain directly employed by the Service (Davies, 2004). More recently, in 2005, unions and the Department of Health reached an agreement with private contractors that hospital cleaners, porters and catering staff would, in future, receive pay and conditions on a par with those agreed under the Agenda for Change programme for internally employed health service staff (Bewley, 2006).

The fact, nevertheless, remains that while these initiatives go someway to restricting the development of a 'two-tier workforce' engaged in public sector work, they do so in a way that is distant from the activities of workplace trade union organisations. As a result, it may well be that they do little to demonstrate the value of union membership to those, particularly new recruits, employed by external contractors. In addition, they also do nothing to preclude unions being derecognised by such contractors. Or to overcome the difficulties that unions can face in both maintaining membership and effective workplace organisation among staff transferred to them and, for that matter, obtaining recognition from those that do not recognise unions and have no obligation to do so because of the absence of relevant TUPE staff transfers.

There consequently remains a clear potential for externalisation to lead to lower levels of membership among those employed in *public sector work* as a whole and to also reduce the role that unions play in influencing not only their pay and other basic terms of employment but such aspects of their employment as the nature of shift patterns, staffing levels, and workloads. How far these potential impacts are occurring in practice, however, remains difficult to determine in the absence of relevant systematic and broadly based research. In the following section, therefore, an attempt is made to shed some light on them by drawing on the findings of recent research undertaken by one of the present authors in the social care voluntary sector (Cunningham, 2006).[6]

## Trade unions and the regulation of 'public service work' – the case of the social care voluntary sector

The UK voluntary sector represents a potentially fertile ground for union organisation. Thus, not only does it currently employ 608,000 employees, representing 2.2 per cent of the UK paid workforce, but its workforce increased by 10,000 a year between 2000–4 (Wainwright *et al.*, 2006).

Much of this growth in employment has occurred in the context of a significant contracting out of social services from the state to the point where it has grown to become the voluntary sector's main source of employment (Kendall and Knapp, 1996; Wilding *et al.*, 2004). The contribution of this 'contracted out' workforce can be further illustrated at a regional level. For example, between 1994 and 2003 employment in the Scottish social care sector increased by some 23 per cent (96,000 in 1994 to 118,000 in 2003), with the independent sector (private and voluntary combined) growing by 76 per cent, and now accounting for more than half of social care employment in Scotland (*Scottish Executive*, 2005).

This growth of employment in the voluntary sector as a result of contracting out exists alongside evidence suggesting that changes to terms and conditions of employment within it are also potentially supportive of union recruitment. It also, however, further exists alongside other evidence providing a mixed picture with regard to the present capacity of unions to regulate these terms and conditions and to successfully organise in the sector.

### Changing terms and conditions

There is clear evidence that workers in voluntary organisations undertaking public sector work are increasingly in need of unions to protect their employment security and terms and conditions. For example, funding pressures from contracting have led to a greater reliance on atypical/temporary forms of employment in the sector (Cunningham, 2000). In addition, a recent study of trade union workplace representatives found how 76 per cent of them felt short-term funding was increasing and that this was often linked to greater stress and anxiety in the workplace, and a lowering of morale, with subsequent detrimental effects on service provision (Amicus, 2005)

Another key area of detrimental change is pay. Here, prior to the development of the quasi-market, rewards were traditionally aligned to local authority scales (Ball, 1992). However, since the early 1990s this has unravelled as pressure from the quasi-market has intensified (Ford *et al.*, 1998; Cunningham, 2001; Knapp *et al.*, 2001; Barnard *et al.*, 2004; Cunningham, 2006). As a result, it is estimated that the proportion of voluntary organisations still using such pay scales has declined to 20 per cent (Remuneration Economics, 2002).

Research has further highlighted how this change in pay arrangements, as well as other changes to terms and conditions, has been prompted by pressures exerted by client local authorities. For example, it has been found that a common practice on the part of authorities has been to refuse, through the widespread use of opt-out clauses in contracts, to award, in relation to existing contracts, annual increases in line with inflation for staff budgets. In addition, even where local authorities have paid inflationary increases, contractual negotiations have been found to focus on other aspects of the staff budget such as holidays, pension entitlements, management fees and training (Cunningham, 2006). Findings which would, in turn, seem to go some way to explaining why there have been reports indicating that voluntary organisations are less likely to provide other benefits such as higher rates of pay for achieving accreditation under the National Vocational Qualification (NVQ) schemes (IDS, 2005).

There are also concerns regarding working time. Specifically, regulatory pressures from central, notably the Care Commission,[7] and local government agencies means that care for the vulnerable involves providing 24 hour services, a situation that has, inevitably, had significant implications for the organisation of working time, staff flexibility and work loads (Leat and Ungerson, 1994). The previously referenced study by Cunningham (2006), for example, found that union officials were becoming increasingly concerned with regard to the widespread use of sleepovers and on-call responsibilities in the voluntary sector to cover nightshifts. In particular, these concerns related to the strain such arrangements placed on union members, and the tensions they created with regard to compliance with both working time and 'family friendly' employment legislation. Tensions that are of considerable relevance given that the majority of the workforce in the sector is female and hence likely to need some flexibility in working time to match their childcare responsibilities (Almond and Kendall, 2000).

## Union regulation of employment conditions

Despite the above, there is a mixed picture of union regulation of employment in the UK voluntary sector at the workplace level. The Labour Force Survey, for example, has revealed that 37 per cent of voluntary workplaces had a trade union presence in 1998, which was higher than the private sector at 28 per cent, but significantly lower than the public sector at 89 per cent. Meanwhile, it would seem that membership density is not only low but has also been declining as membership has failed to keep pace with the rise in the voluntary sector workforce (Passey *et al.*, 2000). A scrutiny of membership figures on union websites, moreover, confirms this picture of low membership density, with estimates of it standing at approximately

15 per cent (Unison, 2006). It would also seem that a substantial proportion of this membership comes from staff who have involuntarily entered the sector because of the contracting out of public services, especially from transfers of housing stock from local authorities to the social housing sector (Unison, 2006).

As regards the proportion of workplaces that recognise trade unions, the available information is patchy. Several studies, however, suggest steady progress in new recognition deals since the election of the Labour Government and the introduction of a statutory recognition procedure under the Employment Relations Act 1999. In particular, a positive shift in attitudes to recognition has reportedly occurred among some employers in the sector in response to their experiencing rapid employment growth and having to deal with subsequent communication and consultation issues (Cunningham, 2000; Simms, 2003). These developments, though, have also coincided with an increase in union organising efforts from the late 1990s, with Unison, Amicus, and the Transport and General Workers Union (TGWU) establishing dedicated national officers and campaign resources to service current members and gain recognition (Cunningham, 2000). Efforts which appear to have supported the conclusion of partnership agreements with some employers in the sector (IDS, 2005; Unison, 2006; Amicus, 2006a) and which presumably go some way to explaining why union recognition in the social care sub-sector of the voluntary sector appears to be greater than that among private organisations delivering care services (IDS, 2006).

While information from the above studies is useful, it nevertheless tells us little about the capacity of unions, where they have a presence, to regulate the employment relationships of those employed on 'public sector work' in the voluntary sector. Although some of the aforementioned studies relating to pay, for example, reveal that some voluntary organisations are still wedded to public sector pay scales (Cunningham, 2001; IDS, 2005), they tell us little about the union contribution to maintaining this linkage.

The study by Cunningham (2006), however, does shed some light on this last issue and, in doing so, suggests a mixed picture with regard to union workplace influence. Thus, this found that in some organisations with union agreements there was evidence suggesting management were finding it problematic to transform their terms and conditions to suit the demands of funders and the Care Commission, such as with regard to pension rights, skills dilution and cuts to unsocial hours payments. However, in other cases there were signs of weakness in union organisation with regard to protecting pay and working conditions, with less than half of unionised workplaces retaining the link with local authority pay and conditions. Indeed, the study revealed how in a number of the cases where organisations had partially or wholly moved away from public sector pay scales, union input into these decisions had been very limited. This failure of unions to effectively mobilise worker interests was also evident from a scrutiny of membership density, with only one of the voluntary sector organisations with union recognition studied reporting membership above 50 per cent of the workforce (Cunningham, 2006).

This same study also gives some insight into local authority perspectives in relation to the situation prevailing in the sector with regard to union organisation. In particular, it suggests that weak unionisation across the sector was considered by some authorities to be advantageous to them. Specifically, in contrast to situations where work was still undertaken by public sector employees, it was sometimes felt to be easier to achieve the desired degree of workforce flexibility and cuts in wage costs in services through contracting with the voluntary sector. Moreover, where older, unionised, voluntary organisations insisted on retaining the link to public sector pay and conditions, it is reported that some local authorities deliberately expanded the care market in order to bring in non-union private or non-profit providers. The purpose of this being to use these new entrants to replace the more established voluntary organisations or encourage them to restructure their own working hours and terms and conditions (Cunningham, 2006).

## Explanations for union success and failure

In searching for explanations for the mixed success of union regulation of employment in the voluntary sector, the study by Cunningham (2006) revealed a combination of factors. The first related to the difficulties for leaders and activists to emerge in the workplace, which is seen as crucial to achieve the successful mobilisation of union strength (see Kelly, 1998). For example, on a general level, all union representatives interviewed made reference to the scarce resources available to them to service members and organise in the sector relative to those that existed in other areas of activity such as the public sector. This lack of resources was, in turn, seen to be aggravated by a proliferation of contracts with local authorities that led to the establishment of numerous, small and geographically dispersed, workplaces and consequent problems with regard to the recruitment of activists/shop stewards and wider membership. These findings therefore echo those of other studies which have highlighted how employee voice can become 'disconnected' in networked organisations marked by extensive contractual relations and outsourcing (Marchington *et al.*, 2005).

In addition to weak organising ability, an interlinked restraint on unions successfully regulating employment in the sector highlighted in the study by Cunningham (2006) concerns the constraints on their activity arising from having an external third party (in this case local authorities) influencing pay and conditions. For its findings revealed that workplace and regional union officials invariably faced a dilemma when seeking to challenge voluntary organisations that wished to move away from public sector pay comparability, namely the risk that this comparability might only be maintained at the cost of their losing contracts and, even, going out of business.

More generally, Cunningham's study therefore suggests strongly that, in addition to strong grassroots activism, union success or failure, in particular voluntary sector organisations is intimately connected to their wider position in the quasi-market. Thus, unions appeared to be more successful in the larger voluntary organisations because they were less resource dependent on one or two funding sources and hence better able to generate surpluses to subsidise pay and conditions, including a link with public sector comparability. Moreover, this financial stability further seemed to be built on the likelihood that these organisations were 'providers of choice' with good reputations for delivering quality services, filling a particular niche and/or delivering innovation.

## Conclusion

Union membership, recognition and organisation remain high *within* the public sector and have proved remarkably resilient in the face of the major changes that have occurred in the sector over the last quarter of a century. Membership density has, however, declined somewhat overall and it would seem likely that this decline has been associated with a growth in the number of staff who do not see membership as part of the social norms in the workplaces where they work and/or do not view it as being of instrumental value. This growth, in turn, would further appear to be linked to a lack of effective workplace organisation in parts of the sector.

Research evidence suggests that this problem relating to workplace union organisation has been growing. Therefore, despite the continued resilience of union organisation compared to the private sector, a major challenge for public sector unions is to find ways of addressing this area of weakness and in doing so establish on a wider basis a virtuous circle between local trade union activism and membership recruitment and retention.

Meanwhile, it would seem that unions face a further challenge in maintaining membership levels in a context of the growing externalisation of work and the related transfer of staff to private and non-for-profit organisations. The evidence on the voluntary social care sector in this chapter suggests that there are some grounds for believing that this challenge can be potentially met given the aforementioned modest growth of union recognition agreements in the sector and the way in which the financial pressures being exerted by public sector commissioning bodies are placing a downward pressure on terms and conditions of work and thereby engendering widespread staff dissatisfaction.

At the same time, however, the evidence also suggests that this ground for optimism exists alongside significant barriers to the further development of membership, recognition and workplace organisation in the sector. These difficulties mirror the issues faced by unions in the public sector. However, there is, comparatively, even less in-depth knowledge as to why density remains low in the voluntary sector despite an expanding workforce, and hence the relative role played by such factors as 'social custom', instrumental calculations and a lack of representatives at the workplace level. Moreover, we know little about how far these barriers have been exacerbated by the problems that unions have faced in protecting staff terms and conditions within severely financially constrained contractor organisations. We also, more generally, know little about the degree to which the interests of these two union constituencies, that is those directly employed in the public sector and those working for external contractors, are in harmony and hence the extent to which the protection of them is the subject of internal competition for resources within unions.[1]

## Notes

1.  It is important, however, to note that some unions which have historically only recruited in the public sector no longer do so as they have 'followed' members and work transferred to external contractors in the private and not-for-profit sectors. This development is clearly exemplified by the decision taken when several civil service unions merged to call the new combined organisation the Public and Commercial Services Union.
2.  One consequence of this fragmentation of union members across a large number of unions is that it is invariably the case that employers deal with a number of different unions. This 'multi-unionism' may, and perhaps most commonly does, involve the presence of different unions representing different categories of staff. However, it can also encompass situations, such as are found in teaching and nursing, where more than one union represents the same category of staff.
3.  It should be borne in mind that unions exert an influence over the outcomes of the deliberations of pay review bodies, notably by submitting evidence to them and pressuring governments to implement their recommendations in full.
4.  It should, however, be noted that the history of some of these centralised bargaining arrangements, such as those existing in the civil service and education and in relation to local authority manual workers, can be traced back to the period immediately following the First World War. See Beaumont (1992).
5.  Some discussion of the schemes established in the NHS and local government is provided in Chapter 6 of this volume.
6.  The financial support for this research provided by the Carnegie Trust is gratefully acknowledged.
7.  The Care Commission has a regional infrastructure and has taken over the responsibility from local authorities for the inspection of registered care homes in the public, private and voluntary sectors. It also has powers to introduce and amend standards of care expected in these homes, and has powers of accreditation over the care workforce under National Vocational Qualifications (NVQs) or Scottish Vocational Qualification (SVQs) in Scotland.

# 11

# Partnership: Transforming the Employment Relationship in Public Service Delivery

*Damian Grimshaw and Ian Roper*

Current reform agendas in public service delivery have moved away from what have been seen as adversarial buyer-supplier relationships based on cost-only tendering processes for public service delivery. Instead, an alternative approach is claimed to foster long-term inter-organisational relations, encouraging a high trust, partnership approach to mutually beneficial investment. Influenced by Le Grand (2003), the 'public-private partnership' approach emphasises the way quasi-markets can address principal-agent problems between public service worker (whether employed in the public or private sector) and commissioning body to maximise value for the service-user. But numerous studies point to tensions in this new governance model. These include questions about the individualisation of the public service user, the intangible costs of separating policy knowledge from responsibility over implementation and, critically, unanticipated problems arising from applying a principle-agent model to an employment relationship traditionally governed through an open-ended contract.

This chapter examines the rationale for this emerging hybridised public/private organisational form and examines the impact of this on employment relations in the sector. Initially, the political/ideological developments that have informed its evolution are examined; an examination which proceeds by, firstly, highlighting the key features of the way in which public services were organised prior to the election of the Thatcher Government in 1979 and the way in which these were amended following its coming to power, and then examining the impact of New Labour's approach to public sector reform and the way in which this can be linked to the work of Le Grand. Attention then moves on to an exploration of the employment-related rationales and assumptions that have underpinned the establishment of public-private partnerships (CPPP) and the extent to which these receive endorsement from existing empirical evidence.

## Transforming the employment relationship in the delivery of public services

One of the features of public services reform over the past two decades has been a changing of the structure of relationships between those delivering public services. If we were to conceptualise ideal-type characteristics for the organisation of public services, we could say that the (pre-Thatcher) model involved service delivery through the discretion of the public service professional who, in turn, was accountable to (hierarchical) management within the same organisation, which itself was tempered by accountability to joint union/management consultative bodies and, ultimately, to publicly elected representatives.[1]

The Thatcherite ideal-type was informed – sometimes retrospectively, often inconsistently (Gamble, 1994) – by new right thinking on the role of the state, whereby the interests of tax-payers were deemed paramount, while büro-professionals, unions and the overloading tendencies of political pluralism were to be mistrusted (see Thompson, this volume). This approach favoured frontline staff being answerable to the line-management of a financially accountable contractor, who itself was accountable to a slimmed-down publicly-owned commissioner which had justified the cost of service levels required to tax-payers *via* directly elected representatives, and to central government through a variety of quangos and independent scrutineers.

### A Third Way?

If the New Labour approach were to be similarly idealised, it would be based on its mission to reestablish the legitimacy of public services in the face of the Conservative attempt to undermine their very existence. For the first two terms of office this involved, after an initial period of maintaining inherited targets of government spending, a step change in financial resources being made available for public services. This boost was important not only on its own terms, but also in terms of it providing the justification for further reforms as *quid pro quo*. It also involved the continuation of market-based solutions inherited from the previous government, combined with top-down performance management driven by centrally determined targets. Since 2005, however, the emphasis has shifted more in favour of the former: the key words describing reform since then being (service user) 'choice' and 'partnership' (with private or non-profit external organisations). Whatever the nuances of the balances between these two elements, however, it is clear that the traditional notion that the public service professional can be broadly trusted to deliver good quality work is now viewed as irresponsibly naïve: mistrust is now built into the mechanism of public service management. To exemplify this a recent government document (Cabinet Office, 2006a: 5) cites the following four elements as being at the heart of its public service reform agenda:

- Top-down performance management (pressure from government);
- The introduction of greater competition and contestability in the provision of public services;
- The introduction of greater pressure from citizens... through choice and voice; and
- Measures to strengthen the capability and capacity of civil servants and of central and local government to deliver improved public services.

More generally, New Labour's reform agenda has been informed by 'third way' prescriptions for the renewal of social democracy intended to address the 'five dilemmas' facing progressive governments aiming to reform public services, notably those relating to globalisation, individualism and political agency. Giddens (1998; 2000) contends that globalisation challenges the ability of the nation-state to offer relatively generous universal welfare provision because of the consequences on fiscal stability caused by capital mobility; that individualism has created a more demanding citizen that ceases to value universalised state provision; and that the legitimacy of the political process – of which public services are key manifestation – has been undermined through the mistrust of political parties and their representatives and institutions.

In this context, modernising public services is centred on enhancing legitimacy by tailoring services more towards the aspirations and expectations of users: making services more akin to those private services that consumers value. In turn, these aims are to be achieved through a more dynamic and responsive service provider which is provided by a transformation of leadership style from a professional public service ethos to one of 'social entrepreneur'. The key mechanisms for reform are, hence, the involvement of external agencies and consumer choice.

## Knights and knaves; pawns and queens

Perhaps the most influential academic associated with the recent reform agenda has been Julian Le Grand, who has been an advocate of the use of 'quasi-markets' as a key reform mechanism in public service reform from the 1980s. The basis of Le Grand's (2003) theoretical advocacy of quasi-markets is principal-agent theory relating to the motivation of frontline staff and the implications that this has for the relationship between them and service users. Le Grand breaks with public choice theory in rejecting the notion that all acts conducted in the name of public service are necessarily selfish ('knavish') acts and allows for the important contributory motivating factor of altruism ('knightly acts'). However, in dealing with a situation where knights and knaves coexist, Le Grand is led to promote mechanisms that get the best from both. The consequent adoption of principal-agent theory leads to the assertion that public service organisations will function more efficiently when disaggregated into quasi-markets. In this way the agent (the contracted service worker) can be motivated more effectively by the principal (the commissioner of the service) through careful contractual arrangements that appeal to the knavish motivation of those that are purely self-interested, while not demotivating the knightly behaviour of those who are purely altruistic.

The other element to Le Grand's conceptualisation of public service work is in the degree of agency that can be attributed to service users: they are assumed to be either 'queens' or 'pawns'; queens are deemed to be fully self-actualising individuals operating with perfect knowledge whereas pawns are disempowered individuals subject to the paternalistic judgement of professional service providers. For Le Grand, optimising the best outcomes requires the user to be assumed to be a queen, redressing the imbalance in power held by professionals by access to information and by greater options for exit. Overall, this view provides the basis of current government thinking for the reform of organisations delivering public services: the greater use of internal (quasi-) markets; the provision of greater information and choice to service users; and the greater use of external organisations and/or management to bring in expertise and cultural values closely associated with more 'customer-focused' approaches to service delivery.

## Partnership as a mechanism for reform

Much of the Blair Government's reform agenda is replete with references to 'partnership'. In part, this could be seen as a pragmatic attempt to establish a workable system of 'governance' in a situation where a public body now has to deal with a whole range of external organisations and stakeholders where previously a single unified body existed. However, such monolithic structures have not existed since the imposition of compulsory competitive tendering (CCT) and market testing from as far back as 1980.

The clamour for partnership, then, is more than pragmatic: it is based on a developing theoretical base. Chief among these has been the development of PPP as a replacement for the more rigid and antagonistic mechanisms involved in CCT. PPP, it is claimed, benefits both parties through the reduction in transaction costs and the development of 'human capital' (Erridge and Green, 2002), which is contrasted to traditional public sector management behaviour which is characterised as being 'resistant to change and risk averse' (*ibid.*: 56). Further, initiatives like PPP are said to emphasise a shift towards a 'joint enterprise' or 'preferred supplier' approach that emphasises longer contractual periods as a means to establish a basis for investment (Lyons and Mehta, 1997). Relational contracting assumes the existence of trust between parties – a trust primarily built upon a shared commitment to common values, familiarity, and the exchange of information and personnel between parties. However, Fischbacher and Beaumont (2003) point out that such arrangements tend to underestimate the costs associated with separating policy from implementation, the heavy transaction costs associated with knowledge transfer and the heavy opportunity costs in effort.

Where PPP may be more contentious, however, is in its implications for the employment relationship. With public services being labour intensive, there could be seen to be a direct incentive to gain cost-savings at the expense of staff terms and conditions (Walsh, 1995; Geddes, 2001). Partnership could be seen as being different, in respect of the above factors, through its emphasis on collaborative working whereby the delivery of a particular service could be seen as a 'shared task with shared management and supervision or staff' (Flynn, 2002: 165). However, even here there may be problems. In parallel with the Government's promotion of PPP in the delivery of public services, Labour has also been pursuing a neo-pluralist 'third way' agenda in employment relations (Ackers, 2002) which is also defined in terms of partnership. Given the high-trust nature of this model, it is not easy to see how it can effectively be pursued while also attempting high commitment relationships with external partners, and 'customers'. Indeed, it has been observed that managerial commitment to staff interests are consistently undervalued when compared to the commitment made to the benefits of outsourcing (Roper *et al.*, 2005, 2007).

## Public-private partnership in practice: reshaping the employment relationship

Implicit in the conventional reasons used to support the adoption of the PPP model is a set of assumptions about the role of employment relationships that are rarely acknowledged or proven. A first reason given is that publicly controlled organisations are sheltered from market discipline and therefore lack incentives to control costs or improve service quality. As a result, as noted above, the public sector is said to suffer from a principal-agent problem. However, implicit in this argument is the untested assumption that public sector managers face relatively large difficulties in exercising regulatory control over a highly organised (through unions or professional associations) workforce, who enjoy sheltered employment conditions, and therefore are party to a power imbalance that favours the workforce. A second reason given for the PPP model is that public sector organisations can exercise greater regulatory control over performance by managing a contract agreed with a private sector firm than is possible by managing directly employed workers. The unstated assumption is that managerial authority in directing services provision through use of the traditional open-ended employment contract is weaker than use of a contract for services provision that specifies job tasks and performance penalties and targets. Again, this is a strong assumption and deserves further interrogation. A third reason is that private sector firms are more innovative than public sector organisations owing to their greater market experience. Here, a major implicit assumption is that private sector firms have greater expertise in introducing innovative forms of work organisation that can both reduce costs and improve service quality and have the capacity to success-fully integrate workers who transfer from the public sector to the private sector as part of the contracting arrangement. And fourth, the model of PPP is claimed to promote more collaborative working where services delivery is a shared task among managers, supervisors and staff across the blurred public-private sector boundaries. This claim can be seen to rest on the assumption that the associated blurring of boundaries can support seamless working and avoid new lines of fragmentation and disordering across managers and workers in partner organisations.

In this section, we address these assumptions drawing on empirical evidence of change in public sector working conditions and employment relationships associated with PPPs, as well as examples of related trade union campaigns and policy reform in the UK.

## Do public sector workers enjoy too much bargaining power?

For the public sector organisation, PPPs involve replacing the traditional contract for employment with a contract for services (Domberger, 1998). The benefits of doing so depend upon a reading of how much bargaining power public sector workers exert over their public sector employers and what impact a shift towards greater numbers of workers employed in the private sector will have.

One indication of public sector workers' bargaining power is their ability to extract a wage premium from working in the public sector. Given the direction of government policy, one might anticipate a growing wage premium during the 1980s and 1990s. In fact the reverse is true. For men, the wage premium fell from 13 per cent in 1976 to just 3 per cent in 2002 and for women the premium fell from 42 per cent to 13 per cent (Dolton and McIntosh, 2003). A possible reason is that wages in the private sector increased in response to technology-led demands for professional and highly skilled labour (*op. cit.*). But perhaps more important is the fact that the public sector employer exercises strong monopsony control over many occupations (especially in teaching and nursing, for example) and can, as a result, pay less than workers with similar skills in the private sector since their alternative employment options are limited (Grout and Stevens, 2003: 222). The problems caused by this declining wage premium were witnessed especially during the late 1990s with recruitment problems for teachers and nurses. As an indicator of relative bargaining power, therefore, the declining wage premium suggests it was the public sector employers, not the collective workforce, who enjoyed greater control during this period.

The rising use of PPPs means the government will no longer be the dominant employer for some public service occupations and, instead, the growing number of private sector firms (including some very large multinational companies) will shape the dynamics of the labour market for public service workers. Perversely, greater competition among potential employers may drive up wages where public and private sector providers bid for those employees in strong demand, increasing costs for the Treasury since it finances all public services provision, whether provided by public or private sectors. However, in the situation where private sector firms compete against each other to win contracts with a public sector client, wages are likely to fall. The net result for the public purse is not obvious. What is likely, however, is a polarisation of wage trends between low skilled and high skilled groups.

A second indicator of workers' bargaining power in the public sector might be their ability to preserve relatively strong conditions of job security and more generous secure pension schemes than private sector workers. Here the evidence is generally supportive, despite the recent trends of a decline in job security among public sector workers (Morgan *et al.*, 2000; Dibben, this volume) and new policies to increase the retirement age from 60 years old in the public sector. However, the costs to the employer of providing stable tenure and generous pensions must be balanced against the benefits of worker retention and stability. These benefits include the mutual incentives for worker and employer to invest in education and training, since both parties can anticipate a stable period during which they recoup the returns on their investments. Greater competition among public and private sector employers for public services workers, coupled with the equation of contract tenure with employment tenure, are likely, therefore, to undermine the incentives to bear training costs.

A third indicator concerns direct evidence of collective worker bargaining power – unionisation and strike action. There are indeed more trade union members in the public sector than in the private sector (3.7 million and 2.7 million, respectively, in 2005) and trade union density is far higher (59 per cent and 17 per cent respectively) (Grainger, 2006: Table 3). Crucially, this means public sector employers are more likely to have to engage in a jointly regulated process involving negotiation and consultation with unions and professional associations (Bach and Winchester, 2003). Compared to the capacity for flexible change in the private sector, such 'deliberative institutions' tend to be slow (Hall and Soskice, 2001), and for some managers this may be a cause for frustration in implementing public sector reforms. However, as the lessons of post-War Germany show, a slow jointly negotiated process of reform is also more likely to achieve consensus to change, establishing mutual commitment to organisational goals and minimising the costs of adversarial industrial relations disputes.

## Are there benefits from replacing a contract for employment with a contract for services?

Although the benefits of contracting for services over directly managing employment are often assumed among advocates of PPPs, research points to key limitations. One issue that is highlighted by employment scholars is that the open-ended employment contract provides a range of benefits that are under-appreciated. Commons (1924), Simon (1951), and, more recently, Marsden (1999), among others, provide strong theoretical foundations for the relative effectiveness of the open-ended employment contract over other forms of contracting arrangements, and empirical studies point to its continued wide popularity among developed countries (Auer and Cazes, 2000). Rather than a coordinator of spot contracts, the employing organisation develops a platform of rules that can contain sources of conflict and tensions to deliver more cooperative production and lower transaction costs than the alternative of market coordination. In particular, open-ended employment contracts are seen to facilitate agreed notions of how job tasks are designed, as well as how job demands are matched with worker skills.

Contracting with private sector firms and outsourcing workers from one employer to another clearly marks a radical break to the open-ended contract and its tradition of job security in the public sector. The question is whether this is justifiable. Research on new forms of project-based work, which are similar to PPPs since they involve successive contracts for fixed periods of work, suggests not. Marsden (2004), for example, asks whether the employment relationship in project-based networking firms offers a functional equivalent to open-ended employment and finds it lacking in this respect. In particular, the functional equivalent to a stable job under an open-ended employment contract would be membership of an occupational or professional community. In the case of workers with low and intermediate skills outsourced from public sector organisations, the absence of a well-developed apprenticeship structure in the UK limits their potential for inter-firm mobility. This condition adds an element of labour market vulnerability and reduces the mutual commitment of employer and worker to future investment in training. Also, in the case of high skill employees such as IT professionals, PPPs may generate new tensions in the management of skill development. The transfer of IT professionals through outsourcing to multinational computer services firms may widen career horizons, but it also creates new opportunities for skill-mix and task specialisation (often involving second-tier subcontracting and off-shoring), which are not necessarily in line with employee expectations. Moreover, the uncertainties of repeat contracting for projects may generate peaks and troughs in IT skills investment, as well as conflicts between IT firm and public sector client regarding responsibility for investment costs and how to share dividends (Grimshaw and Miozzo, 2005).

A further assumed benefit of managing a contract for services concerns the power of market competition to drive down prices. Studies of CCT in the 1990s demonstrated that market competition reduced costs, regardless of whether services were outsourced or provided in-house (e.g. Escott and Whitfield, 1995; Szymanski, 1996; Domberger and Jensen, 1997). But evidence of the impact on service quality has been more difficult to demonstrate. A focus on employment, however, provides some insight. For example, detailed case-study evidence from a Private Finance Initiative (PFI) outsourcing contract showed that costs were reduced at the expense of work intensification and employee morale. Commenting on the staffing cuts following the staff transfer, a porter working for a private sector firm described the situation vividly:

> They are running us ragged. They've only got half the amount of porters [compared to pre-outsourcing], but patients are sat there waiting for two hours while they try and get a porter (cited in Grimshaw and Hebson, 2005: 127).

It is also important to note that in many cases of outsourcing the assumed market competition does not even exist – both because of a shortage of firms competing for the contract and due to the long duration of contracts. The large costs of bidding for what are often enormous public sector contracts impose serious limits to the number of firms that can enter the bidding process. Also, long duration contracts carry the risk that the public sector becomes locked in to a partnership arrangement that is sheltered from the market – due to the costs of exiting the contract early and the practical impossibility of regular benchmarking of costs through market comparisons (Grimshaw *et al.*, 2002). And, as Crouch (2003: 12–13) notes, the problem of a small number of giant firms operating in essentially closed markets is that they engage in privileged lobbying of political authorities. In the case of IT outsourcing, for example, the strong role of US multinationals, EDS and IBM, suggests they have been successful in shaping the rules and conduct of the IT outsourcing market, limiting the ability of public sector organisations to adapt a given set of contract standards to suit their particular needs (Miozzo and Grimshaw, 2006).

## Are private sector firms more innovative in their approach to employment?

The wisdom underpinning PPPs associates innovation, expertise and diversity of employment policy and practice with private sector markets, not with large, bureaucratic public sector organisations (Cutler and Waine, 1994). The ability to implement more flexible systems of staffing, new forms of skill-mix and work design and incentive-improving payment systems is perceived to be greater within the private sector than the public sector. But this view ignores key features of PPPs and needs correcting in light of recent policy developments.

A curious feature of PPPs is that some private sector firms that bid for contracts have no expertise, or very limited expertise, in the areas of service provision involved. They are, however, experts in contract design. What they understand is that they need (a) to poach managers and professionals from related public authorities to design and manage the contract, and (b) to organise very well the transfer of staff involved in the delivery of public services to be outsourced. What this illustrates is that these firms in fact offer very little value-added. Crouch sums up the issue:

> What [private sector contracting firms] possess rather is a specialist skill in winning and possibly managing government contracts from politicians and civil servants. This is not necessarily a skill which passes value-added and service quality to the ultimate customers. After all, the need for the skill could have been avoided simply by not bringing in the private agent at all (Crouch, 2003: 16).

Staff transfer is critical to the ability of private sector contracting firms to establish expertise in the area of services provision. It provides the tacit knowledge of how the outsourced activity has been traditionally organised, as well as how it 'fits' with other services activities in the public sector client organisation. Thus, a relatively seamless handover of services delivery is to some extent guaranteed. One concern, however, is that as contracts near their end, private sector firms have a strong incentive to redeploy the more expert transferred staff to other positions in the firm. Where this involves managers and supervisors with lengthy work experience, the risk is that their redeployment denies the public sector client access to a valuable stock of organisational memory.

Throughout the duration of a contract, the private sector firm may, nevertheless, introduce various employment innovations. One popular change has been the introduction of lower rates of pay for new recruits to the firm, resulting in the widely publicised problem of a two-tier workforce (since transferred workers' terms and conditions are generally protected under the Transfer of Undertakings (Protection of Employment) legislation, commonly referred to as TUPE. This 'innovation' in wage-setting has widely been viewed as a failure. A long-running trade union campaign resulted in the New Labour Government announcing a form of wage extension agreement across the public sector in March 2005 (an extension to the 'Code of Practice on Workforce Matters', known as 'The Two-Tier Code'). This rolled out the existing agreement in local government, and obliges private sector firms to pay new recruits hired to work on a public service contract 'fair and reasonable terms and conditions which are, overall, no less favourable than those of transferred employees.' (Cabinet Office, 2006b).

Nevertheless, it is possible that the private sector is at the vanguard of other areas of employment policy and practice – such as work organisation, for example. For low skilled work, which constitutes the bulk of activities outsourced from the public sector to the private sector, there would appear to be great potential for a new employer to dismantle old legacies and introduce more effective, enhanced forms of working, such as multi-skilling, team-working and job rotation. Unfortunately, there is very little research evidence on the issue of job design in PPPs. Evidence from one small-scale case-study of a PFI contract finds that innovation in work organisation was undermined by disregard for other pillars of the traditional employment relationship such as job security and joint negotiation. In this case study, the private firm intended to introduce a new integrated job post at the ward level, combining the tasks of the cleaner, caterer and porter. However, trials of the new post demonstrated that it was not attractive to male porters because it conflated 'male' and 'female' work tasks, nor to many of the caterers (whether male or female) since they disagreed with the integration of hygiene tasks with catering tasks involving patient contact. Moreover, part-timers were anxious that they would be made redundant because only full-time hours were available, and many staff across the occupational groups argued a higher wage offer was needed to match the wider range of skills required. Unilateral implementation was not assisted by accompanying job cuts (including 75 per cent of chefs) and obligatory re-application for a job in the new post (Cooke *et al.*, 2004; Hebson and Grugulis, 2005).[2] Overall, while innovative job redesign may be needed to boost the working conditions of low wage jobs in UK public sector hospitals, this snap-shot evidence suggests the private sector is not a guarantor of positive transformation.

A further potential source of innovation concerns a greater willingness of the private sector to experiment with non-standard employment contracts. Key areas of the UK public sector have agreed partnerships with private sector temporary employment agencies in a quest to inject greater flexibility and efficiency into the delivery of public services. In the National Health Service (NHS) and education, partnerships with agencies were designed to replace 'in-house' systems for organising the temporary replacement of nursing and teaching staff, respectively. In education, the market grew quickly in the 1990s with more than 60 agencies competing for a market of around £200–400m by 2001 (Hutchings, 2000; Dean, 2001) and quickly made the traditional role of Local Education Authorities (LEAs) in organising temporary cover redundant. Their rapid growth might suggest private temp agencies are more fit for purpose than LEAs. But their role is controversial. There are conflicting findings as to whether the privatisation of supply teachers has lessened or exacerbated teacher shortage problems, and while agencies claim to meet the needs of teachers opting for alternative career routes, trade unions point to the fast growth in fees and problems of performance checks on recruits (Grimshaw *et al.*, 2003). A similar pattern of fast-rising agency costs has occurred in the NHS, but here there has been an innovative policy response in the form of a new national organisation, NHS Professionals (NHSP). Established in 2000, this not-for-profit organisation has operated nationally since April 2004 and had 52,000 staff on its books by 2005 (nurses, administrative staff and locum doctors). It charges half the fees of a private sector temp agency (7.5 per cent compared to a 15 per cent average), and extends all NHS benefits to temps, including the final salary scheme and access to training. Unlike a for-profit agency, NHSP does not seek to grow revenue by maximising the placement of agency temps; instead it cooperates with NHS trusts to minimise agency expenditure and also, through the NHS Skills Escalator programme, assists in the recruitment and induction of persons with limited employment experience into permanent NHS employment. Thus the real innovation appears to be on the side of the public sector in the shape of an organisation that can meet both the needs of workers wishing to enjoy the flexibility of agency employment and NHS trusts wishing to economise on agency costs, without having to meet the conflicting demands of private shareholders.

## Do PPPs promote more collaborative working?

The success of networked organisations, such as found in PPPs, is sometimes claimed to rest on the opportunities they provide for enhanced cooperation among partners, especially where they are willing to invest in strong goodwill trust through sharing tacit and codified knowledge (e.g. Dyer and Singh, 1998). The wider 'relational contracting view' to understanding an organisation's competitive advantage stresses the need for organisations to exploit the capabilities and resources located in the surrounding network of organisations through appropriate relational contracting (Milgrom and Roberts, 1992; Adler, 2001). However, while the relational approach underpins pressures to establish trusting, partnership arrangements, the associated implications for collaborative working tend to be assumed rather than demonstrated. The problem is that there is, in fact, very little analysis of how alternative forms of organisational structures impact upon the employment relationship within these accounts. Rather than consider the potential for conflicts and contradictions associated with employment relationships established within and between networked partner organisations, there is instead an assumed unity of interest (for a critique see Child and McGrath, 2001). The implicit assumption is that the 'human assets' or 'individual members', as described in such accounts, fit unproblematically into a rational inter-organisational network design and can therefore be ignored.

But empirical research demonstrates the limitations to this unitarist view and paints a picture of disorder and fragmentation that may undermine the opportunities for collaborative working within PPPs. Table 11.1 summarises some of the key findings in studies of the employment effects of PPPs.

These studies, taken together, suggest a change in the wage-effort bargain to the disadvantage of workers transferring from the public sector to the private sector provider of services. Moreover, there is fragmentation among workers in many cases due to the accumulation of complex mixes of differ-

**Table 11.1   Disorder and fragmentation in working conditions in PPPs**

| Employment condition: | Impact of public private partnership | Study |
| --- | --- | --- |
| Pay | Deterioration in manual workers' pay following transfer to private firm | Ascher (1987); Bach (1989); Colling (1993); Escott and Whitfield (1995); Unison (2000) Walsh and O'Flynn (2000) |
| | Teams of workers in private firm experience a range of different rates of pay and payment systems including protected pay (where TUPE applies) and new firm rates | Rubery and Earnshaw (2005) |
| | Improvements in pay among transferred white-collar workers | Kessler *et al.* (1999) |
| Work effort | Work intensification following transfer to private sector firm | Kessler *et al.* (1999); Cooke *et al.* (2004) |
| Job ladders | Transferred low wage workers face weakened bridges to more extended internal labour market in public sector organisation | Grimshaw and Carroll (2006) |
| | Improvement in perceived career prospects | Kessler *et al.* (1999) |
| Skill development | Specialist private sector firms narrow range of skills required in jobs and strengthen monitoring of work effort | Grugulis *et al.* (2003) |
| Empowerment | Multiple layers of control and authority, caused by involvement of multiple contracting partners, reduce potential for worker empowerment | Rubery and Earnshaw (2005) |
| Worker commitment | Emphasis on private sector profit-related values conflicts with traditional public sector ethos for some workers | Hebson *et al.* (2003) |
| Job security | Direct negative impact caused by redundancies associated with outsourcing | Escott and Whitfield (1995); Walsh and Davis (1993) |
| | Negative qualitative impact on perceived job security caused by change in employer and recurrent contracting | Morgan *et al.* (2000), Rubery and Earnshaw (2005) |

ent rates of pay, reflecting protected terms and conditions from various ex-employers, as well as individually negotiated conditions with the new private employer (Rubery and Earnshaw, 2005). Such disordering can clearly undermine the potential for intra- and inter-organisational collaboration.

Studies also identify potential problems in the area of skill development and career progress. A study comparing conditions of NHS employed domestic assistants with domestics outsourced to private cleaning firms found considerable frustration with disrupted job ladders among the latter workforce group (Grimshaw and Carroll, 2006). A common career route within the NHS is from domestic assistant to healthcare assistant. However, in NHS trusts with outsourced services, Human Resource (HR) managers were reluctant to poach domestics from the private sector firm for posts as healthcare assistants due to a fear of losing goodwill trust (*op. cit.*). In this case, collaborative working between managerial partners was prioritised over maximising career progress for outsourced low wage workers due to the difficulties of reconciling partner goals.

Other employment conditions that might underpin effective collaborative working in a partnership model include the degree of empowerment, commitment and job security experienced by the worker. While PPPs do not have a universal impact on these conditions, studies suggest a whittling away of customary practices associated with public sector employment. Transferred workers may be subject to new regulatory controls on their performance by the public sector client organisation (their ex-employer), reducing their scope to exercise discretion (Hebson *et al.*, 2003; Rubery and Earnshaw, 2005). Confusions in lines of control and authority between private sector provider and public sector client can lead to serious disciplinary problems – for example, in the case of supply teachers who do not meet the performance standards of a client school (Grimshaw *et al.*, 2003). And, finally, collaborative working would appear to be seriously compromised by replacing the open-ended employment contract with recurrent rounds of contracting and staff transfer, which effectively places staff on fixed-term contracts.

## Conclusion

This chapter has examined the developing evidence on the issue of how far public private partnerships are transforming the employment relationships of the people that deliver public services in the way intended. The general claim made is that the 'traditional' assumption built into the employment relationship was that the public service worker was altruistically motivated and adhered to a public service ethos; and that this assumption was false as public service workers were as likely to be selfishly motivated and needed incentive structures built into the employment relationship to realise optimum outcomes. However, creation of a contract culture in the 1980s was found to create a cost-only mentality that discouraged collaborative working. Therefore the creation of PPPs was seen as being capable of optimising the principal-agent outcomes whilst encouraging collaboration. However, despite the explicit desire of PPP to curtail the assumed 'knavish' behaviour of the public service worker, it is strangely claimed not to result in negative outcomes for the said workers.

From an employment perspective, evidence presented in this chapter indicates that the supposed benefits of PPP have not been realised. First, the notion that the traditional open-ended employment contract granted too much bargaining power to public sector workers during the 1980s and 1990s seems to have been greatly exaggerated. Not only were public sector workers unable to extract a wage premium for high unionisation and scarce skills, but also the proposed PPP solution would be likely to polarise wage differentials among the low and high skilled. Secondly, it is not clear that replacing the open-ended employment contract with a contract for services provision delivers the anticipated benefits. The uncertainties of repeat contracting, coupled with the conflicting goals of partner organisations, may generate disincentives to training provision and obstruct inter-organisational career paths – especially problematic in the UK where the institutional foundations for vocational training are known to be weak. Thirdly, while more research is needed, PPPs do not appear to have generated substantive innovation in employment relations. The use of market rates in setting pay led to the widely derided problem of a two-tier workforce and new government policies (for example, the Two-Tier Code) signal the rejection of such private sector practices. Finally, research on the implications for employment relations demonstrates that the goal of fostering partnership relations between employing organisations must also integrate the need for partnership with the different workforce groups. While PPPs may be more likely to encourage collaborative working than short-term tendering processes such as those utilised under CCT, it is nonetheless overly optimistic to expect working relationships of this type to become widespread given the erosion of trust created by the kinds of employment 'innovations' described above.

Overall, given the multifaceted vision of 'partnership' – one where the workforce are considered as 'partners', as is the governments stated wish – then traditional direct employment on an open-ended contract would seem preferable to the low-trust basis of partnership contracts, certainly from the point of view of the public service worker, but also quite probably in terms of the public service itself.

## Notes

1. Elected representatives being from either the local council, the local health authority or members of parliament.
2. Both papers report evidence from the same case-study since they derive from the same research project, funded as part of the (ESRC) 'Future of Work' programme (see Marchington *et al.*, 2005).

# 12
# Conclusion: The Logic of Work and Employment Reforms in the Public Services – A Comparative Reflection

*Geoffrey Wood and Ian Roper*

This book centres on the changing nature of work and employment in British public services. Following the global recession of the 1980s, governments worldwide have experimented with wide ranging neoliberal reforms, in the hope of unleashing a new period of growth. For the most part, this has been unsuccessful – neoliberalism is less a coherent growth regime, than a series of experiments that have at certain times and places proved highly functional for specific segments of capital, and indeed provided periodic upsurges of growth. At the same time, the neoliberal age has been characterised by great volatility, and an inability to provide enduring prosperity or even geographically dispersed growth. Central to neoliberal reforms has been a redefinition of the role of the public sector. This has combined a simple reduction in the range of services and benefits offered by the state, with the greater provision of services by private operators. Crucially, it has meant a redefinition of the roles and relationships involved for the people involved in providing those services. Nowhere has this been more evident than in Britain and this has been the focus of this book. This chapter reflects on the contributions made in this book and uses this to examine the underlying logic of neoliberal reforms.

## The logic of neoliberal reforms

Contemporary *regulationist* thinking points to the importance of institutions and embedded practices in providing the basis for stable, yet always temporally and spatially confined, accumulation. The ending of the long post-war period of growth in the 1970s led to intense policy contestations, arguably a process most pronounced in traditional liberal market economies such as the United Kingdom. In most cases, neoliberal reforms represented less of a coherent policy agenda and more of a series of experiments. Whilst generally-speaking, the track record of such reforms has been at best mixed, this process remains an ongoing one, as Geoffrey Wood points out in Chapter 3. This would reflect the ideological hegemony of neoliberalism, and the fact that whilst the neoliberal age cannot in any sense be seen as a coherent growth regime at all (Wolfson, 2003), such reforms have proven highly beneficial to sections of the elite. Again, whilst neoliberal reforms are clearly not *supermodular* (that is demonstrably better than any alternative), clusters of reforms may unleash a certain *complementarity* (in other words, reforms working together better than on their own) (c.f. Boyer, 2006). For example, the package of legal reforms that made for the liberalisation of financial markets, allowed for a wave of finance capital-driven accumulation, centring on redefinition of financial services, and the reprioritisation of the generation of shareholder value reflected by consecutive waves of corporate downsizing and redistribution (Grahl and Teague, 2000). Alternatively we can also see the complementarity of imposing compulsory outsourcing on public service providers in conjunction with applying restrictive measures upon organised labour in the 1980s through to the mid-1990s.

Packages of reforms within the public sector have proved highly beneficial to elite interests for four distinct reasons. Firstly, public sector reforms have opened up whole new areas of activity to commercialisation. Private firms have been able to market a vast range of new products through preferential access to users of public services, thus being able to offer a range of other public services outright. To give only one example, private sector media providers have been able to benefit from the provision of pay-per-view entertainment to hospital patients, whilst the private healthcare sector has gained lucrative contracts to help redress National Health Service (NHS) backlists.

Secondly, public sector reforms have fulfilled an ideological role; by moving public sector employment practices more closely into line with those in the private – whether through internal measures to enhance managerial control or outright outsourcing – the state can help legitimate the dominant private sector managerial paradigms of the day. As Kelly (1998) notes, adverse economic turnarounds are associated with labour repression, as employers seek to claw back the gains secured by employees during better times. Public sector employees are more sheltered from the vicissitudes of markets. Within national employment systems, similar 'ways of doing things' tend to diffuse across economies, owing to the accumulation of expectations, and lower transaction costs, including in the operationalisation of the employment contract. Private sector employers are freer to innovate in the direction of cost cutting labour repressions – most states face a range of political pressures to be seen to be promoting 'good practice' in employment relations. However, whilst innovations that prove their utility may disseminate rapidly, the persistence of an alternative more 'worker friendly' employment relations paradigm in the public sector may help shore up employee interests more generally. Individual employees retain the option of seeking public sector work, whilst private sector workers can point to the persistence of better conditions elsewhere when bargaining with their employer. Hence, in promoting the coalescence of a neoliberal cluster of institutions and practices, elites will favour the promotion of less worker-friendly private sector employment practices in the public sector, in order to make such practices more justifiable and sustainable in the private. More broadly speaking, if governments are committed to neoliberalism, it makes logical sense for them to promote such reforms within their own immediate domain.

A third reason for neoliberal public sector reforms centres on the logic of financialisation. Privatisation places public assets in the hands of the private sector, often on highly beneficial terms. Private firms are then in a position to downsize and distribute assets that may have been accumulated over centuries: 'selling the family silver' as a former Conservative prime minister famously put it in the 1980s. Recent examples of the latter include the sale of former rail and canalside properties, reservoirs and school playing fields. This category also includes the policy of the Private Finance Initiative (PFI) which is currently the dominant means of investment for public transport, for schools and for the NHS. Alternatively, public services may be pared back to what is 'strictly necessary', the latter being defined either on cost grounds, or when public resistance remains weak.

A fourth reason is suggested by John K. Galbraith's concept of 'bezzling', corruption and quasi-corruption (Blackburn, 2006: 54). All systems incorporate a degree of bezzling that may, in fact, ameliorate the unresponsiveness of formal institutions to day-to-day needs. However, bezzling may reach such a scale as to prove totally dysfunctional (*ibid.*). A significant number of beneficiaries of public sector outsourcing or sub-contracting are firms that have gained their contracts not because they are demonstrably the best potential provider on the grounds of costs, proven efficiency or objectively measurable expertise, but simply because of political influence. Perhaps some of the most notorious examples can be found in the selection of certain private sector firms through 'no bids contracts' by the US armed forces, although many equally dubious examples can be found in the United Kingdom. Such firms have been able to use their political influence simply to help themselves to public sector resources. Indeed, as Colin Crouch (2004a) notes, a key trend has been the rise of organisations that are neither strictly state nor market. On the one hand, they are formally independent of government, seek to make profits and seek to evade public scrutiny and accountability. On the other hand, they are incapable of competing on a commercial playing field, and seek state protection and/or persistently solicit government handouts in order to return profits to shareholders. The increasingly self referential political class becomes more concerned about building links with wealthy private interests than in formulating political programmes that genuinely meet the needs of the masses (Crouch, 2004b). For example, the British government has already committed £42 billion to PFIs, many of which have been characterised by chronic cost overruns and other problems. The public is inevitably presented with a stark choice of a PFI or no expenditure in the area at all. Firstly, the nature of specific PFIs are tailored to meet the needs of private contractors (Monbiot, 2006). Secondly, civil servants are under great pressure to generate a:

> ... 'public sector comparator' figure to show that PFI delivers best value for money...As Jeremy Colman, at the time the UK's assistant auditor-general, said, 'If the answer comes out wrong you don't get your project. So the answer doesn't come out wrong very often' (Monbiot, 2006).

Thirdly, whilst 'risk transfer figures' are often used to justify claims that PFIs are cheaper than the state doing it on its own, the costing often appears to overstate the real risks to contractors (Monbiot, 2006).

Similarly controversial are Public-Private Partnerships (PPPs) for the delivery of basic public services. The scale and debilitating nature of dubious costing, let alone corruption and quasi-corruption and its essentially cannibalistic nature – expropriating and liquidating existing assets, rather than generating new value, may help explain why neoliberalism has failed to become a coherent growth regime at all (c.f. Wolfson, 2003).

## The politics of public service reform in Britain

The specifically British context of reform is important. For Gamble (2003) the reform of public services in Britain has been part of a wider restructuring of the British state; firstly, in the 1980s, as a cathartic conclusion to the narrative of British imperial decline; then, from 1997, as part of an, as yet unclear, post-decline agenda that is now devoid of the previously dominant alternative narratives of 'empire' and 'socialism'. The ideological logic of the Thatcher reform agenda was concerned with halting decline by attacking the mutually supportive structures of the welfare state and trade unionism. It was, of course, additionally inspired by partisan reasons and aimed specifically at the institutions that bound the Labour Party together. While general success was achieved in privatising and deregulating the 'commanding heights' of industry and of undermining the power of trade unionism, success on welfare reform was hampered by the persistent public legitimacy of institutions such as the NHS, not to mention its immense scale. The paradox of Thatcherism was that in attacking Britain's 'socialist' institutions, the logic of this process went on to undermine the institutions that held together those institutions close to the Conservative Party – those linked with 'Empire' and 'the British Union'. Indeed the logic came to undermine the legitimacy of the Conservative Party itself as a binding British institution, and it eventually fell from grace in 1997. The lasting legacy of this period was the transformation of the Labour Party and in Chapter 1, Noel Thompson explores some of the ideological continuities of New Labour with its Conservative predecessors.

The reform agenda being pursued by the Blair Governments since 1997 is further seen by Gamble as being the response of 'constitutional modernisers' to broader state restructuring: where the 'big issues' concern balancing 'the four circles' of Europe, Anglo-America, (post) Empire and the British Union, the constitutional modernisers see those issues as being resolved on pragmatic, rather than principled, grounds: be the issue devolution, the unelected second chamber, the Euro or the Atlantic (military) Alliance. The focus of attention for the constitutional modernisers therefore switches from the big issues, to the issues of legitimacy of what the state does domestically and this means reforming and modernising public services. In Chapter 5, Catherine Needham reappraises the changing nature of the public sector ethos in the context of such reforms.

## Alternative HR paradigms and neoliberal reforms

The existing literature has highlighted five dominant alternative paradigms defining employment and work relations (see Whitley, 1999; Guest, 2000; Brewster *et al.*, 2006) – each of these may serve as a basis for viable commercial activity. These are sophisticated 'hard Human Resource Management (HRM)', 'soft' more pluralist HRM, traditional pluralism, traditional patriarchal approaches, and hardline or 'bleak house' approaches (Guest, 2000: 96). The defining features of each are summarised in Table 12.1 on page 000.

Hard HRM represents a paradigm that came into particular prominence in the United States in the 1980s. This paradigm centres on a vision of employees as simply another resource to be used of and disposed of as necessary. At the same time, as with any other resources, people need to be husbanded, and utilised in the best manner possible. This may entail both investing in skills that cannot be obtained externally, and focusing on individually orientated and direct involvement and participation, aimed at harnessing their knowledge and skills in pursuit of overall organisational objectives. Such approaches are typically encountered in areas of 'high tech' industry involving relatively large numbers of highly skilled workers. Aspects of this model have been infused into areas of outsourced public functions involving relatively highly skilled workers – most notably in terms of greatly reduced security of tenure, focused involvement, and individual performance-based pay systems. In practice however, evidence is far from conclusive as to how much these strategic objectives are actually met. For example, the effect on job security not only significantly degrades the

**Table 12.1  Alternative paradigms for work and employment relations**

| Relationships | Hard HRM | Soft HRM | Traditional pluralism | Traditional patriarchal | Bleak house |
| --- | --- | --- | --- | --- | --- |
| **Interdependence** | | | | | |
| Security of tenure | Low | High | High | Informal centring on notions of mutual obligations | Low |
| Investment in training and development | Development a imed at plugging gaps in external labour market. Primary focus in induction | Systematic, aimed at enhancing human capital | Job specific skills | Informal | Low, basic induction training only |
| **Delegation** | | | | | |
| Involvement | High | High | Limited | General staff meetings, etc. | Low |
| Participation | Direct and individually orientated | Partnership with employee collectives | High, centring on collective bargaining | Low | Low |
| **Reward** | Individual performance-based pay | Collective and individual performance-based pay systems | Pay setting *via* collective contracts | In line with long-term practice, relatively low pay ameliorated by informal benefits | Individual output based or minimum legal wage |

*Source*: Adapted from Whitley, 1999; Guest, 2000; Brookes *et al.*, 2005; Brewster *et al.*, 2006.

experience of work in these areas – as explained by Pauline Dibben in Chapter 8 – but it is having tangibly negative effects on recruitment and retention of staff in some crucial areas of public service delivery, as Philip Beaumont, Judy Pate and Moira Fischbacher point out in Chapter 4; to take another example, while the principle of performance related pay remains politically popular, David Marsden points out in Chapter 7 that without employee participation in such schemes, both legitimacy for such schemes and any potential benefits are likely to continue to be unproven.

Softer HRM combines aspects of the hard HRM model with a recognition of the importance of employee collectives – however, the latter should be firmly subordinated to overall organisational interests. Moreover, established collective bargaining will be supplemented by a range of other mechanisms for promoting employee involvement, which may or may not involve the union. Whilst this paradigm may represent a relatively benign alternative to hard HRM, in reality, as suggested by Miguel Martínez Lucio and Mark Stuart in Chapter 9, there are serious problems in making 'partnership models' work in the public sector.

The patriarchal model is most commonly encountered among long established small scale private sector operatives, and has little relevance to work and employment in the public domain. Again, private firms seeking to perform functions previously carried out by the public sector are unlikely to experiment with a model that imposes some obligations on the employer in terms of commitment to long serving staff, yet that lacks modern devices for people management.

Increasingly common in outsourced public sector functions is the bleak house paradigm. This model is particularly likely to be encountered in basic frontline service occupations with limited skills prerequisites, such as catering and call centres. Firms may be encouraged to make use of this model given that outsourcing will inevitably weaken established collective bargaining practices, even if the outsourced jobs are carried out by former public sector staff that retain their union membership. The bleak house model centres on paring back labour costs to the bare minimum, again particularly attractive in those instances where state contracts are relatively short term, necessitating an immediate emphasis on the bottom line. Moreover, the ideological commitments of successive governments to outsourcing will mean that, even if the quality of the outsourced service greatly deteriorates as a result of low employee morale, firms will be unlikely to be fully held to account, other than in the case of extreme incompetence, a good example of the latter being Railtrack. Again, only limited efforts seem to have been made to innovate in these areas – many private contractors have focused on labour repression as the basis of profitability, rather than innovative forms of work organisation (Toynbee, 2003), an issue further examined by Damian Grimshaw and Ian Roper in Chapter 11.

The established pluralist model has traditionally underpinned work and employment in the public sector. However, this model has come under attack on a range of fronts. Successive governments – even Labour under Blair – have publicly criticised public sector unions as protectors of privilege rather than guarantors of service. Private sector contractors have tended to favour more unitarist employment relations paradigms, on account of the greater numerical flexibility it accords them. In Chapter 10, Ian Cunningham and Phil James explore the challenges that unions face in attempting to regulate the employment relationship in the public sector. Moreover, even in remaining areas of the public sector, this model has been eroded both through greatly reduced security of tenure, and the adoption of new non-union-based mechanisms for employee involvement, and the gradual dissemination of aspects of performance-based pay. In Chapter 6, Susan Corby, explores barriers – in terms of cost considerations and organisational restructuring – to the state promoting greater equality in the public sector.

The above alternative models simply represent archetypes. In most areas of the public – and private – sectors, organisations adopt policy mixes, albeit that these mixes are invariably more orientated towards one or other of these archetypes. It might seem that, given a strong legacy of pluralism, there would be a natural move towards more advanced forms of collective participation. Such advanced pluralism has underpinned incremental innovation in high value-added manufacturing industry in coordinated market economies. Incremental improvement might seem particularly welcome in the public services, given the proud tradition of the Welfare State, and overwhelming public sentiment in favour of gradual improvements rather than wholesale dismantling.

However, it remains extremely difficult to promote such models in liberal market economies such as the United Kingdom. Firstly, employers are invariably hostile to far-reaching social compromises unless all other viable alternatives have been exhausted (Wood and Harcourt, 2001) – most will naturally opt for more immediate returns and fewer restraints on managerial power (c.f. Iles, 2000). Secondly, the kind of private firms seeking public sector contracts or concessions are likely to be under intense pressures to maximise shareholder value (Lazonick and O'Sullivan, 2000). This is likely to impel them towards greater short-termism, which again would require ever fewer restraints on managerial power, and a reluctance to invest in the long term, both in terms of employees and physical infrastructure. Thirdly, and ironically, given the British Right's hostility to all things European, whilst some EU policy directives have promoted social democratic practices, others have the potential to force greater liberalisation, a topic discussed by John Grahl in Chapter 2. Figure 12.1 summarises trends in the drift towards the erosion of the traditional pluralist paradigm in the public sector.

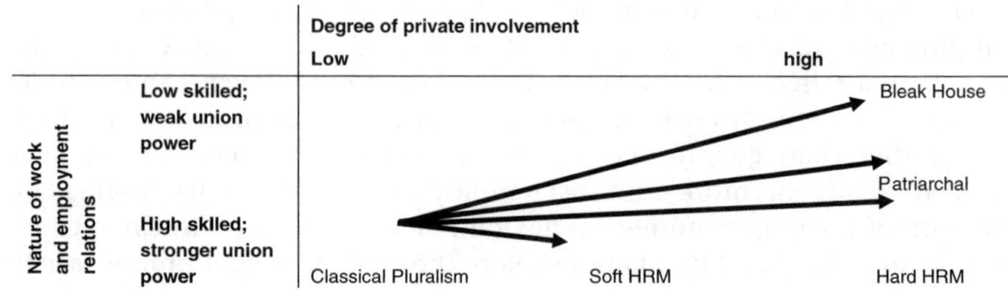



*Figure 12.1*   The fracturing of traditional public sector pluralism

## Resisting public sector reforms? – manifestations and possibilities

Union resistance to public sector reforms in work and employment have been most effective in core frontline services offered by professions that have traditionally had a high regard in the public esteem. Examples of this would be teachers, police, nurses, and firefighters. Yet, even here, the results of collective action are uneven. Whilst the British Medical Association seems capable of extracting premium wages for its members, the firefighters strike of 2002–3 yielded very mixed results. Again, union resistance to PFIs and privatisation seems to have been generally uneven and unsuccessful. Perhaps the area where the unions have been most successful has been in raising public awareness to the fragility of public services: so much so that it has allowed the Conservatives to attempt a somewhat implausible defence of public service values – as Catherine Needham points out in Chapter 5.

## Conclusion

Central to public sector reforms has been increased labour repression. There have been few examples where private sector *concessionaires* have brought much to the public sector either in terms of innovative high quality service delivery or long-term investment, other than when relatively high rates of return on investment have been guaranteed. Rather, such firms have sought to maximise their return through cost cutting, including in the scale and conditions of employment, and by reforming work relations. Nor have such innovations been focused on promoting incremental innovation through deepening mutual commitment and the promotion of organisation specific human capital. Such forms of innovation would be particularly welcome in the public sector, owing to continued overwhelming public support for high quality service provision. Whilst alternative involvement-based models may, in some instances, be conducive to blue skies innovation (Anderson, 2004), there is little evidence of the latter in areas of outsourced public functions other than in the areas of cost cutting and short-term profit maximisation. Rather, the remaking of work and employment has been towards the 'bleak house' model in those instances where employees are in a particularly weak position – though with some qualification. While New Labour's reform project has been based on a continuation of an institutionalised mistrust of professional and union interests in public services, it has not been total. The government has sought to dispel the worst fears of 'bleak house' outcomes from outsourcing through introducing a series of baseline protections to benefit transferred workers – the national minimum wage, enhanced individual employment rights for part-time and temporary workers, and national agreements with unions on curbing some of the excesses of 'two-tier workforce' iniquities – making the New Labour approach somewhat of a hybridised version of the 'market state' vision of Thatcherist Conservatives (Roper *et al.*, 2007).

Nevertheless, given that in the United Kingdom, all three main political parties remain unashamedly neoliberal in their approach to public service reform, it is evident that resisting the hollowing out of the state – in many cases, little more than 'bezzling' – will have to come from the unions and civil society. Whilst specific union campaigns have had very mixed results, opinion polls would indicate a growing public unease as to the dilution of public services (ICM, 2005). Yet still political parties continue to renew commitments to 'radical reforms' that simply entail more marketisation whilst issuing vapid platitudes as to the value of public services. The change in the public mood since the 1980s is of considerable significance, and could provide the foundations for new challenges to an increasingly unworkable *status quo* from both within and without the mainstream political discourse.

# Bibliography


ACAS (1990) *Appraisal Related Pay*. ACAS Advisory Booklet No. 14, London: HMSO.

Ackers, P. (2002) 'Reframing Employment Relations: the Case for Neo-Pluralism', *Industrial Relations Journal*, 33(1): 2–19.

Ackers, P. and Payne, J. (1998) 'British Trade Unions and Social Partnership: Rhetoric, Reality And Strategy', *International Journal of Human Resource Management*, 9(3): 529–49.

Ackers, P., Marchington, M., Wilkinson, A. and Dundon, T. (2005) 'Partnership and Voice, With or Without Trade Unions: Changing UK Management Approaches to Organisational Participation', in M. Stuart and M. Martínez Lucio (eds), *Partnership and Modernisation in Employment Relations*, London: Routledge.

Adler, P. (2001) 'Market, Hierarchy and Trust: the Knowledge Economy and the Future of Capitalism', *Organization Science*, 12(2): 214–34.

AIM (Association Internationale de la Mutualité) (2004) *The Proposal for a Directive on Services in the Internal Market: Position Paper*, www.aim-mutual.org

Alatrista, J. and Arrowsmith, J. (2004) 'Managing Employee Commitment in the Not-for-Profit Sector', *Personnel Review*, 33(5): 536–48.

Aldridge, R. and Stoker, G. (2002) *Advancing a New Public Service Ethos*, London: New Local Government Network.

Almond, S. and Kendall, J. (2000) 'Taking the Employees' Perspective Seriously: An Initial United Kingdom Cross-Sectoral Comparison', *Nonprofit and Voluntary Sector Quarterly*, 29(2): 205–31.

Amable, B. (2003) *The Diversity of Modern Capitalism*, Oxford: Oxford University Press.

Amicus (2005) *Short Term Funding, Short Term Thinking*, London: Amicus.

Amicus (2006a) www.amicustheunion.org, accessed 19.5.06.

Andersen, T.J. (2004) 'Integrating the Strategy Formation Process: an International Perspective', *European Management Journal*, 22(3): 263–72.

Andrews, G. (2004) *Endgames and New Times: The Final Years of British Communism 1964–1991*, London: Lawrence and Wishart.

Annual Staff of Scottish Local Authority Social Work Service Census, 2005. Scottish Executive, 2005. Staff of Scottish Local Authority Social Work Services, 2004. 23 June 2005. A Scottish Executive National Statistics Publication ISSN 1479–7569 (online).

Armstrong, M. and Murlis, H. (1994) *Reward Management: A Handbook of Remuneration Strategy and Practice*, 3rd edn, London: Kogan Page.

Armstrong-Stassen, M. (1994) 'Coping with Transition: A Study of Lay-off Survivors', *Journal of Organisational Behaviour*, 15: 597–621.

Ashford, S., Lee, C. and Bobko, P. (1989) 'Content, Causes and Consequences of Job Insecurity: A Theory-based Measure and Substantive Test', *Academy of Management Journal*, 32(4): 803–29.

Atkinson, J. (1984) 'Manpower strategies for flexible organizations', *Personnel Management*, August 28–31.

Auer, P. and Cazes, S. (2000) 'The Resilience of the Long-Term Employment Relationship: Evidence from Industrialised Countries', *International Labour Review*, 139: 379–408.

Bach, S. (1989) *Too High a Price to Pay? A Study of Competitive Tendering in the NHS*, Warwick Papers in Industrial Relations No. 25, Industrial Relations Research Unit.

Bach, S. (2002) 'Annual Review Article 2001: Public Sector Employment Relations Reform under Labour: Muddling through on Modernisation?', *British Journal of Industrial Relations*, 40(2): 319–39.

Bach, S. and Winchester, D. (2003) 'Industrial Relations in the Public Sector', in P. Edwards (ed.), *Industrial Relations: Theory and Practice* (2nd edition), Oxford: Blackwell.

Bach, S., Bordogna, L., Della-Rocca, G. and Winchester, D. (1999) *Public Service Employment Relations in Europe: Transformation, Modernization or Inertia?*, London: Routledge.

Bach, S., Kessler, I. and Heron, P. (2006) 'Changing Job Boundaries and Workforce Reform: The Case of Teaching Assistants', *Industrial Relations Journal*, 37(1): 2–21.

Bacon, N. and Blyton, P. (2004) 'Trade Union Responses to Workplace Restructuring: Exploring Union Orientations and Actions', *Work, Employment and Society*, 18(4): 749–73.

Bacon, N. and Blyton, P. (2006) 'Union Co-operation in a Context of Job Insecurity: Negotiated Outcomes from Teamworking', *British Journal of Industrial Relations*, 44(2): 215–37.

Bacon, N. and Storey, J. (2000) 'New Employee Relations Strategies in Britain: Towards Individualism or Partnership?', *British Journal of Industrial Relations*, 38(3): 407–27.

Bacon, R. and Eltis, W. (1976) *Britain's Economic problems, Too Few Producers*, London: Macmillan.

Ball, C. (1992) 'Remuneration Policies and Employment Practices: Some Dilemmas in the Voluntary Sector', in J. Batsleer, C. Cornforth and R. Paton, R. (eds), *Issues in Voluntary and Non-profit Management*, Wokingham: Addison-Wesley.

Barber, B. (2003) 'Successful change must build on the public service ethos', *The Guardian*, 1 October.

Barnard, C. and Hepple, B. (2000) 'Substantive Equality', *Cambridge Law Journal*, 59(3): 562–85.

Barnard, J., Broach, S. and Wakefield, V. (2004) *Social Care: The Growing Crisis*, Report on Recruitment and Retention Issues in the Voluntary Sector by the Social Care Employers Consortium, London.

Barry, N. (1984) 'Ideas versus Interests: The Classical Liberal Dilemma', in N. Barry *et al.*, *Hayek's 'Serfdom' Revisited: Essays by Economists, Philosophers and Political Scientists on 'The road to Serfdom' after 40 Years*, London: Institute for Economic Affairs.

Beale, D. (2005) 'The Promotion and Prospects of Partnership at Inland Revenue: Employer and Union Hand in Hand?', in M. Stuart and M. Martínez Lucio (eds), *Partnership and Modernisation in Employment Relations*, London: Routledge.

Beaumont, P. (1992) *Public Sector Industrial Relations*, London: Routledge.

Beer, M., Spectator, B., Lawrence, P.R., Quinn Mills, D. and Walton, R.E. (1984) *Managing Human Assets*, New York: Free Press.

Bevir, M. and Rhodes, R. (2003) 'Searching for civil society: changing patterns of governance in Britain', *Public Administration*, 81: 41–62.

Bewley, H. (2006) 'Raising the Standard? The Regulation of Employment and Public Sector Employment Policy', *British Journal of Industrial Relations*, 44(2): 351–72.

Bichard, M. (2006) 'There's only one team to play for', *Society Guardian*, 21 June, http://society.guardian.co.uk/societyguardian/story/0,,1801816,00.html

Bird, D. and Corcoran, L. (1994) 'Trade Union Membership and Density 1992–93', *Employment Gazette*, June, 189–97.

Biggs, D., Burchell, B. and Millmore, M. (2006) 'The Changing World of the Temporary Worker: The Potential HR Impact of Legislation', *Personnel Review*, 35(2): 191–206.

Blackburn, R. (2006) 'Finance and the Fourth Dimension', *New Left Review*, 39: 39–70.

Blair, T. (1998) *The Third Way*, London: Fabian Society.

Blair, T. (2001) 'Speech on Public Service Reform', 16 October, http://www.number10.gov.uk/output/Page1632.asp

Blair, T. (2002) 'Interview on the Today Programme', 3 October, http://news.bbc.co.uk/1/hi/business/2291361.stm

Blair, T. (2003) 'Speech to the Fabian Society', 17 June, http:// politics.guardian.co.uk/speeches/story/0,,979507,00.html

Blair, T. (2006) '21st Century Public Services', Speech, 6 June, http://www.number-10.gov.uk/output/Page9564.asp

Bolkestein, F. (2002) 'Europe, America and the Middle East', speech in Amsterdam, 12th December, http://www.fritsbolkestein.com

Bolkestein, F. (2003) 'EU Competitiveness: actions speak louder than words', speech to VNO-NCW symposium, Aalsmeer, 3rd November, http://www.fritsbolkestein.com

Bolkestein, F. (2005) 'The Services Directive', http://www.fritsbolkestein.com

Bosch, G. (2004) 'Towards a New Standard Employment Relationship in Western Europe', *British Journal of Industrial Relations*, 42(4): 617–36.

Boyne, G., Jenkins, G. and Poole, M. (1999) 'Human Resource Management in the Public and Private Sectors: An Empirical Comparison', *Public Administration*, 77(2): 407–20.

Boyne, G., Kirkpatrick, I. and Kitchener, M. (2001) 'Introduction to the Symposium on New Labour and the Modernisation of Public Management', *Public Administration*, 79(1): 1–4.

Boyer, R. (2006) 'How do Institutions Cohere and Change?', in P. James and G. Wood (eds), *Institutions, Production and Working Life*, Oxford: Oxford University Press.

Boyne, G., Martin, S. and Walker, R. (2004) 'Explicit Reforms, Implicit Theories and Public Service Improvement', *Public Management Review*, 6(2): 189–210.

Brereton, M. and Temple, M. (1999) 'The New Public *Service* Ethos: An Ethical Environment for Governance', *Public Administration*, 77(3): 455–74.

Brett, S. and Milsom, S. (2004) *Monitoring Progress on Equal Pay Reviews*, Manchester: Equal Opportunities Commission.

Brewer, G.A., Selden, S.C. and Facer, R.L. (2000) 'Individual Conceptions of Public Service Motivation', *Public Administration Review*, 60(3): 254–64.

Brewster, C., Wood, G. and Brookes, M. (2006) 'Varieties of Capitalism and Varieties of Firm', in G. Wood and P. James (eds), *Institutions, Production and Working Life*, Oxford: Oxford University Press.

British Household Panel Survey (BHPS) http://www.iser.essex.ac.uk/bhps

Brittain, S. (1973) *Capitalism and the Permissive Society*, London: Macmillan.

Brockner, J., Grover, S., Reed, T.F. and DeWitt, R.L. (1992) 'Layoffs, Job Insecurity and Survivors' Work Effort: Evidence on an Inverted-U Relationship', *Academy of Management Journal*, 32(2): 413–25.

Brodie, M. (2006) 'Equal Pay Crisis in Local Government', *Diversity at Work*, 22, April, 23–4.

Brookes, M., Brewster, C. and Wood, G. (2005) 'Social Relations, Firms and Societies: A Study in Institutional Embeddedness', *International Sociology*, 20(4): 403–26.

Brown, G. (2003) 'State and Market: Towards a Public Interest Test', *Political Quarterly*, 74: 266–84.

Brown, G. (2004) 'Prosperity and Justice for All', Speech to the Labour Party Conference, Brighton, 27 September, http://www.labour.org.uk/ac2004news?ux_news_id=ac04gb

Bruun, N. (2004) 'Memorandum on Employment Issues', contributed to a Public Hearing on the Proposal for a Directive on Services in the Internal Market, European Parliament, Brussels, 11th November.

Bryson, A. and Gomez, R. (2005) 'Why Have Workers Stopped Joining Unions? The Rise in Never-Membership in Britain', *British Journal of Industrial Relations*, 43(1): 67–92.

Buchanan, J. and Wagner, R. (1977) *Democracy in Deficit*, London: Academic Press.

Buchanan, J. (1972) 'Towards Analysis of Closed Behavioural systems', in J. Buchanan and R. Tollinson (eds), *The Theory of Public Choice, Political Applications of Economics*, Michigan: University of Michigan Press.

Bunting, M. (2005) *Willing Slaves*, London: Harper Perrenial.

Burchell, F. (2002) 'The Prevalence and Redistribution of Job Insecurity and Work Intensification', in F. Burchell, D. Ladipo and F. Wilkinson, *Job Insecurity and Work Intensification*, London: Routledge, pp. 61–76.

Burchell, F., Lapido, D. and Wilkinson, F. (2002) *Job Insecurity and Work Intensification*, London: Routledge.

Burgess, S. and Rees, H. (1998) 'A Disaggregate Analysis of the Evolution of Job Tenure in Britain, 1975–1993', *British Journal of Industrial Relations*, 36(4): 629–55.

Burton, J. (1984) 'The Instability of the "Middle Way"', in N. Barry *et al.*, *Hayek's 'Serfdom' Revisited: Essays by Economists, Philosophers and Political Scientists on 'The road to Serfdom' after 40 Years*, London: Institute for Economic Affairs.

Cabinet Office (1994) *The Civil Service: Continuity and Change*, Cmnd. 2627, London: HMSO.

Cabinet Office (1998) *Equal Opportunities in the Civil Service 1995–9*, London: Stationery Office.

Cabinet Office (1999) *Modernising Government*, Cm 4310, London: Stationery Office.

Cabinet Office (2004) *News Release*, CAB 051/04, 21 October.

Cabinet Office (2005a) *Delivering a Diverse Civil Service: a 10-point plan*, London: Cabinet Office.

Cabinet Office (2005b) *Transformational Government*, Cm 6683, London: Cabinet Office.

Cabinet Office (2006a) *The UK Government's Approach to Public Service Reform*.

Cabinet Office (2006b) http://archive.cabinetoffice.gov.uk, accessed June 2006.

Cabinet Office/TUC (2006) 'Drive for Change', http://www.driveforchange.org.uk/

Callaghan, H. and Höpner, M. (2005) 'European Integration and the Clash of Capitalisms: Political Cleavages Over Takeover Liberalisation', *West European Politics*, 26(4): 179–98.

Cameron, D. (2006) 'Public Service Ethos – Learning from the Frontline', 6 June, http://www.conservatives.com/tile.do?def=news.story.page&obj_id=130222

Campbell, I. (2005) 'Trade Unions and Temporary Employment: New Initiatives in Regulation and Representation', Centre for Applied Social Research Working Papers No. 2005-3, July 2005.

Capelli, P. (1999) *The New Deal at Work: Managing the Market-driven Workforce*, Boston: Harvard Business School Press.

Chapman, R. (1993) 'Ethics in Public Service', in R. Chapman (ed.), *Ethics in Public Service*, Edinburgh: Edinburgh University Press, pp. 155–72.

Charles, N. and James, E. (2003) 'The Gender Dimensions of Job Security in a Local Labour Market', *Work, Employment and Society*, 17(3): 531–52.

Child, J. and McGrath, G. (2001) 'Organizational Form in an Information-Intensive Economy', *Academy of Management Journal*, 44(6): 1135–48.

CIPD (2005a) *Absence Management: Annual Survey Report*, London: CIPD.

CIPD (2005b) *Recruitment, Retention and Turnover: Annual Survey Report*, London: CIPD.

Civil Service Department (1971) *The Employment of Women in the Civil Service*, London: HMSO.

Clark, A. (2005) 'Your Money or Your Life: Changing Job Quality in OECD Countries', *British Journal of Industrial Relations*, 43(3): 377–400.

Claydon, T. (1998) 'Problematising Partnership: The Prospects for a Co-Operative Bargaining Agenda', in P. Sparrow and M. Marchington (eds), *Human Resource Management: The New Agenda*, London: Financial Times Pitman Publishing.

Cockett, R. (1995) *Thinking the Unthinkable: Think-Tanks and the Economic Counter-Revolution*, London: HarperCollins.

Cohen, S. (2001) 'A Strategic Framework for Devolving Responsibility and Functions from Government to the Private Sector', *Public Administration Review*, 61(4): 432–40.

Cole, A. (2006) 'More Money, More Problems?', *Guardian*, Society Guardian, April, 12.

Colling, T. (1993) 'Contracting Public Services: the Management of Compulsory Competitive Tendering in Two County Councils', *Human Resource Management Journal*, 3(4): 1–15.

Colling, T. (1997) 'Managing Human Resources in the Public Sector', in I. Beardwell and L. Holden (eds), *Human Resource Management: A Contemporary Perspective*, 2nd edition, London: Pitman.

Commission for Racial Equality (2002) *Code of Practice on the Duty to Promote Race Equality*, London: Commission for Racial Equality.

Commission for Racial Equality (2003a) *Race Equality and Public Procurement*, London: Commission for Racial Equality.

Commission for Racial Equality (2003b) *Race Equality in Prisons: A Formal Investigation into HM Prison Service of England and Wales, Part 2*, London: Commission for Racial Equality.

Commission for Racial Equality (2005a) *The Police Service in England and Wales: Final Report of a Formal Investigation by the Commission for Racial Equality*, London: Commission for Racial Equality.

Commission for Racial Equality (2005b) *Procurement and the Duty*, www.cre.gov.uk/duty/procurement.html.pr [accessed 23 April 2006].

Commons, J.R. (1924) *Legal Foundations of Capitalism*, New York: Macmillan.

Conley, H. (2002) 'A State of Insecurity: Temporary Work in the Public Services', *Work Employment and Society*, 16(4): 725–37.

Conley, H. (2006) 'Modernisation or Casualisation? Numerical Flexibility in Public Services', *Capital & Class*, 31–57.

Conservative Party (1976) *The Right Approach, a Statement of Conservative Aims*, London.

Conservative Party (1979) *The Conservative Manifesto*, London.

Cooke, F., Earnshaw, J., Marchington, M. and Rubery, J. (2004) 'For Better and For Worse: Transfer of Undertakings and the Reshaping of Employment Relations', *International Journal of Human Resource Management*, 15(2): 276–94.

Cooke, W.N. (1990) *Labor-Management Cooperation: New Partnerships or Going in Circles?*, Kalamazoo, MI: W.E. Upjohn Institute.

Corby, S. and White, G. (1999) *Employee Relations in the Public Services: Themes and Issues*, London: Routledge.

Corby, S. (1994) 'The Rise and Fall of Equal Opportunities', *Personnel Management*, December, 34–6.

Corby, S. (1995) 'Opportunity 2000 in the NHS: A Missed Opportunity for Women', *Employee Relations*, 17(2): 23–37.

Corby, S. (1998) 'Industrial Relations in the Civil Service Agencies: Transition or Transformation?', *Industrial Relations Journal*, 29(3): 194–206.

Corby, S. (2000) 'Employee Relations in the Public Services: A Paradigm Shift?', *Public Policy and Administration*, 15(3): 60–74.

Corby, S., Stanworth, C. and Green, B. (2005) *Gender and the Labour Market in South East England, Volume 2: Employers' Policies and Practices*, London: University of Greenwich.

Coyle, A. (1989) 'The Limits of Change: Local Government and Equal Opportunities for Women', *Public Administration*, 67: 39–50.

Coyle-Shapiro, J. and Kessler, I. (2002) 'Contingent and Non-contingent Working in Local Government: Contrasting Psychological Contracts', *Public Administration*, 80(1): 77–101.

Cremers, J. and Donders, P. (eds) (2004) *The Free Movement of Workers in the European Union*, CLR/Reed Business Information, Brussels.

Cropanzano, R. and Greenberg, J. (1997) 'Progress in Organizational Justice', in C. Cooper and I. Robertson (eds), *International Review of Industrial and Organizational Psychology*, New York: John Wiley, pp. 317–72.

Crouch, C. (2003) *Commercialisation or Citizenship? Education Policy and the Future of Public Services*, Fabian Ideas, London: Fabian Society.

Crouch, C. (2004a) 'Presidential Address', Society for the Advancement of Socio-Economic Annual Conference, George Washington University, Washington D.C.

Crouch, C. (2004b) *Post Democracy*, Cambridge: Polity.

Cully, M. and Woodland, S. (1996) 'Trade Union Membership and Recognition: An Analysis of Data from the 1995 Labour Force Survey', *Labour Market Trends*, June, 231–9.

Cully, M., Woodland, S., O'Reilly, A. and Dix, G. (1999) Britain at Work: As Depicted by the 1998 Workplace Employee Relations Survey, London: Routledge.

Cunningham, I. (2000) 'Prospects for Union Growth in the UK Voluntary Sector: The Impact of the Employment Relations Act, 1999', *Industrial Relations Journal*, 31(3): 192–206.

Cunningham, I. (2001) 'Sweet Charity! Managing Employee Commitment in the UK Voluntary Sector', *Employee Relations Journal*, 23(3): 226–40.

Cunningham, I. (2006) *Struggling to Care: Voluntary Sector Work Organization and Employee Commitment in the Era of the Quasi-Market*, unpublished Phd Thesis, University of Strathclyde.

Cunningham, I., James, P. and Dibben, P. (2004) 'Bridging the Gap between Rhetoric and Reality: Line Managers and the Protection of Job Security for Ill Workers in the Modern Workplace', *British Journal of Management*, 15: 273–90.

Cutler, T. and Waine, B. (1994) *Managing the Welfare State*, Berg: Oxford.

Danford, A., Richardson, M. and Upchurch, M. (2002) '"New Unionism", Organising and Partnership: A Comparative Analysis Of Union Renewal Strategies in the Public Sector', *Capital and Class*, 76: 1–27.

Davies, R. (2004) 'Contracting Out and the Retention of Employment Model in the National Health Service', *Industrial Law Journal*, 33(2): 95–120.

Davies, S. (2006) *Third Sector Provision of Employment-Related Services*, London: PCS.

Deakin, N. and Walsh, K. (1996) 'The Enabling State: The Role of Markets and Contracts', *Public Administration*, 74: 33–47.

Deakin, S. and Morris, G. (2005) *Labour Law*, 4th edition, Oxford: Hart.

Deakin, S., Hobbs, R., Konzelmann, S. and Wilkinson, F. (2005) 'Working Corporations: Corporate Governance and Innovation in Labour Management Partnerships in Britain', in M. Stuart and M. Martínez Lucio (eds), *Partnership and Modernisation in Employment Relations*, London: Routledge.

Dean, C. (2001) 'Hire Staff and Win a Toaster', *The Times Educational Supplement*, 8 June.

Dean, H. (1998) 'Undermining Social Citizenship', paper presented at the ISSA Second International Conference on Social Citizenship, Jerusalem.

Department of Health (1999) *Agenda for Change: Modernising the NHS Pay System*, London: Department of Health.

Department of Health (2000a) *The NHS Plan*, London: Department of Health.

Department of Health (2000b) *Improving Working Lives Standard*, London: Department of Health.

Department of Health (2003) *Equalities and Diversity Strategy & Delivery Plan to Support the NHS*, London: Department of Health.

Dibben, P. (2006) 'The "Socially Excluded" and Local Transport Decision-making: Voice and Responsiveness in a Marketised Environment', *Public Administration*, 84(3): 655–72.

Dibben, P., James, P. and Cunningham, I. (2001) 'Absence Management in the Public Sector: An Integrative Model?', *Public Money and Management*, 21(4): 55–60.

Dibben, P., Wood, G. and Roper, I. (2004) *Contesting Public Sector Reforms: Critical Perspectives: International Debates*, London: Palgrave.

Dickens, L. (1994) 'The Business Case for Equality: Is the Carrot Better than the Stick?', *Employee Relations*, 16(8): 5–18.

Dickens, L. (2006) 'Re-regulation for Gender Equality: From "Either/or" to "Both"', *Industrial Relations Journal*, 37(4): 299–309.

*Diversity at Work* (2004) 'Councils Move to Fund Equal Pay', *Diversity at Work*, 2, August, 3.

*Diversity at Work* (2006a) 'Prison Service Settles Equal Pay Claims for £50m', *Diversity at Work*, 21, March, 2.

*Diversity at Work* (2006b) 'Equal Pay Claims to Cost £560m, Says Scottish LAs', *Diversity at Work*, 22, April, 3–5.

*Diversity at Work* (2006c) '£30m for NHS Equal Pay', *Diversity at Work*, 23, May, 2.

Doig, A. and Wilson, J. (1998) 'What Price New Public Management', *Political Quarterly*, 69(3): 267–80.

Doig, A. (1995) 'Mixed signals? Public Sector Change and the Proper Conduct of Government Business', *Public Administration*, 73: 191–212.

Doig, A. and Wilson, J. (1998) 'What Price New Public Management', *Political Quarterly*, 69(3): 267–80.

Dolton, P. and McIntosh, S. (2003) 'Public and Private Sector Labour Markets', in R. Dickens, P. Gregg and J. Wadsworth (eds), *The Labour Market under New Labour: the State of Working Britain*, London: Palgrave.

Domberger, S. (1998) *The Contracting Organisation: a Strategic Guide to Outsourcing*, Oxford: OUP.

Domberger, S. and Jensen, P.H. (1997) 'Contracting out by the Public Sector: Theory, Evidence, Prospects', *Oxford Review of Economic Policy*, 13(4): 67–78.

Doogan, K. (2001) 'Insecurity and Long-term Employment', *Work, Employment and Society*, 15(3): 419–41.

Downs, A. (1956) *An Economic Theory of Democracy*, New York: Harper and Row.

Dräger, K. (2006) 'Sozial oder marktradikal? Die Zukunft der Dienstleistungen in der europäischen Binnenmarkt', in Bsirke *et al. Die EU-Dienstleistungsrichtlinie: ein Ansclag auf das europäische Sozialmodell*, Hamburg: VSA Verlag.

Dräger, K. (2006a) 'Wut auf die Idee von gestern? Die EU-Dienstleistungsrichtlinie geht in die zweite Runde'.

Dräger, K. and Wagenknecht, S. (2005) *Der Bolkesteinhammer muss weg! Europa braucht zukunftsfähige Dienstleistungen*, GUE/NGL and PDS, www.pds-europa.de

Druker, J. and Stanworth, C. (2004) 'Mutual Expectations: A Study of the Three-way Relationship between Employment Agencies, Their Client Organisations and White-collar "Temps"', *Industrial Relations Journal*, 35(1): 58–75.

Duncan, C. (2001) 'The Impact of Two Decades of Reform of British Public Sector Industrial Relations', *Public Money & Management*, Jan–March 2001: 27–34.

Dunleavy, P. (1991) *Democracy, Bureaucracy and Public Choice: Economic Explanations in Political Science*, London: Harvester Wheatsheaf.

Dyer, J.H. and Singh, H. (1998) 'The Relational View: Cooperative Strategy and Sources of Interorganizational Competitive Advantage', *Academy of Management Review*, 23(4): 660–79.

*Economic Trends*, Nos 626, January 2006–04–28.

*Economist* (2006) Labour and the Health Service: Trimming the Fat, 29 April: 32.

Edwards, P. (2001) 'The Puzzle of Work: Autonomy and Commitment plus Discipline and Insecurity', *Skope Research Paper No. 16*. Summer 2001. ISSN 1466–1535.

Egan, J. (2003) 'Aspiring to Equal Pay in Higher Education', *Equal Opportunities Review*, 115, March, 10–15.

Equal Opportunities Review (2004a) 'Civil Service acts on Equal Pay', *Equal Opportunities Review*, 125, January, 3.

Equal Opportunities Review (2004b) 'Mixed Progress on Diversity in Civil Service', *Equal Opportunities Review*, 130, June, 3.

Erridge, A. and Greene, J. (2002) 'Partnerships and Public Procurement: Building Social Capital through Supply Relationships', *Public Administration*, 80(3): 503–22.

Escott, K. and Whitfield, D. (1995) *The Gender Impact of CCT in Local Government*, Manchester: Equal Opportunities Commission.

European Commission (2002) 'The State of the Internal Market for Services', COM (2002) 441 final, Brussels, 30th July.

European Commission (2004) 'Proposal for a Directive of the European Parliament and of the Council on Services in the Internal Market', COM (2004) 2 final/3 Brussels, 5th March.

European Commission (2004a) *White Paper on Services of General Interest*, COM (2004) 374, Brussels.

European Parliament (2006)*Texts Adopted at the Sitting of Thursday 16 February 2006:* Part 1, European Parliament legislative resolution on the proposal for a directive of the European Parliament and of the Council on services in the internal market, PE 369.553\I.

Ewing, K. (2006) *Global Rights in Global Companies: going for Gold at the UK Olympics*, London: Institute of Employment Rights.

Fairbrother, P. (2000) *Trade Unions at the Crossroads*, London: Mansell.

Farnham, D. and Horton, S. (1996) 'Continuity and Change in the Public Services', in D. Farnham and S. Horton (eds), *Managing People in the Public Services*, London: Macmillan Business Press, pp. 3–42.

Ferner, A. (2002) 'The State as Employer', Kelly, J. (ed.), *Industrial Relations: Critical Perspectives on Business and Management – Volume III*, London: Routledge.

Fielding, S. (2003) *The Labour Party, Continuity and Change in the Making of New Labour*, London: Palgrave.

Fischbacher, M. and Beaumont, P. (2003) 'PFI, Public-Private Partnership and the Neglected Importance of Process: Stakeholders and the Employment Dimension', *Public Money and Management*, 23(3): 171–6.

Flynn, N. (2002) 'Explaining the New Public Management: The Importance of Context', in K. McLaughlin, S. Osborne and E. Ferlie, *New Public Management: Current Trends and Future Prospects*, London: Routledge, pp. 57–76.

Flynn, N. (2002) *Public Sector Management* (4th edition), Harlow: Pearson.

Flynn, R., Williams, G. and Pickard, S. (1996) *Markets and Networks: Contracting in Community Services*, Buckingham: Open University Press.

Folger, R. and Cropanzano, R. (1998) *Organizational Justice and Human Resource Management*, Thousand Oaks, CA: Sage.

Ford, J., Quiglars, D. and Rugg, J. (1998) *Creating Jobs: The Employment Potential of Domiciliary Care*, Joseph Rowntree Foundation, Community Care into Practice Series, Bristol: Policy Press.

Foster, J., Newburn, T. and Souhami, A. (2005) *Assessing the Impact of the Stephen Lawrence Inquiry*, Home Office Research Study 294, London: Home Office.

Fulton, Lord (1968) *The Civil Service: Report of the Committee, 1966–68*, Cmnd. 3638, London: HMSO.

Fung, A. and Wright, E.O. (2003) 'Thinking About Empowered Participatory Governance', in A. Fung and E.O. Wright (eds), *Deepening Democracy – The Real Utopias Project IV*, London: Verso.

Galbraith, J.K. (2004) *The Economics of Innocent Fraud: Truth for our Time*, Boston: Houghton Mifflin.

Gall, G. (2005) 'Breaking with, and breaking, "Partnership": The Case of the Postal Workers and Royal Mail in Britain', in M. Stuart and M. Martínez Lucio (eds), *Partnership and Modernisation in Employment Relations*, London: Routledge.

Gallie, D., White, M. and Cheng, Y. and Tomlinson, M. (1998) *Restructuring the employment relationship*, Oxford: OUP.

Gamble, A. (1994) The *Free Economy and the Strong State: The Politics of Thatcherism* (2nd Edition), Basingstoke: Macmillan.

Gamble, A. (2003) *Between Europe and America*, Palgrave Macmillan: London.

Garstka, T., Hummert, M. and Branscombe, N. (2005) 'Perceiving Age Discrimination in Response to Intergenerational Inequity', *Journal of Social Issues*, 61(2): 321–42.

Geddes, M. (2001) 'What about the Workers? Best Value, Employment and Work in Local Public Services', *Policy and Politics*, 29(4): 497–508.

Gershon, P. (2004) *Releasing Resources to the Front Line: Independent Review of Public Sector Efficiency*, London: HMSO.

Giddens, A. (1998) *The Third Way. The Renewal of Social Democracy*, Cambridge: Polity.

Giddens, A. (2000) *The Third Way and its Critics*, Cambridge: Polity.

Gill, D. (2000) 'New Zealand Experience with Public Sector Reform', *International Public Management Journal*, 3(1).

Glennerster, H. (2002) 'United Kingdom Education 1997–2001', *Oxford Review of Economic Policy*, 18(2): 120–36.

Godwin, K. (2004) 'Contracting for Equality', *Equal Opportunities Review*, 130, June, 8–14.

Gold, J. (2003) 'Human Resource Planning', in J. Bratton and J. Gold (eds), *Human Resource Management: Theory and Practice*, London: Palgrave.

Gordon, R. (2005) 'Europe-Etats-Unis: un siècle de crossance économique comparée', *Problèmes Économiques*: Dossier Productivité et Temps du Travail, no. 2870, March 2nd.

Gould-Williams, J. (2004) 'The Effects of "High Commitment" HRM Practices on Employee Attitude: The Views of Public Sector Workers', *Public Administration*, 82(1): 63–81.

Grahl, J. and Teague, P. (2000) 'The Regulation School, the Employment Relation and Financialization', *Economy and Society*, 29(1): 160–78.

Grahl, J. (2006) 'Labour Market Policies in the European Union' forthcoming in P. Arestis and M. Sawyer (eds), *Alternative Perspectives on Economic Policies in the European Union*.

Grainger, H. (2006) *Trade Union Membership 2005 – Employment Market Analysis and Research*, London: DTI.

Gray, J. (1984) 'The Road to serfdom forty years on', in N. Barry *et al.*, *Hayek's Serfdom Revisited: Essays by Economists, Philosophers and Political Scientists on 'The road to Serfdom' after 40 Years*, London: Institute for Economic Affairs.

Greater London Authority (n.d.) *Core GLA Procurement Strategy*, London: Greater London Authority.

Green, F., Felstead, A. and Burchell, B. (2000) 'Job Insecurity and the Difficulty of Regaining Employment: An Empirical Study of Unemployment Expectations', *Oxford Bulletin of Economics and Statistics*, 62, Special issue 0305–9049.

Greenaway, J. (1995) 'Having the Bun and the Half-Penny: Can Old Public Service Ethics Survive in the New Whitehall?', *Public Administration*, 73(3): 357–74.

Gregg, P., Knight, G. and Wadsworth, J. (2000) 'Heaven Knows I'm Miserable Now: Job Insecurity in the British Labour Market', in E. Heery and J. Salmon (eds), *The Insecure Workforce*, London: Routledge, pp. 39–56.

Grimshaw, D. and Carroll, M. (2006) *Low Wage Work in the UK Public Hospital Sector*, Report for the Russell Sage Foundation Programme on 'Low Wage Work in Europe' (July).

Grimshaw, D. and Hebson, G. (2005) 'Public Private Contracting: Performance, Power and Change at Work', in M. Marchington, D. Grimshaw, J. Rubery and H. Willmott (eds), *Fragmenting Work: Blurring Organizational Boundaries and Disordering Hierarchies*, Oxford: Oxford University Press.

Grimshaw, D. and Miozzo, M. (2005) 'Trading IT workers: New Employment Principles in a Fast-Growing Business Services Sector', Paper presented at the *International Working Party on Labour Market Segmentation*, Berlin (September).

Grimshaw, D., Earnshaw, J. and Hebson, G. (2003) 'Private Sector Provision of Supply Teachers: a Case of Legal Swings and Professional Roundabouts', *Journal of Education Policy*, 18(3): 267–88.

Grimshaw, D., Marchington, M. and Rubery, J. (2006) 'The Blurring of Organisational Boundaries and the Fragmentation of Work', in G. Wood and P. James (eds), *Institutions, Production and Working Life*, Oxford: Oxford University Press.

Grimshaw, D., Vincent, S. and Willmott, H. (2002) 'Going Privately: Partnership and Outsourcing of Public Sector Services', *Public Administration*, 80(3): 475–502.

Grout, P. and Stevens, M. (2003) 'The Assessment: Financing and Managing Public Services', *Oxford Review of Economic Policy*, 19(2): 215–34.

Grugulis, I., Vincent, S. and Hebson, G. (2003) 'The Rise of the "Network" Organization and the Decline of Discretion', *Human Resource Management Journal*, 13(2): 45–59.

Grunberg, I. (1999) *Jobs for All: What Have We Learnt Since the Social Summit?*, UNESCO, Oxford: Blackwell, pp. 483–91.

Guest, D. (1997) 'Towards Jobs and Justice in Europe: A Research Agenda', *Industrial Relations Journal*, 28(4): 344–52.

Guest, D. (2000) 'Industrial Relations and Human Resource Management', in J. Storey (ed.), *Human Resource Management: A Critical Text*, London: Thomson Learning.

Guest, D. (2000) 'Management and the Insecure Workforce', in E. Heery and J. Salmon (eds), *The Insecure Workforce*, London: Routledge, pp. 140–54.

Guest, D. and Peccei, R. (1998) *The Partnership Company: Benchmarks for the Future*, London: Involvement and Participation Association.

Guest, D. and Peccei, R. (2001) 'Partnership at Work: Mutuality and the Balance of Advantage', *British Journal of Industrial Relations*, 39(2): 207–36.

Gumplowicz, L. (1889) *Outlines of Sociology*, Philadelphia.

Gunderson, M. (2003) 'Age Discrimination in Employment in Canada', *Contemporary Economic Policy*, 21(3): 318–28.

Hacker, J. (2004) 'Dismantling the Health Care State?', *British Journal of Political Science*, 34: 693–724.

Hall, P. and Soskice, D. (eds) (2001) *Varieties of Capitalism: the Institutional Foundations of Comparative Advantage*, Oxford: Oxford University Press.

Hall, S. (2003) 'Sticky Times for NHS Glue', *The Guardian*, 1 October.

Hallier, J. (2000) 'Security Abeyance: Coping with the Erosion of Job Conditions and Treatment', *British Journal of Management*, 11: 79–89.

Haque, M.S. (2001) 'The Diminishing Publicness of Public Service under the Current Mode of Governance', *Public Administration Review*, 61(1): 65–82.

Haque, M.S. (1996) 'Public Service Challenge in the Age of Privatisation', *Governance*, 9(2): 186–216.

Harris, L., Doughty, D. and Kirk, S. (2002) 'The Devolution of HR Responsibilities – Perspectives from the UK's Public Sector', *Journal of European Industrial Training*, 26(5): 218–29.

Harris, R. (1980) *The End of Government?*, London: Institute of Economic Affairs.

Harvey, D. (2003) *The New Imperialism*, Oxford: Oxford University Press.

Hayek, F. (1979) *Law, Legislation and Liberty*, Vol. 3, *The Political Order of a Free People*, Chicago: University of Chicago Press.

Hayek, F. (1960) *The Constitution of Liberty*, London: Routledge and Kegan Paul.

Hayek, F. (1986) [1944] *The Road to serfdom*, London: Ark.

Haynes, P. and Allen, M. (2001) 'Partnership as Union Strategy: A Preliminary Evaluation', *Employee Relations*, 23(2): 164–87.

Heap, D. (2005) 'Characteristics of People Employed in the Public Sector', *Labour Market Trends*, 113(12), December, 489–500.

Hebson, G. and Grugulis, I. (2005) 'Gender and New Organizational Forms', in M. Marchington, D. Grimshaw, J. Rubery and H. Willmott (eds), *Fragmenting Work: Blurring Organizational Boundaries and Disordering Hierarchies*, Oxford: Oxford University Press.

Hebson, G., Grimshaw, D. and Marchington, D. (2003) 'PPPs and the Changing Public Sector Ethos: Case Study Evidence from the Health and Local Authority Sectors', *Work Employment and Society*, 17(3): 481–501.

Heery, E. (1998) 'A Return to Contract? Performance Related Pay in a Public Service', *Work, Employment & Society*, 12(1): 73–95.

Heery, E. and Abbot, B. (2000) 'Trade Unions and the Insecure Workforce', in E. Heery and J. Salmon (eds), *The Insecure Workforce*, London: Routledge, pp. 155–80.

Heery, E. and Salmon, J. (2000) 'The Insecurity Thesis', in E. Heery and J. Salmon (eds), *The Insecure Workforce*, London: Routledge, pp. 1–24.

Heery, E., Simms, M., Conley, H., Delbridge, R. and Stewart, P. (2002) *Trade Unions and the Flexible Workforce: A Survey Analysis of Union Policy and Practice.* Working Paper no. 22, ESRC Future of Work Programme, June 2002.

Herzog, H.W. (1997) 'Ethnicity and Job Tenure in a Segmented Labour Market: The Case for New Zealand', *The Australian Economic Review*, 30(2): 167–84.

Hicks, S. and Lindsay, C. (2005) 'Public Sector Employment', *Labour Market Trends*, 13(4): 139–47.

Higgins, P., James, P. and Roper, I. (2004) Best Value: Is It Delivering? *Public Money and Management*, 24(4): 243–258.

Hindmoor, A. (2005) 'Public Policy: Targets and Choice', *Parliamentary Affairs*, 58(2): 272–86.

Hirst, P. and Zeitlin, J. (2001) 'Flexible Specialization versus Post-Fordism', Jessop, B. (ed.), *Regulationist Perspectives on Fordism and Postfordism – Regulation Theory and the Crisis of Capitalism Volume 3*, London: Edward Elgar.

Hood, C. (1991) 'A Public Management for All Seasons', *Public Administration*, 69(1): 3–19.

Hood, C. (1991) 'Beyond the Public Bureaucracy State? Public Administration in the 1990s', Inaugural Lecture, London: LSE.

Howe, G. (1982) *Conservatism into the Eighties*, London: Conservative Political Centre, http://www.hm-treasury.gov.uk/media/B2C/11/efficiency_review120704.pdf

http://www.lse.ac.uk/collections/LSEPublicLecturesAndEvents/events/2006/2005120 6t1246z001.htm#generated-subheading1

Hughes, M. (2005) *Evaluation of the Procurement Agenda – Baseline Survey Report*, London: Office of the Deputy Prime Minister.

Hutchings, M. (2000) 'The role of agencies in teacher supply in London', Institute for Policy Studies in Education.

Hutton, J. (2005) 'Public Service Reform: the Key to Social Justice', Speech to the Social Market Foundation, 24 August, http://www.cabinetoffice.gov.uk/chartermark/downloads/doc/jh_smf_speech_24aug 05.doc

Hyman, R. (1997) 'The Future of Employee Representation', *British Journal of Industrial Relations*, 35(3): 309–31.

ICM (2005) Guardian Poll http://www.icmresearch.co.uk/reviews/2005/Guardian %20Poll%20-%20September/Guardian%20Poll%20-%20September.asp

IDS Pay Report 935, August 2005.

Iles, P. (2000) 'Employee Resourcing', in J. Storey (ed.), *Human Resource Management: A Critical Text*, London: Thomson Learning.

Incomes Data Services (IDS) (2005) 'Pay and Conditions in Social Care', *IDS Pay Report 926*, April, 15–18.

Incomes Data Services (2005a) 'Will Public Authorities Rise to the Challenge of Real Equality?', *IDS Brief 774*, February.

Incomes Data Services (2005b) 'Local Government Equality Indicators', *Diversity at Work*, 14, August, 22–4.

Income Data Services (2006) 'Pay in housing and social care', IDS Pay Report, March, Incomes Data Services, London.

Independent Review (2002) *The Future of the Fire Service: Reducing Risk, Saving Lives*, London: Independent Review of the Fire Service.

Institute of Personnel Management (1987) *Contract Compliance: The UK Experience*, London: Institute of Personnel Management.

Involvement and Participation Association (IPA) (2001) 'Definitions of Partnership', http://www.Partnership-at-work.com/pardefs.html accessed on 17/10/2001.

ISD Scotland Workforce Figures, www.isdscotland.org

Jenkins, P. (1989) *Mrs. Thatcher's Revolution: The Ending of the Socialist Era*, London: Pan.

Jenkins, S., Noon, M. and Martínez Lucio, M. (1995) 'Negotiating Quality: The case of TQM in Royal Mail', *Employee Relations*, 17(3): 87–98.

Jennex, M.E., Olfman, L. and Addo, T.B.A. (2003) 'The Need for an Organisational Knowledge Management Strategy', *Proceedings of the 36th Hawaii International Conference on Systems Sciences*, Hawaii.

Jessop, B. (2001) 'Series Preface', in Jessop, B. (ed.), Regulation Theory and the Crisis of Capitalism Volume 5 – Developments and Extensions, London: Edward Elgar.

Johnston, P. (2006) 'Reid blasts management failures at Home Office', *The Telegraph*, 24 May.

Joseph, K. (1975) *Monetarism is Not Enough*, London: Centre for Policy Studies.

Joseph, K. (1976) *Stranded on the Middle Ground? Reflections on Circumstances and Policies*, London: Conservative Political Centre.

Katz, H., Kochan, T.A. and Gobeille, K.R. (1983) 'Industrial Relations Performance, Economic Performance and QWL Programs: An Interplant Analysis', *Industrial and Labour Relations Review*, 37(1): 3–17.

Kelliher, C. (1996) 'Competitive Tendering in NHS Catering: A Suitable Policy?', *Employee Relations*, 18(3): 62–76.

Kelly, J. (1998) *Rethinking Industrial Relations*, London: Routledge.

Kelly, J. (2004) 'Social Partnership Agreements in Britain', in M. Stuart and M. Martínez Lucio (eds), *Partnership and Modernisation in Employment Relations*, London: Routledge.

Kendall, J. and Knapp, M. (1996) *The Voluntary Sector in the UK*, John Hopkins Nonprofit Sector Series, Manchester: Manchester University Press.

Kersely, B., Alpin, C., Forth, J., Bryson, A., Bewley, H., Dix, G. and Oxenbridge, S. (2004) *Inside the Workplace: First Findings from the 2004 Workplace Employment Relations Survey*, London: Department of Trade and Industry.

Kersely, B., Alpin, C., Forth, J., Bryson, A., Bewley, H., Dix, G. and Oxenbridge, S. (2006) *Inside the Workplace*, London: Routledge.

Kessler, I., Koyle-Shapiro, J. and Purcell, J. (1999) 'Outsourcing and the Employee Perspective', *Human Resource Management Journal*, 9(2): 5–19.

King, A. (1975) 'Overload: Problems of Governing in the 1980s', *Political Studies*, 23: 284–96.

Kirkpatrick, I. and Hoque, K. (2005) 'The Decentralisation of Employment Relations in the British Public Sector', *Industrial Relations Journal*, 36(2): 100–20.

Kirkpatrick, I. (2006) 'Post Fordism and Organisational Change within the State Administration', in L.E. Alonso and M. Martínez Lucio (eds), *Employment Relations in a Changing Society*, London: Palgrave Macmillan.

Kirkpatrick, I., Ackroyd, S. and Walker, R. (2005) *The New Managerialism and Public Service Professions*, London: Palgrave.

Knapp, H., Hardy, B. and Forder, J. (2001) 'Commissioning for quality: ten years of social care markets in England', *Journal of Social Policy*, 30(2): 283–306.

Kochan, T., Locke, R., Osterman, P. And Piore, M. (2004) 'Extended Networks: A Vision for the Next Generation Unions', in A. Verma and T. Kochan, *Unions in the 21st Century: An International Perspective*, London: Palgrave, pp. 30–43.

Kochan, T.A. and Osterman, P. (1994) *The Mutual Gains Enterprise: Forging a Winning Partnership Among Labour, Management and Government*, Boston: Harvard University Press.

Koike, K. (1997) *Human Resource Development*. Japanese Economy & Labor Series, Formatted: Font: Italic no. 2, Japan Institute of Labour, Tokyo.

Kok, W. (2004) *Report from the High Level Group: Facing the Challenge – the Lisbon Strategy for Growth and Employment*, European Communities, Brussels.

Kreiner, G.E. and Ashforth, B.E. (2004) 'Evidence Toward an Expanded Model of Organizational Identification', *Journal of Organizational Behaviour*, 25: 1–27.

Krugman, P. (2004) *The Great Unraveling: Losing Our Way in the New Century*, New York: W.W. Norton.

Labour Market Trends, April 2005.

Labour Market Trends, February 2006.

Labour Market Trends, July 2004.

Ladipo, D. and Wilkinson, F. (2002) 'More Pressure, Less Protection', in F. Burchell, D. Ladipo and F. Wilkinson, *Job Insecurity and Work Intensification*, London: Routledge, pp. 8–38.

Lafferty, G. and Rou, A. (1999) Public Sector Outsourcing: Implications for Training and Skills, *Employee Relations*, 22(1): 76–83.

Laidler, D. (1976) 'United Kingdom Inflation and its Background: a Monetarist Perspective', in M. Parkin and M. Sumner (eds), *Inflation in the United Kingdom*, Manchester: Manchester University Press.

Lazonick, W. and O'Sullivan, M. (2000) 'Maximizing Shareholder Value: A New Ideology for Corporate Governance', *Economy and Society*, 29(1): 13–35.

Le Grand, J. (1999) 'Competition, Co-operation or Control? Tales from the British National Health Service', *Health Affairs*, 18: 27–39.

Le Grand, J. (2003) *Motivation, Agency and Public Policy*, Oxford: Oxford University Press.

Le Grand, J. (2006) 'The Blair Legacy? Choice and Competition in Public Services', Public Lecture, London School of Economics, 21 February.

Leach, B. (1989) 'Disabled People and the Implementation of Local Authorities' Equal Opportunities Policies', *Public Administration*, 67: 65–77.

Leat, D. and Ungerson, C. (1994) 'Payments for Care: The Case of Britain', in A. Evers, M. Pijl and C. Ungerson (eds), *Payments for Care: A Comparative Overview*, Aldershot: Avebury.

Le Grand, J. and Bartlett, W. (eds) (1993) *Quasi-markets and Social Policy*, London: Macmillan.

Leys, C. (2001) *Market-Driven Politics: Neoliberal Democracy and the Public Interest*, London: Verso.

Local Government Commission on Pay (2003) *Report*, London: Local Government Commission on Pay.

Lyons, B. and Mehta, J. (1997) 'Private Sector Business Contracts: the Text Between the Lines', in S. Deakin and J. Michie (eds) *Contacts, Co-operation and Competition*, Oxford: Oxford University Press.

Macais, E. (2003) 'Job Instability and Political Attitudes towards Work: Some Lessons from the Spanish Case', *European Journal of Industrial Relations*, 9(2): 205–22.

Makinson, J. (Chair) (2000) *Incentives for Change: Rewarding Performance in National Government Networks*, Public Services Productivity Panel, HM Treasury, London.

Maley, J. (2006) 'Sexual Harassment Rife in Armed Forces', *Guardian*, 26 May, 5.

Mann, M. (2003) *Incoherent Empire*, London: Verso.

March, J.G. and Olsen, J.P. (1989) *Rediscovering Institutions: the Organisational Basis of Politics*, New York: Free Press.

Marchington, M., Grimshaw, D., Rubery, J. and Willmott, H. (eds) (2005) *Fragmenting Work: Blurring Organizational Boundaries and Disordering Hierarchies*, Oxford: Oxford University Press.

Marsden, D. and French, S. (1998) *What a Performance: Performance Related Pay in the Public Services*. Centre for Economic Performance Special Report, London School of Economics, London, available online from www.cep.lse.ac.uk

Marsden, D. (1999) *A Theory of Employment Systems: Micro-Foundations of Societal Diversity*, Oxford: Oxford University Press.

Marsden, D. (2004) 'The Role of Performance Related Pay in Renegotiating the "Effort Bargain": The Case of the British Public Service', *Industrial and Labor Relations Review*, 57(3): 350–70.

Marsden, D. and Belfield, R. (2007) 'Pay for Performance where Output is Hard to Measure: The Case of Performance Pay for School Teachers', *Advances in Industrial and Labor Relations*, 15: 1–37.

Marsden, D. and Richardson, R. (1994) 'Performing for Pay? The Effects of "Merit Pay" on Motivation in a Public Service', *British Journal of Industrial Relations*, 32(2): 243–62.

Martínez Lucio, M. and Stuart, M. (2002) 'Assessing the Principles of Partnership: Workplace Trade Union Representatives' Attitudes And Experiences', *Employee Relations*, 24(3): 305–20.

Martínez Lucio, M. and Stuart, M. (2004) 'Swimming against the Tide: Social Partnership, Mutual Gains and the Revival of "Tired" HRM', *International Journal of Human Resource Management*, 15(2): 404–18.

Martínez Lucio, M. and Stuart, M. (2005) 'Partnership and New Industrial Relations in a Risk Society: An Age of Shotgun Weddings and Marriages of Convenience?', *Work, Employment and Society*, 19: 797–817.

Massey, A. and Pyper, R. (2005) *Public Management and Modernisation in Britain*, London: Palgrave Macmillan.

Mather, G. (2003) 'Beyond Targets, Towards Choice', *Political Quarterly*, 74(4).

Maurin, E. and Postel-Vinay, F. (2004) 'The European Job Security Gap', *Work and Occupations*, 32(2): 229–52.

Mayhew, C. and Quinlan, M. (2006) 'Economic Pressure, Multi-tiered Subcontracting and Occupational Health and Safety in Australian Long-haul Trucking', *Employee Relations*, 28(3): 212–29.

Mayo (ed.) (2006) 'More than Words', *Society Guardian*, 12 April. http://society.guardian.co.uk/secondopinion/story/0,,1751573,00.html

McBride, J. and Stirling, J. (2002) 'Partnership and Process in the Maritime Construction Industry', *Employee Relations*, 24(3): 290–304.

McDougall, M. (1998) 'Devolving Gender Management in the Public Sector: Opportunity or Opt-out?', *International Journal of Public Sector Management*, 11(1): 71–80.

Milgrom, P. and Roberts, J. (1992) *Economics, Organization and Management*, Englewood Cliffs, NJ: Prentice Hall.

Miliband, D. (2006) Speech to the National Council of Voluntary Organisations annual conference, 21 February http://www.communities.gov.uk/index.asp?id=1163772

Millward, N., Bryson, A. and Forth, J. (2000) *All Change at Work? British Employment Relations 1990–1998, as Portrayed by the Workplace Industrial Relations Survey Series*, London: Routledge.

Ministry of Defence (2006) *Key Facts: Diversity and Equality in the Armed Forces*, www.mod.uk/DefenceInternet/AboutDefence/Organisation [accessed 21 March 2006].

Minogue, M., Polidano, C. and Hume, D. (eds) (1998) Beyond the New Public Management: Changing Ideas and Practices in Governance, Cheltenham: Edward Elgar.

Mintzberg, H., Ahlsftrand, B. and Lampel, J. (1998) *Strategy Safari*, London: Pearson Education.

Miozzo, M. and Grimshaw, D. (2006) 'Capabilities of Computer Services Firms', Paper presented at the *Academy of Management Conference*, Atlanta (August).

Monbiot, G. (2006) *Our Very Own Enron*. http://www.monbiot.com/archives/2005/06/28/our-very-own-enron/

Morgan, P. and Allington, N. (2002) 'Has the Public Sector Retained its 'Model Employer' Status?', *Public Money & Management*, Jan–March 2002: 35–42.

Morgan, P., Allington, N. and Heery, E. (2000) 'Employment Security in the Public Services', in E. Heery and J. Salmon (eds), *The Insecure Workforce*, London: Routledge, pp. 78–111.

Morgan, R. (2003) 'Outsourcing: Towards the Shamrock Organization?', *Journal of General Management*, 29(2): 35–52.

Morris Inquiry (2004) *Report: The Case for Change: People in the Metropolitan Police Service*, London: Metropolitan Police Service.

National Audit Office (2004) *Delivering Public Services to a Diverse Society*, London: Stationery Office.

Needham, C. (2006) 'Customer Care and the Public Service Ethos', *Public Administration*, 84(4).

Neumark, D. (2003) 'Age Discrimination Legislation in the United States', *Contemporary Economic Policy*, 21(3): 217–317.

NHS Employers (2005) *Quick Guide: Positively Diverse*, London and Leeds: NHS Employers.

NHS Executive (1998) *Working Together*, Leeds: NHS Executive.

NHS Executive (1999) *Agenda for Change*, London: Department of Health.

NHS Executive (2000a) *The Vital Connection: An Equalities Framework for the NHS*, London: Department of Health.

NHS Executive (2000b) *Positively Diverse*, London: Department of Health.

Niskanen, W. *et al.* (1973) *Bureaucracy: Servant or Master?*, London: Institute of Economic Affairs.

Nolan, J., Wichert, I.C. and Burchell, B. (2000) 'Job Insecurity, Psychological Well-Being and Family Life', in E. Heery and J. Salmon (eds) *The Insecure Workforce*, London: Routledge, pp. 181–209.

Nolan, Lord (1995) *First Report of the Committee on Standards in Public Life*, London: The Stationery Office.

Nolan, P. (1989) 'Walking on Water? Performance and Industrial Relations under Thatcher', *Industrial Relations Journal*, 20(2): 81–92.

O'Cinneide, C. (2003a) 'Extending Positive Duties Across the Equality Grounds', *Equal Opportunities Review*, 120, August, 12–16.

O'Cinneide, C. (2003b) 'Making Use of Positive Duties: The UK Experience', in C. Costello and E. Barry (eds), *Equality in Diversity: The New Equality Directives*, Dublin: Irish Centre for European Law.

O'Cinneide, C. (2005) 'Positive Duties and Disability Rights', in A. Lawson and C. Gooding (eds), *Disability Rights in Europe*, Oxford: Hart.

O'Toole, B. (1993) 'The Loss of Purity: The Corruption of Public Service in Britain', *Public Policy and Administration*, 8.

OECD (Organisation for Economic Cooperation and Development) (2000) 'The Service Economy', *Business and Industry Policy Forum Series*, OECD, Paris.

OECD (2005) *Performance related pay policies for government employees: an overview of OECD countries* by D. Landel and D. Marsden, Organisation for Economic Cooperation and Development, OECD, Paris.

Office for Public Management (1996) *Ministry of Defence: Review of Ethnic Minority Initiatives*, London: Office for Public Management.

Office of Public Services Reform (2002) *Principles into Practice*, London: Office of Public Services Reform.

ODPM (Office of the Deputy Prime Minister) (2003) *National Procurement Strategy for Local Government*, London: Office of the Deputy Prime Minister.

Olson, M. (1982) *The Rise and Decline of Nations, Economic Growth, Stagflation and Social Rigidities*, New Haven: Yale University Press.

ONS (August 2006) Labour Market Overview: August 2006.

Oxenbridge, S. and Brown, W. (2002) 'The Two Faces of Partnership? An Assessment of Partnership and Co-operative Employer-Trade Union Relationships', *Employee Relations*, 24(3): 262–276.

Oxenbridge, S. and Brown, W. (2005) 'Developing Partnership Relationships: Case of Leveraging Power', in M. Stuart and M. Martínez Lucio (eds), *Partnership and Modernisation in Employment Relations*, London: Routledge.

PASC (Public Administration Select Committee) (2002) *A Public Service Ethos*, Seventh Report, Session 2001-02m, http://www.publications.parliament.uk/pa/cm200102/cmselect/cmpubadm/263/26302.htm

Passey, A., Hems, L. and Jas, P. (2000) *The UK Voluntary Sector Almanac*, London: NCVO Publications.

Peng, B. and Kleiner, B. (1999) 'New Developments in Age Discrimination', *Equal Opportunities International*, 18(2–4): 72–5.

Perri, G. and Peck, E. (2004) 'New Labour's Modernisation in the Public Sector', *Public Administration*, 82(1): 83–108.

Perry, J.L. and Wise, L.R. (1990) 'The Motivational Bases of Public Service', *Public Administration Review*, 50(3): 367–73.

Peters, T. and Waterman, P. (1987) *In Search of Excellence: Lessons from America's Best-run Companies*, London: Harper and Row.

Pfeffer, J. (1994) *Competitive Advantage through People*, Boston: Harvard Business School Press.

Philpott, J. (2005) 'Work Audit: Public Sector: Jobs, Pay and Productivity', CIPD Impact, London, May: 30–5.

Plant, R. (2003) 'A Public Service Ethic and Political Accountability', *Parliamentary Affairs*, 56(4): 560–79.

Pollert, A. (1991) 'The Orthodoxy of Flexibility', in A. Pollert (ed.), *Farewell to Flexibility?*, Oxford: Blackwell, pp. 3–31.

Pollert, A. (2005) 'The Unorganised Worker: The Decline in Collectivism and New Hurdles to Individual Employment Rights', *Industrial Law Journal*, 34(3): 217–38.

Pollin, R. (2003) *Contours of Descent*, London: Verso.

Pollitt, C. (1987) 'Performance Measurement and the Consumer: Hijacking a Bandwagon?', in *Performance Measurement and the Consumer*, London: National Consumer Council.

Pollitt, C. and Summa, H. (1997) 'Trajectories of Reform: Public Management Change in Four Countries', *Public Money and Management*, 17(1): 7–18.

Pratchett, L. (1999) 'The New Ethics of Modern Public Service', *British Journal of Politics and International Relations*, 1(3): 366–76.

Pratchett, L. and Wingfield, M. (1996) 'Petty Bureaucracy and Woolly-minded Liberalism?', *Public Administration*, 74(4): 639–56.

Prentis, D. (2004) 'Profit Motive', *The Guardian*, 29 October.

Prowse, P. and Prowse, J. (2006) 'Are Non-union Workers Different to their Union Colleagues? Evidence from the Public Services', *Industrial Relations Journal*, 37(3): 222–41.

Public Services Forum (2005) *Pay and Reward Principles*, London: Cabinet Office.

Purcell, K., Hoggarth, T. and Simm, C. (1999) 'Whose Flexibility? The Costs and Benefits of "Non-standard" Working Arrangements and Contractual Relations', York: Joseph Rowntree Foundation, *Work and Opportunity Series No. 12*. ISBN 1-902633-37-7.

Purcell, K. (2000) 'Gendered insecurity', in E. Heery and J. Salmon (eds), *The Insecure Workforce*, London: Routledge.

Reich, R. (1993) *The Work of Nations*, New York: Simon and Schuster.

Reid, J. (2004) 'We Can be Consumers and Citizens', *The Guardian*, 13 November.

Remuneration Economies (2002) *15th Annual Voluntary Sector Salary Survey*, http://www.celre.co.uk

Rhodes, R. (1996) 'The New Governance: Governing without Government', *Political Studies*, 44: 41–62.

Richardson, M., Tailby, S., Danford, A., Stewart, P. and Upchurch, M. (2005) 'Best Value and Workplace Partnership in Local Government', *Personnel Review*, 34(6): 713–28.

Ridley, F. (1996) 'The New Public Management in Europe: Comparative Perspectives', *Public Policy and Administration*, 11(1): 16–29.

Ridley, N. (1991) *My Style of Government, the Thatcher Years*, London: Hutchinson.

Robinson, P. (2000) 'Insecurity and the Flexible Workforce', in E. Heery and J. Salmon (eds) *The Insecure Workforce*, London: Routledge, pp. 25–38.

Rohr, J. (1989) *Ethics for Bureaucrats: an Essay on Law and Values*, 2nd edition, New York: Marcel Dekker.

Roper, I., James, P. and Higgins, P. (2005) 'Workplace Partnership and Public Service Provision: The Case of the "Best Value" Performance Regime in British Local Government', *Work, Employment and Society*, 19(3): 639–49.

Roper, I., Higgins, P. and James, P. (2007) 'Shaping the Bargaining agenda? The Audit Commission and Local Government Industrial Relations', *International Journal of Human Resource Management*, 18(9).

Rosenberg, N. (2005) 'Economic Experiments', in G. Dosi, D. Teece and J. Chytry (eds), *Understanding Industrial and Corporate Change*, Oxford: Oxford University Press.

Rubery, J. and Earnshaw, J. (2005) 'Employment Policy and Practice; Crossing Borders and Disordering Hierarchies', in M. Marchington, D. Grimshaw, J. Rubery and H. Willmott (eds), *Fragmenting Work: Blurring Organizational Boundaries and Disordering Hierarchies*, Oxford: Oxford University Press.

Sachdev, S. (2001) *Contracting Culture: From CCT to PPPs: The Private provision of public services and its impact on employment relations*, London: Unison.

Sanchez-Runde, C. (2001) 'Strategic Human Resource Management and the New Employment Relationships: A Research Review and Agenda', in J. Gual and J. Ricart (eds), *Strategy, Organization and the Changing Nature of Work*, London: Edward Elgar.

Sauter, R. (1988) 'Union View: Subcontracting the Work of Union Members in the Public Sector', *Labor Law Journal*, August, 487–92.

Seldon, A. (2000) 'Editorial note', Tullock *et al. Government Whose Obedient Servant?*, London: Institute of Economic Affairs.

Simms, M. (2003) 'Union Organizing in a Not-for-profit Organization', in G. Gall (ed.), *Union Organizing: Campaigning for Trade Union Recognition*, London: Routledge, pp. 97–113.

Simon, H.A. (1951) 'A Formal Theory of the Employment Relationship', *Econometrica*, 19.

Sisson, K. (2001) 'Human Resource Management and the Personnel Function – A Case of Partial Impact?', Storey, J. (ed.), *Human Resource Management: A Critical Text*, London: Thomson.

Skarpelis-Sperk, S. (2006) Eine radikale Abkürzung auf dem Weg in ein marktradikales Europa, in Bsirke *et al.* (eds), *Die EU-Dienstleistungsrichtlinie: ein Ansclag auf das europäische Sozialmodell*, Hamburg: VSA Verlag.

Smeaton, D. and March, A. (2006) *Maternity and Paternity Rights and Benefits: Survey of Parents 2005*, Employment Relations Research Series 50, London: Department of Trade and Industry.

Smith, D. (1987) *The Rise and Fall of Monetarism*, London: Penguin.

Smith, J. (1991) 'The Public Service Ethos', *Public Administration*, 69(4): 515–23.

Social Care Labour Market (2005) National Workforce Group, Scottish Executive (2005) *Scotland's Social Care Labour Market*, 24th February, mimeographed.

Standing, G. (1999) Global Labour Flexibility: Seeking Distributive Justice, London: Macmillan.

Stigler, G.J. (1975) *The Citizen and the State*, Chicago: University Chicago Press.

Stredwick, J. and Ellis, S. (2005) (2nd edn) *Flexible Working*, London: CIPD.

Stuart, M. and Martínez Lucio, M. (2000) 'Renewing the Model Employer: Changing Employment Relations and Partnership in the Health And Private Sector', *Journal of Management in Medicine*, 14(5/6): 310–25.

Stuart, M. and Martínez Lucio, M. (2002) 'Social Partnership and the Mutual Gains Organisation: Remaking Involvement and Trust at the British Workplace', *Economic and Industrial Democracy*, 23(2): 177–200.

Stuart, M. and Martínez Lucio, M. (2005a) 'Introduction', in M. Stuart and M. Martínez Lucio (eds), *Partnership and Modernisation in Employment Relations*, London: Routledge.

Stuart, M. and Martínez Lucio, M. (2005b) 'Trade Union Representatives' Attitudes and Experiences of the Principles and Practices of Partnership', in M. Stuart and M. Martínez Lucio (eds), *Partnership and Modernisation in Employment Relations*, London: Routledge.

Stuart, M. and Martínez Lucio, M. (2006) 'A Bridge over Troubled Water: The Role of the British Advisory, Conciliation and Arbitration Service (ACAS) in Facilitating Labour-Management Consultation in Public Sector Transformation', paper presented to the *IIRA World Congress*, Lima, Peru, September.

Supiot, A. (2001) *Beyond Employment*, Oxford: Oxford University Press.

Sverke, M. and Hellgren, J. (2002) 'The Nature of Job Insecurity: Understanding Employment Uncertainty on the Brink of a New Millenium', *Applied Psychology: An International Review*, 51(1): 23–42.

Szymanski, S. (1996) 'The Impact of Compulsory Competitive Tendering on Refuse Collection Services', *Fiscal Studies*, 17(3): 1–19.

Taylor, P. and Ramsay, H. (1998) 'Unions, Partnership and HRM: Sleeping with the Enemy?', *International Journal of Employment Studies*, 6(2): 115–43.

Taylor, R. (2002) *Britain's World at Work- Myths and Realities*, Swindon: ESRC.

Taylor, R. (2004) 'Partnership at Work: The Way to Corporate Renewal', ESRC Future of Work Programme Commentary Series, No. 7, Swindon: ESRC.

Terry, M. and Smith, J. (2003) *Evaluation of the Partnership at Work Fund*, Employment Relations Research Series No. 17, London: Department of Trade and Industry.

Thatcher, M. (1977) *Let Our Children Grow Tall, Selected Speeches, 1975–77*, London: Centre for Policy Studies.

Thompson, G. (1990) *The Political Economy of the New Right*, London: Pinter.

Thompson, M. (1993) *Pay and Performance: The Employee Experience*, IMS Report 218, Institute of Manpower Studies, Brighton.

Thompson, N. (2002) *Left in the Wilderness, the Political Economy of British Democratic Socialism since 1979*, Acumen.

Torres, L. and Pina, V. (2002) 'Changes in Public Service Delivery in EU Countries', *Public Money and Management*, 22(4): 41–8.

Toynbee, P. (2002) *Hard Work: Life in Low-Pay Britain*, London: Bloomsbury.

Toynbee, P. (2003) *Hard Work: Life in Low-Pay Britain*, London: Bloomsbury Publishing.

TUC (2004) *Things Have Got Better – Labour Market Performance 1992–2002.*

TUC (2005) *The EU Temp Trade: Temporary Agency Work Across the European Union*, June 2005.

Tullock, G. *et al.* (2000) *Government: Whose Obedient Servant?*, London: Institute of Economic Affairs.

Tullock, G. (1976) *The Vote Motive, an Essay in the Economics of Politics, with Applications to the British Economy*, London: Institute of Economic Affairs.

Tullock, G. (1998) 'Public choice', in J. Eatwell, M. Milgate and P. Newman (eds), *New Palgrave Dictionary of Economic Thought*, Vol. 3, London: Macmillan.

Turnbull, P. and Wass, V. (2000) 'Redundancy and the Paradox of Job Insecurity', in E. Heery and J. Salmon (eds), *The Insecure Workforce*, London: Routledge, pp. 57–77.

Ugboro, I. and Obeng, K. (2001) *Managing the Aftermaths of Contracting in Public Transit Organizations: Employee Perceptions of Job Security, Organizational Commitment and Trust*. Report for U.S. Department of Transportation, Washington. DTRS93-G-0018. August 2001.

Unison (2000) *Contracting Out and the Two-Tier Workforce*, London: Unison.

Unison (2006) www.unison.org.uk/voluntaryindex, accessed 19.5.06.

Upchurch, M. (2003) 'Public Sector Employment', in G. Hollinshead, P. Nicholls and S. Tailby (eds), *Employee Relations*, London: Prentice Hall, pp. 531–59.

Veltz, P. (2000) *Le Nouveau Monde Industriel*, Paris: Gallimard.

Voos, P.B. (1987) 'The Influence of Cooperative Programs on Union-management Relations Programs', *Industrial and Labor Relations Review*, 40(2): 195–208.

Waddington, J. and Kerr, A. (1999) 'Trying to Stem the Flow: Union Membership Turnover in the Public Sector', *Industrial Relations Journal*, 30: 184–96.

Wainwright, S., Clark, J., Griffith, M., Jochum, V. and Wilding, K. (2006) *The UK Voluntary Sector Almanac*, London: NCVO.

Waldegrave, W. (1994) 'The Reality of Reform and Accountability in Today's Public Service', in Norman Flynn (ed.), *Public Finance Foundation Reader: Change in the Civil Service*, CIPFA, 81–8.

Walsh, J. and Davis, H. (1993) *Competition and Service: the Impact of the Local Government Act 1988*, London: HMSO.

Walsh, K. (1995) Quality Through Markets: the New Public Service Management, in A. Wilkinson and H. Willmott (eds), *Making Quality Critical New Perspectives on Organisational Change*, London: Routledge.

Walton, R.E. and McKersie, R.B. (1965) *A Behavioral Theory of Labour Negotiations: An Analysis of a Social Interaction System*, New York: McGraw-Hill.

Ward, K., Grimshaw, D., Rubery, J. and Beynon, H. (2001) 'Dilemmas in the Management of Temporary Work Agency Staff', *Human Resource Management Journal*, 11(4): 3–21.

Watt, N. (1999) 'Blair Berates Old Labour "Snobs"', *The Guardian*, 7 July.

Webb, J. (2001) 'Gender, Work and Transitions in the Local State', *Work, Employment and Society*, 15(4): 825–44.

Wesselius, E. (2002) 'GATS 2000: Corporate Power at Work', TNI Briefing Series 2002/6, www.tni.org

White Paper (1989) *Working for Patients*, London: HMSO.

Whitley, R. (1999) *Divergent Capitalisms*, Oxford: Oxford University Press.

Wickert, I. (2002) 'Job Security and Work Intensification', in F. Burchell, D. Lapido and F. Wilkerson, *Job Security and Work Intensification*, London: Routledge, pp. 92–111.

Wilding, K., Collins, G., Jochum, V. and Wainwright, S. (2004) *The UK Voluntary Sector Almanac 2004*, London: NCVO Publications.

Wilensky, H. (2003) 'Postindustrialism and Postmaterialism? A Critical View of the "New Economy", the "Information Age", the "High Tech Society", and All That'. In *Rich Democracies: Political Economy, Public Policy and Performance*, Berkeley: University of Carolina Press, pp. 187–208.

Wilkinson, F. and Ladipo, D. (2002) 'What Can Governments Do?', in F. Burchell, D. Ladipo and F. Wilkinson, *Job Insecurity and Work Intensification*, London: Routledge, pp. 172–84.

Willetts, D. (1992) *Modern Conservatism*, Harmondsworth: Penguin.

Williams, S. (2004) 'Accounting for Change in Public Sector Industrial Relations: The Erosion of National Bargaining in Further Education in England and Wales', *Industrial Relations Journal*, 35(3): 233–48.

Wolfson, M. (2003) 'Neoliberalism and the Social Structure of Accumulation', *Review of Radical Political Economics*, 35(3): 255–62.

Women and Equality Unit (2005) *Advancing Equality for Men and Women: Government Proposals to Introduce a Public Sector Duty to Promote Gender Equality*, London: Department of Trade and Industry.

Wood, G. and Harcourt, M. (2001) 'The Consequences of Neo-Corporatism: A Syncretic Analysis', *International Journal of Sociology and Social Policy*, 20(8): 1–22.

Wood, G., Wilkinson, A. and Harcourt, M. (2006) 'Age Discrimination and Working Life: Perspectives and Contestations', Working Paper, School of Management, University of Sheffield.

Woodhams, C. and Corby, S. (2006) 'Then and Now: Disability Legislation and Employers' Practices', *Academy of Management Annual Meeting*, Atlanta, Georgia, 11–16 August.

Wright, T. (2003) 'Defining the Ethos', *The Guardian*, 1 October.

# Index